RONAN KEATING

LIFE IS A
ROLLERCOASTER

Ronan teamed up with his close friend, Irish author and journalist Eddie Rowley, to co-write his story.

Eddie is the chief entertainment correspondent on Ireland's biggest-selling newspaper, the *Sunday World*.

RONAN KEATING

LIFE IS A ROLLERCOASTER

with Eddie Rowley

EBURY
PRESS

This edition first published in Great Britain in 2001

1 3 5 7 9 10 8 6 4 2

Hardback edition first published in 2000
Copyright © Ronan Keating 2001

Ronan Keating has asserted his right under the Copyright, Designs and
Patents Act 1988 to be identified as the author of this work.

Ebury Press
Random House · 20 Vauxhall Bridge Road · London SW1V 2SA

Random House Australia Pty Limited
20 Alfred Street · Milsons Point · Sydney · New South Wales 2061 · Australia

Random House New Zealand Limited
18 Poland Road · Glenfield · Auckland 10 · New Zealand

Random House (Pty) Limited
Endulini · 5A Jubilee Road · Parktown 2193 · South Africa

The Random House Group Limited Reg. No. 954009

www.randomhouse.co.uk

Papers used by Ebury Press are natural, recyclable products
made from wood grown in sustainable forests.

A CIP catalogue record for this book is available from the British Library.

ISBN 0 09 187848 9

Designed by Lovelock & Co.

Printed and bound in Great Britain by
Bookmarque Ltd, Croydon, Surrey

CONTENTS

Where would ya be with
no bell on ya bike and
ya knickers ringing?

ACKNOWLEDGEMENTS

How's it going?

Welcome to my first book. Let me start off by saying – I'm only twenty-three, so this is not exactly what you'd call an autobiography! It's too soon to start writing my memoirs. That would be like me saying that I have come to the end of my career. And I feel it's anything but that. It's only the beginning.

But I found the book really rewarding to write, and I hope you find it as rewarding to read. This is a book about what I'm doing now, a little about where I've been and all about where I hope I'm going.

None of this would have been possible without my good friend Eddie Rowley, supremos Hannah MacDonald and Jake Lingwood and all at Ebury Press, and researcher Sarah Hamilton. Also my friends in the band – Duster, Shanno, Steo and Mikey. Thanks also to my management, Louis Walsh and Mark Plunkett. Most importantly thanks to my family and friends at home, especially Yvonne and Jack. I love you all.

And finally thanks again to the fans. Enjoy the book and keep listening …

Thanks and God bless you all.

RONAN

FLYING SOLO

13 JANUARY 2000

'Ronan! Ronan!'

I hear a voice and, very gingerly, I prise open an eyelid. 'Yee-aah?' I groan.

'Ronan!'

'What? What!' I sit bolt upright on the couch. Ugh! My stomach lurches and my head spins. 'Oh, please, tell me it's not morning.'

'It was morning when you got in, Ronan,' Yvonne says with a laugh.

I squint at her through bleary eyes and catch her smiling. Unlike me, Wivvy (as I call her) was the sensible one last night. I, on the other hand, was the party animal and now I'm getting my comeuppance. My tongue seems to be magnetically attached to the roof of my mouth and my throat feels like it's had a desert sand storm blowing through it. It all seemed like such a good idea in the early hours of this morning. Why didn't someone stop me at a sensible time?

I rub my head and try to remember how I ended up in this state. The evening before comes back to me with all its mixed emotions. It had been a strange night of highs and lows. It had almost felt like the end of an era …

Boyzone had been playing at The Point Depot, the former train station out in the grim, windswept docklands area of Dublin. Even through my hangover, the memory of the concert brings a groggy smile to my face. What a buzz! The place was awash with colour and on every side, draped on balconies or waved by the fans over the heads of the crowd, there were banners declaring undying love, and some saucy suggestions, for us lads (Jeez! Did that group of girls really want to do those things to Shanno?). Strobe lights spanned the sea of happy young faces, like candles flickering on a birthday cake. It had been party time in Dublin for Boyzone and the six thousand fans who had come out on a chilly January night. They were there to soak up the raw excitement of a live show, to lose themselves in the full Boyzone experience. They weren't disappointed.

We've done this type of concert hundreds of times in the six years we've been together, but last night was different for many reasons. Over the past few years Boyzone have broken new ground in Ireland. Last night was another first as we set a new record for the biggest number of shows ever staged at The Point Depot. We beat Dire Straits! We beat Cliff Richard! We even beat the man they call 'The Cat In The Hat', the massive country star Garth Brooks. As I stumble to my feet, using the edge of the couch as a lever, I feel a glow of pride. Jesus, we really did make a little bit of history in Ireland yesterday! What a sweet feeling. We've had to fight hard to gain respect here, but it has gradually come over the years, and last night was the ultimate acknowledgement of that as we completed nine nights of successive concerts at The Point. Was it really *nine nights*? My God! I can hardly believe it.

It was the end of our UK and Irish winter tour, but it was also a major landmark in Boyzone's career. After last night, things will never, ever, be the same again for us. A few months ago we all agreed to fly the nest and follow our own solo dreams. There is no acrimony, no one member putting a gun to the heads of the other guys. Six years on a non-stop rollercoaster ride in the pop world is an eternity for any band. The time has come to search out new pastures for ourselves and discover the big wide world outside the band.

Last night we all went away with happy hearts, relieved that, unlike other groups, we have survived as a complete unit. There is no Robbie or Geri scenario. We are all still talking to each other. And we are all agreed that Boyzone will be back. We've made a pact on that.

If there was excitement in the crowd last night, there was emotion on stage, too, as our lives in Boyzone over the last six years flashed before us. We all sensed it. Most of all, I remembered those early days on the road, travelling the small lanes of Ireland in a battered white Transit van. But how could six years pass so quickly? It felt like someone had pressed the fast-forward button.

For six years the five of us experienced everything together. We've often lived and worked together twenty-four hours a day. Now we are going to take on new challenges away from each other and inevitably things between us will change. So last night, along with the adrenaline rush of a live performance, there was a definite sadness too, simmering underneath the surface. We all knew we were coming to the end of a part of our lives that could never be relived, except in our memories.

Now, through the swirling fog of the morning after, I find

myself remembering how it finally hit me as I was singing the lyrics of 'Everyday I Love You' and the line 'together we are the very best'. Glancing over at Keith and seeing that the words were not lost on him, I added the line, 'the five of us together' and I put my hands out across the stage. It just sort of came to me.

Catching Keith's eye, I saw his look that said, 'Feck, wouldn't it be great to be starting out all over again, having the craic on the road in the van!' I was thinking exactly the same thing. My eyes filled up with water and I just wanted the song to end before the tears really started to flow. But it's a moment I will hold on to forever – my ultimate memory of Boyzone.

Last night, despite the fact that it wasn't the opening performance, there was a large media presence at The Point. During the finale, I could sense them waiting in anticipation of a big announcement. I spotted one or two of them near the stage, their notebooks at the ready. The rumour factory had been working overtime and there had already been a lot of speculation in the newspapers about Boyzone finally calling it a day. I knew those guys wanted a story, but I couldn't deliver the one they were expecting. Instead, I was determined finally to put a nail in the coffin of those false reports. So in my best Arnie Schwarzenegger voice I promised 'We'll be back!'

Then there was *that* party. The one which has left me with a jack-hammer working at full blast inside my head. The memory of it causes me to slump back on the couch and shut my eyes. There was no post-mortem after the show, no wake and no time to get all sentimental. It was straight on to our very personal after-show party in the Chocolate Bar, a funky but intimate Dublin café-bar, owned by Boyzone's co-manager John. It was totally different to the normal Boyzone parties, which are usually attended by all sorts of people from the media and music biz. Last night we had wanted it to be just the five of us. Together.

We locked the doors, the drinks flowed and soon the banter between us became more and more nonsensical. I can remember laughing, and then laughing some more. None of it makes any sense in the painfully bright light of this morning, but I do remember having a very long and very funny conversation with Keith Duffy, all of which is now a complete blur. If a Martian had landed and infiltrated the Chocolate Bar last night, he would surely have reported back to High Command: 'These Earthlings are very, very strange beings.'

I try to remember what hour of the morning I finally left. Was it five o'clock? Six o'clock? Of course, when I got home I decided it was far too early to stop the party, so I headed straight to the bar in the house. Somewhere along the line I dozed off on the couch.

I'm drifting off again as a familiar voice shakes me out of my reverie. 'Jeez, Ronan, are you still pissed? You gotta move or you're going to miss the flight!'

Flight? Christ! The flight! I'm going to LA this morning. 'Oh man, I don't need this now!'

'C'mon brother, shift your ass!'

My older brother Gar is standing over me. He'd been partying with us last night and I've seen him having better days too. 'Jesus, Gar,' I say, struggling to my feet again. 'How am I going to get my act together for this LA trip? I'm in ribbons.'

My brother seems to be coping with his hangover better than

me. I suppose he's had five more years' practice. 'Listen, don't worry, Ro,' he says. 'Everything is taken care of. The luggage is in the Range Rover. You'll get there in plenty of time, no problem. Grab a quick shower, but make it fast.'

There's nothing in the world to beat the sensation of a full-force hot shower, especially when you feel like you've just been dragged through a hedge by a runaway horse. I feel half-human again as I towel myself dry, but what on God's earth must I look like? I rub the towel across the steamed-up mirror and catch a glimpse of two bloodshot eyes. Liam Gallagher, eat your heart out.

'Have we got everything, Wiv?' I call out, hurriedly dressing.

'Yeah hon, stop worrying, it's all there.' At least someone seems to be in control.

Outside the house, a sharp breeze helps to refresh my senses, and I examine the mountain that is our luggage. I look over at Jack, who's snug as a bug in his car seat. 'For a little guy, you create as much baggage as the whole of Boyzone on tour,' I laugh. He's like a little mascot, and suddenly it hits me how glad I am that he and Yvonne are coming with me to LA.

Dublin Airport is milling with people, many of them emigrants heading away again after Christmas at home. The baseball cap comes down over my eyes as we wade through the throng. But I still get stopped.

'Ronan, sorry, would you mind signing this?'

'Sure, no problem.'

We're sitting in the departure lounge and my head is still kicking, when suddenly the full impact of what I'm about to do hits me: *This is it, Ro. Now you gotta get your own act together.* Ever since *Notting Hill* and 'When You Say Nothing at All' I have been dreaming of this moment – the opportunity to make my own album. Whatever success I've been lucky enough to have so far, this challenge is in a different league. This time it is down to me and no one else. I'm excited, but apprehensive as well.

I take a deep breath and, to reassure myself, I run through a mantra: Just let me get to LA. Just let me get a couple of good tracks down. Just let everything go well and I'll be laughing.

It feels like the shortest flight ever to LA. One minute I'm sitting on the runway at Dublin Airport under a dull, grey sky, the next I'm gazing out at sunshine and heat rippling off the tarmac. It looks like an oven out there. I remember waking up a few times on the flight and checking to see if Jack and Yvonne are OK, but for the main part I was out for the count.

I sit there as the other passengers begin to collect their belongings and shuffle off up the aisle. The city awaits, I know. It's here that it will happen for me … or not. But God, do I feel awful! I can't remember ever having a hangover like this. My head is still bursting and I could happily swallow a gallon of water. Do I really have to move? Turning from the window, I look up at Yvonne. 'Do you want me to take Jack?' I ask, wincing.

'No!' she replies, and raises her eyebrows.

Thank God for that! I can hardly lift myself.

Yvonne is brilliant. She knows what I'm like after I've pushed the boat out too far. It doesn't happen very often, but when it does, Wiv gives me the sympathy vote. Not that I deserve it. Businesslike, she gets us all off the plane and I start trying to be of some use, although all I want to do now is be in my hotel room and take another shower. I try feebly to take control of the luggage. 'How many bags did we have? Are they all there?'

As I struggle through Arrivals pushing the mountain of gear, I scan the little placards held up all around. There should be a car to pick us up. I look around again and get that sinking feeling. No Keating. Los Angeles, 'the city of angels', sure doesn't feel like it today. My own guardian angel appears to have deserted me. Perhaps I left it at the Chocolate Bar last night.

We fight our way through the crowd with our piles of luggage in search of the taxi rank and as we come out of the airport building, it feels like someone has opened the door of a furnace. I gasp for air as the overpowering heat of LA drains the little energy I have from my system. Jack had slept for a few hours on the plane, so I was told, but now he's narky as hell. The poor little guy's body clock is all over the place.

'Hey, Jack, I know how you feel.'

Just when I think it can't get any worse, and I'm desperately trying to grab a couple of cabs, I cop a paparazzi guy taking photographs of us. In LA? They don't even know me here. I need this now like a hole in the head. 'Snap away, pal. You'll never sell these pics of me ... far too scary.'

All I'm concerned about is getting two taxis sorted for me, Yvonne, Jack, the nanny we've brought with us and our absurd number of cases. When we are finally organised and in the cabs, the taxi driver turns round and asks, 'OK, guy, where are you going?'

It's a good question. Everyone waits and looks at me. Where *are* we going? I can't remember the name of the bleedin' hotel. 'What's the name of our hotel, Wiv?'

'I thought you knew, Ro!'

'I did know, the alcohol has killed the brain cells.' We head into town anyway, while I trawl my booze-soaked memory. By now there's bedlam in the car. We're crammed in with bags on top of us and poor old Jack is fed up with life and screaming his head off, which isn't helping my head right now. Eventually I remember that the hotel name begins with a P. After another age, the rest of the name – The Peninsula – at last emerges but at that moment I get another sinking feeling.

'I have no dollars, Wiv!'

Aaagh!

I've been fortunate to stay in some of the best hotels in the world during my travels with Boyzone, but today none of them can compare to our suite at The Peninsula. I've never been so happy to see a hotel room. It doesn't have any particularly amazing features, in fact, let's face it, it has no character at all, like most American hotel rooms. But it is exactly what the doctor ordered right now.

As soon as the bags are sorted and Jack is got off to sleep, I think, Right, Ro, get crackin'. This is it. Tomorrow is the start of your solo career. The adrenaline is now pumping as I think about why I'm here. It never takes much to get myself revved up. Work is the best cure for most things. I'm in Los Angeles to put together my solo album with Pat Leonard, who has produced albums for Madonna and Aerosmith. I ring the studio to check in. It's Monday afternoon and I'm due to begin recording there tomorrow. 'Hi, is this the studio?'

'Yeah.'

'It's Ronan Keating here. I'm coming in tomorrow.'

There's a pause and some shuffling of paper. Then the guy says, 'We don't have you in until Thursday.'

'No, it's definitely tomorrow.'

'Sorry, sir, it says here Thursday.'

I put down the phone and suddenly my hangover comes back with a vengeance. Sometimes it doesn't take much to bring me back down, either. I collapse into a chair, holding my head in my hands. I'm totally deflated. This is not good! None of this is good! Why have I come here? I feel like crap and nothing is going right. This is a disaster! Why didn't we just do this in London?

Yvonne is busy sorting out the luggage, organising clothes in wardrobes and drawers. 'Take a shower, Ro. You'll feel better,' she suggests calmly.

She's right, as usual. Life doesn't seem so bad after I've washed and changed into fresh clothes. Yvonne does the same and we decide to get out of the room for a while, to go for a walk and get a feel for the area. Jack is sleeping and we leave him in the capable hands of our nanny. The pavements are empty. Americans don't seem to walk that much, and we don't get far, either. The diner just a block away looks inviting and I have a longing for crispy bacon. Forget everything else. I need crispy bacon, and lots of it. Best hangover cure known to mankind.

I wash it down with gallons of coke as we talk about our new temporary life here in LA. As professional travellers, we're used to the lifestyle of nomads. We can literally create a home anywhere. Once Yvonne and Jack are with me, that's my home. Stick a log fire in there for good measure, although I won't be needing it out here.

I wonder how I'm ever going to survive this heat.

Thursday comes around, although it seems to take forever. I just can't get down to that studio fast enough, even though I'm wary of meeting Pat Leonard. After all, he's one of the top producers in the world, as well as having been Madonna's co-writer and Michael Jackson's musical director.

I'm edgy as I sit in a small office area, while the studio track down Pat for me. Eventually he turns up. My first impression is: this guy looks like a real bulldog. He is a forty-ish, stocky man, a little taller than me, with dark hair and stubble on his face.

'Ronan, hi'ya doin'? We're gonna be workin' together, right?'

'Lookin' forward to it, Pat. It's an honour.'

I'm in awe of Pat, of his reputation and track record, but at the same time, I've come here to record *my* album. I'm feeling kind of wired – excited but nervous. So although it'd be good to spend four hours chatting about the amazing people he's worked with, all I care about right now is my album. Yes, Pat's here to guide me, but I have to take the reins and let him know what I need. I plunge in, tell him everything I want out of my solo debut, my words falling over themselves. And he listens, and listens, and bit by bit I realise I'm in the right hands. By the end of that first day I feel great. We had got to know each other and Pat, I discover, is a really nice guy and has a good sense of humour. I go home happy thinking, yeah, I can work with this guy.

My contented state doesn't last long. The next day they tell me Pat is sick and will be out of action for four whole days! This is turning into my worst nightmare. I'm starting to panic. So much is at stake for me, time is running on and I have nothing to show for it. This is no good at all. It's got to be sorted.

I'm very conscious of the fact that I'm a nobody in America. Boyzone never made it in the States, so Ronan Keating really doesn't mean anything to these guys. I'm just another artiste.

So, I call Pat and say, 'Listen, man, are we going to get this going or are we not? There are a lot of other people that I could have worked with, but I asked to work with you. I want to work with you. You either want to work with me or you don't. Don't beat around the bush, I've spent a fortune on flights over, on hotels, what's going on?'

Pat invites me around to his house and, God love him, he isn't well. He has a very bad 'flu. He has just spent six months of solid work on Elton John's album and that's what happens when you stop: your system goes down – boom! – and you're badly knocked out. But my album is the only thing that is important to me at this moment. So Pat's there struggling through this awful 'flu and he's having to deal with me, a hyper young Irishman talking at ninety – 'What are we going to do? When are we going to start?'

Pat says, very calmly, 'Don't worry. Just let me get back on my feet and we'll be in business. It'll be great. We'll get it done, it'll be fantastic.'

I leave his house feeling reassured. Pat is a good guy, he won't let me down. And, on the positive side, I'm getting to spend some time with Jack and Yvonne while we get settled in. But I can't really relax. This is the beginning of my career as a solo artist. The rest of my life is riding on what happens while I'm here in the States. I am more hungry now for success than I've ever been with Boyzone. I can feel it burning inside. I'm on my own now, which in a way makes me feel strong because if there's one thing I've learnt about myself it's that I'll work and work to get things right. I've made my choices and the last thing I am is a quitter.

But what if it doesn't work out over here with these guys? What if it all goes wrong?

One thing's for certain. I refuse to fail.

CHAPTER 1

IT'S FAR FROM ALL THIS I WAS REARED

The local Garda Sergeant in Raheny on the northside of Dublin was in failing health. In fact, Sgt. James Culleton was staring death in the face. He had just learned that he had cancer and that it was at a very advanced stage. The local policeman was a popular man, well respected in the community and as news of his illness spread, many in the area felt how much he would be missed. Knowing he did not have very much time left, James Culleton took a good, hard look at his life. It had been ordinary but honourable. He had served his community well. But as a father, he felt he had unfinished business. On the spot he resolved to see his offspring settled down and established in their lives before he passed away.

After his daily travels on his creaking bicycle around his patch, the sergeant would head to his local pub, the Raheny Inn, where he'd enjoy a few pints of Guinness and pick up local gossip. There Sgt. Culleton had become friendly with a young barman, Gerry Keating, who had come up from his native County Cavan to find work in the city. He regarded Gerry as 'a nice young fella' with good prospects. He also knew the clean-cut barman was besotted with his beautiful young hairdresser daughter, Marie, so he encouraged the romance, turning a blind eye to whispers on the doorstep and late night walks in the lane.

But as his illness worsened, so Sgt. Culleton's need to see his family settled grew. Finally, taking the bull by the horns, he came right out and said to Gerry, 'Come down to the house, I have a few women below, would you pick one of them?'

Needless to say, Gerry wasn't slow taking the hint. It was the official stamp of approval on a fine romance that eventually led to the wedding of Gerry Keating and Marie Culleton – my mam and dad.

My grandfather didn't survive long enough to lead his beloved young daughter Marie up the aisle. Once the cancer took hold, he quickly weakened. The wedding had been planned before his passing and when he realised he was just too ill to make it, he told Marie to go ahead and on no account postpone the marriage. As he lay in his sickbed at the top of the house, preparations for the large family wedding continued downstairs.

Grandad Culleton died in March 1964 and my parents were married on 10 February 1965. There was a bittersweet feeling amongst the assembled guests. My mother wore some black on her wedding dress in remembrance of the dad she had adored. She was just eighteen years old.

When I was a child they talked a lot in my family about Grandad Culleton and his days in the Garda. There seemed no end to the stories of his bravery, humour and good sense. He was a major figure in my imagination and at one stage I considered joining the Garda myself. Although my parents met in Raheny near Dublin, my father grew up in the empty green spaces of rural Ireland. Grandad Culleton was originally from Kilkenny and his wife, Madeline, my grandmother, was from Freshford nearby. Her maiden name was Hinksman and her family were originally from Germany, emigrating to England around the time of the First World War, from where they made their way to Ireland. So my blood isn't pure Irish!

My paternal grandparents, James and Annie Keating, were small-time farmers from Termon, Kilacar, just outside the town of Virginia in County Cavan, not far from the border with Northern Ireland. So my dad grew up on a remote farm until he emigrated to England at the age of seventeen. He worked in bars all round the country but in the end, like so many do, he returned to Ireland, where he landed the job as a barman in Raheny.

After my parents married, they moved to Cavan, a small town 65 miles northwest of Dublin, where my dad ran another bar and my mother worked as a hairdresser. It was to be the first of a dozen homes they lived in during their married life.

I'm told there was an air of anticipation and excitement around our compact three-bedroomed semi-detached home at 129 Wilson Estate in north County Dublin on 3 March 1977. All the attention was focused on the back bedroom, where a major event was unfolding. Dad was pacing around the house in an agitated state. Eventually, after a flurry of activity, there was white smoke and, more than likely, a fanfare of trumpets.

My sister Linda was tucked up in bed, snuggled into her pink duvet, when Dad popped his head around the door and announced in a euphoric tone, 'Mam has had a baby boy! It's a baby boy!' You'd think it was the first boy that had been born into the family rather than the fourth. My eldest brother Ciaran had a fever and was banned from going down to the room to see 'the new baby'. He kicked up a storm from hell until, in a desperate bid to get some peace and quiet, they eventually allowed him to peep through the doorway at the little bundle in the Moses basket beside Mam's bed.

I was to be the last child in the Keating clan. Ciaran, Linda, Gerard and Gary all came before me. My brothers and sister claim I was spoilt rotten and got away with murder while we were all growing up. But then being the youngest of a large brood is always slightly different. You have to fight for attention, and you always seem to be behind your siblings in experience and achievement. At the same time, though, you are allowed to do things earlier, but you never stop being your mam's little baby. I stood out a mile from the rest of them, all gangly legs and messy snow-white hair. There would always be a fuzzy clump of hair at the back of my head. Mam used to call it 'the bird's nest'. The only time it was normal was when it was just washed, but shortly afterwards it would gather in a matted ball like a Brillo pad.

When I look back it amazes me how my parents supported, let alone spoilt, a gang of five kids. Ireland is going through a boom period at the moment, but it was in a deep depression during those years. To provide uniforms, books, new clothes, Christmas presents and all the rest for five kids was obviously a struggle for them. My dad worked long hours in all sorts of jobs, including some, such as lorry driving, that kept him away from home a lot. Meanwhile Mam made some extra money as a hairdresser.

Although we weren't wealthy, I wasn't conscious of being

poor because I had a comfortable life. I always got what I wanted, within reason. We were never left without and my parents always put us kids first. I remember how one year every one of us got a brand new bicycle for Christmas. Parents would find it hard enough to do that today, let alone back then. I don't know how they did it! I suppose they must have gone without themselves.

There was another Christmas when Ciaran had asked for a stereo music player. Mam and Dad didn't have the money to buy it. Then on Christmas Eve, Dad got an unexpected bonus from work. Not wanting to let his son down, he went out that afternoon to walk the streets of Dublin to find the last remaining 'three-in-one' stereo player that Ciaran just had to have.

I remember another Christmas when Dad went out and laid carpets to make a few extra pounds for our gifts. Because he was away so much of the time, working to support a big family, we would often not see that much of him. The men of today have no problem hugging and kissing their kids, but it was different in my dad's time and I never had that kind of relationship with him. Mam represented the home and gave the emotional support while Dad was the family's main provider.

They were both ambitious for the family, Mam in particular, who wished we were all a bit more prim and proper. All the members of my family, with the exception of Ciaran, ended up with shortened first names. Linda became Lil, Gerard was Ger, Gary became Gar. When I came along, Mam told the others, 'Don't shorten his name. His name is Ronan and you're not to shorten his name.' But, of course, I became Ro. Later on, Mam decided that she wanted to be addressed as 'Mum', which must have sounded a bit posher.

'I'm not going to answer to anyone unless you call me Mum! I won't answer to Mam any more,' she insisted. But, of course, she was wasting her breath talking to our lot. But the one thing she could get perfect was the home. Doing up houses was her passion and there was always some kind of renovation or alteration or addition going on in our homes during my childhood.

My older brother, Ciaran, says that often he'd come home from school and Mam would order, 'Go up to your room and get your dirty clothes on.'

He'd come back down the stairs to find her armed with a sledge hammer pummelling down a wall after deciding to change the sitting room into a sitting room-cum-dining room. Or you might come down on a Saturday morning and she'd be building a wall in the middle of the room. You name the building job and she could do it. She was an amazing woman. Everyone who met her was bowled over by her energy and inspiration.

You never knew what you were going to find when you arrived back at the end of the day. One night my dad arrived in from an evening in the pub. It was late and he was trying not to disturb the rest of the family as he crept through the house without putting on the lights (I've been there a few times myself). Suddenly he let out a roar of pain. In the kitchen he had banged in to a little island my mam had built with red bricks to put her plants on. It wasn't there when Dad left home that day, and no one told him it was going to be there when he returned. Mam never consulted anyone about her plans. She just got an idea into her head and went and did it. I'd come home from school and she'd be in her tracksuit reorganising the rooms. 'Right Ronan,' she'd say. 'I want to move the sofa over there and I want to put the TV there!' That was every other week.

I'll never forget one decorating job she did in the kitchen. She decided on a scheme of red and white squares. Nothing would be allowed to escape. So, first off, the walls were done with red and white crosses. Then she put red sticky tape on the doors of the kitchen units, on the fridge, the washing machine and all the little jars that contained tea, coffee and sugar. By the end, when you walked into the kitchen nothing stood out, everything was red and white. We had to ask, 'Where's the fridge, Mam? Where are the doors, Mam?' You couldn't distinguish anything.

'I think it's lovely,' she'd say, standing back to admire her work.

Once, after she'd knocked the sitting room wall into the dining room, there was an early morning earth tremor in Ireland, which was very unusual. Poor Mam was lying in bed thinking, 'Holy Jesus, I'm after knocking down the wall, I must have disturbed the foundations. What have I done! The whole house is going to come tumbling down.' She was terrified that the house next door was going to fall as well and she'd be responsible for a terrible calamity.

After Mam ran out of creative ideas for a house, it was time to move on. 'I've had enough of this, let's go,' she'd say. Mam then put the house on the market, and the family would be off and the whole process would start again in a new place. Each house would be left in a far better state than she found it and the auctioneers who came out to view them often remarked to her, 'You should go into interior design.' I think she would have been brilliant on one of those before-and-after DIY shows.

Each new house we moved to was better than the last, which was all part of Mam's great ambition. She wanted to provide us with the best that she and Dad could afford and then some. And she showed incredible determination in achieving her ambitions. If Mam wanted something, she went out and got it. But everything she did was done within our budget. If she didn't have the money she'd utilise whatever was there. She'd take a door from upstairs and move it downstairs.

'Take down that wood door, I want a glass door there,' she'd say. And on and on it went.

Woe betide anyone or anything that spoiled one of her beautiful homes. Like most kids, we were always pestering mam and dad for a dog. Mam was adamant that she wasn't going to allow animals into her lovely home. 'There will be no animals in this house, I have five pups and that's enough,' she'd say. But eventually she grew tired of listening to our pleadings and, just for a bit of peace and quiet, she relented. One day we arrived home from school to find a new family member.

I was so excited I could hardly speak. I just stood there wide-eyed. 'Is this ours? Is this really ours?' I squealed.

A terrified little puppy was lying in a box in the sitting room, looking up at me with two big sorrowful eyes. I fell in love straight away. Blondie was a three-month-old sheep dog. I'll never know why I called him Blondie, as he was all black with a white patch.

I hated going off to school the next morning and every

morning after and having to leave him behind. 'Why can't he come with me?' I'd ask sulkily and whisper in his ear that I'd be back soon, before dragging my reluctant feet along the pavement to school. Every evening I'd come bounding through the door shouting, 'Blondie! Blondie! Blondie!', and he'd come racing to meet me.

As Blondie started to get bigger, he would wriggle out of my arms when I was trying to cuddle him. One day he struggled free from my grip and hit the ground hard, letting out a little whine. He limped away feeling sorry for himself. I felt awful that I had hurt him, even though it hadn't been intentional. When I came home from school the following evening, Mam broke the bad news to me. Blondie was gone.

'He went off today and never came back, Ronan,' she told me.

I was devastated. 'It's all my fault for hurting his foot,' I said. 'He's run away from me.'

I insisted that we had to look for him. We did everything except put out a request for 'Missing – Blondie' on *Garda Patrol*. Gar and myself went around the neighbourhood pinning up notices in shop windows and even on trees. We described what he looked like and wrote, 'If you see this dog, please call this number.' Every time the phone rang I'd jump up, hoping it was some good news. But days and then weeks passed without a word. Blondie, my pride and joy, never returned. I knew that was the last we'd see of pets in our house. I was heartbroken and continued to blame myself for his decision to run away. 'I'm sorry, Blondie,' I said to myself over and over again.

It was many years later that I learned the truth. Mam had

been fed up of Blondie messing in every single room in the house, so she had found a new home for him. And I had carried that guilt all those years!

Mam had a restless energy and a strong ambition for all her family. There were always more barriers – or walls – to be knocked down, more goals to achieve. Like her, I believe that taking on new challenges is what makes life worth living. Her burning drive was passed to her children – all my siblings have worked hard and achieved success. As kids we were always on the move, always the new ones in the area and we learnt how to make new friends which, as we've all travelled around the world, we've found a great skill to have. And we've all also joined in the quest for the dream home! Ciaran, who has been married for eight years, is currently on his fourth house and I've already moved a couple of times myself, between the UK and Ireland.

The first of the many moves that happened after my arrival was when I was only a year old. We pulled up our roots in the Wilson Estate and moved to Bayside, also on the northside of the city and closer to Sutton and Howth, both of which were better class areas. So as far as Mam was concerned we were going in the right direction!

Our new home in Bayside was a three-bed semi-detached. It was just a little bigger than the one in the Wilson Estate, which was probably another reason for the move. There was a very large back bedroom, so Dad partitioned it off with timber and turned it into two rooms. Bunk beds were installed in one and that became my room along with Gar. Mam had a great sense of style, so everything matched in the room. Being a boys' room, it had blue wallpaper and blue matching duvets and sheets. One of the advantages of being the only girl in the family was that Linda got a room all to herself. Not that we minded. Everything was pink and, for some odd reason, it always seemed to be a lot neater than our bedroom. I don't think I ever heard Mam scream, 'Linda, would you ever tidy up your room!' But she had a constant battle on her hands trying to get us to sort out the mess we created in our bedrooms.

I have good memories of Bayside. It wasn't a well-to-do area, but neither was it the mean streets of Dublin, nor the stuff of *Angela's Ashes*. Admittedly, it was a concrete jungle, with houses packed closely together. But everyone knew everyone and you'd always see familiar faces at church on Sunday. You'd talk to people in the shops and streets and there was a strong sense of community. We had great neighbours there and I made some good friends that I still see to this day, like Declan Murphy, who always reminds me of rampaging round the neighbourhood.

We were a large family for our street, as most of our neighbours had only two or three kids. We were the real Catholic family – overrun with children! Because of the age gap between each of the Keating siblings, we all had our own set of friends. Between us, we knew everyone in our area. The house was a busy, noisy one, particularly with four boisterous boys and their friends hanging around the place, slamming doors as we came in and out from the street, scrounging food in the kitchen, arguing over the TV or turning up the music. Over the din you'd occasionally hear Mam's voice ringing out with some command: 'If you don't put that coat on a coat hanger I'm throwing it out the back door!'

There was always a terrible row at bedtime because we forever wanted to stay up longer. None of us ever wanted to go to bed. It's totally against the principles of all kids. We used all kinds of tricks to prolong the waking hours. Because the rest of the gang felt that Mam would be more lenient with her youngest boy, they used to send me down from the room to ask her for sandwiches and milk.

'Mam! Ciaran, Linda, Ger and Gar are all starving … and so am I. Can we have some milk and something to eat?'

'That's only an excuse. Now get back up to bed!'

'No Mam, really, they're all starving!'

The poor woman couldn't keep a straight face for long and she'd crack up, giving in to us. She'd always rather say yes to her kids than no. 'Alright, I'll be up in a minute. Now back to bed!'

Loud, rumbling trains raced by on the track at the end of the garden. Just across the road was a cul-de-sac where we played football on the concrete and games like 'squares' and 'tip the can'. There was also a nearby field where games were held on a stretch called the 'lamb chop'. We'd amuse ourselves by playing cops and robbers and cowboys and Indians in the streets and fields, scavenging pieces of wood to use as bows and arrows and make-believe guns.

Perhaps it was an average childhood, mucking around in the streets as trains hurtled by, dodging the odd car, making a noise and getting dirty. But it always felt eventful. Something was always going on and I always ended up having spectacular accidents. My brother Gar, by his own admission, was responsible for most of them. When I was around three years of age, Gar managed to leave me with a broken arm. It wasn't exactly intentional, but he got a slap on the ear for it anyway.

I had crawled underneath one of the bunks, which were at the end of Mam's and Dad's bed. The top one had been removed and I was pushing the base of the other one up and down from underneath. As I did so, for a reason still best known to himself, Gar jumped on to it from our parents' bed and the impact snapped my arm. I screamed out with the pain and bawled my head off.

'What's wrong? What's wrong!' My poor mother came rushing up to the room in a panic.

I was screeching so much I couldn't tell her.

'It wasn't my fault! It wasn't my fault,' Gar was roaring, frantically looking around the room for someone else to blame. Mam picked me up as I continued screaming the roof down.

'Where are you hurt? Where are you hurt?'

As soon as I pointed to my floppy arm she knew it was broken. Then there was a mad dash in to Dublin's Temple Street Children's Hospital where the damage was repaired.

When I arrived home I felt very important with my arm in a plaster. Afterwards, needless to say, I lapped up all the attention, as aunties and sundry local well-wishers dropped by to see the 'poor little fella'.

Gar went into hiding for a long time after that. The rest of the family laugh and claim that today I can look at scars on my body and go, 'That was Gary 1980 … Gary 1981 … Gary 1984 …' Whenever anyone raises the subject, Gar will remark dryly, 'Whatever doesn't kill you makes you stronger.'

To be fair, not all of the accidents were his fault, though. After I got a French-made mountain bike for Christmas, I couldn't wait to get out and do my Evel Knievel stunts on the streets in our neighbourhood. I was flying around corners and showing off to my friends by riding on just the back wheel. But I didn't realise that the brakes were different to my old bike and, as I came to a screeching halt the sudden stop sent me flying over the handlebars. I seemed to hang in the air for an age before landing on the pavement, picking up a serious-looking gash at the back of my head. It was back to the hospital – again! – for a stitch or two and, unfortunately, the cut was in the area of 'the bird's nest', so the doctor had a terrible time trying to cut his way through the thick forest of hair.

The litany of crimes against me continued. One of my friends threw a rock at me when we were out playing and it smashed into my head, splitting it open. He obviously didn't expect to find his target, judging by the look on his face. As he saw the blood gushing from the wound, he was going, 'Oh sorry, Ro! I'm sorry! I'm sorry!' He probably thought he was going to be jailed for attempted murder. Thankfully, all I needed were a couple of stitches and I was fine. I was indestructible.

Gar and myself were closest in age and we hung out together, as we still do. However, there was something about the two of us that created trouble. When I was four or five years of age, Gar and myself were in the bathroom and my dad's electric razor proved to be too much of a temptation to resist. We decided to have a shave – it seemed an amazingly grown-up thing to do. Not deterred by the lack of facial hair to practise on, we set about shaving the small amount of fine, blond fuzz on our arms. When Mam discovered what we'd been up to she was furious. 'That'll grow back ten times thicker and you'll turn into hairy little monkeys,' she said sternly.

I was horrified. Suddenly I had these awful dark visions of becoming Ronan the ugly little monster. Suddenly I started bawling.

No one will like me if I'm a monkey, I thought.

CHAPTER 2

ALL PLAY AND NO WORK

'Star pupil' wasn't a phrase you'd ever hear about me at school. Instead I was constantly told, 'You'll never make anything of yourself, Keating!' I can't say I blame the teachers for forming a low opinion of me. I was one of the class messers; the guy at the back of the school room having a laugh, too busy slagging other guys around me to listen to what the teacher was saying.

In the years I was a student, I don't think the postman ever arrived at my home with a school report that could be flaunted with pride. There was always a comment about 'conduct unbecoming ...'. I wouldn't say I was a teacher's worst nightmare because I wasn't cheeky or disrespectful to the various individuals who had the unenviable job of trying to give me an education. But I wasn't academic in any way. I liked English and was interested in writing poetry, but beyond that I was genuinely and completely bored. It's not something I'm proud of, but that's the way it was.

I started off in Bayside Primary School in Dublin and like a lot of the 'messers' quite enjoyed all that painting and roaring about. I remember one teacher in particular from that school, a Mr Cronin. He was a nice man, very straight and well respected, but I'm not sure he had much time for me because of the giddy way I carried on in class.

But another of my mam's moves took us away from Bayside

and into the country. Lush, rural County Meath was a whole new world for us. The primary school was a tiny little place, with the fourth, fifth and sixth classes all squeezed together in the same room. Although it was only fifty miles from Dublin, to go to County Meath was like going back in time. It was hard for a while, as I had to start making new friends all over again.

Then, just when I'd finally settled in to this funny, small, old-fashioned school, we were back in Bayside after a further move. This now meant another new school – St Fintan's Secondary in Sutton, County Dublin. But after my first year there my family were on the move again back to the country, this time to Dunshaughlin in County Meath. My memories of life in Dunshaughlin are almost entirely happy ones, as I made some good friends in time. But when we first arrived the rural/city divide was *really* evident, even more so than at the primary school. We were older, kids were more judgmental, and from the outset, it was obvious that I wasn't accepted there by many of the guys. To them I was a Dubliner in a country college, with city clothes and a different accent, and they didn't like me straight off.

I'd been there for a few weeks and there'd been comments and cracks but things reached boiling point when one fella in the class challenged me. He was all swagger: 'So you think you're some kind of tough kid? What are you going to do about it?' I remember saying to myself, 'I'm going to have to make my mark here right now or this place will be like a prison. Give your man a hiding and you will be respected, otherwise you'll be ridden for the rest of your life. I'll go for you ... I'll hammer the head off you.'

The guy was about my own height with a skinhead haircut

and he was into the Sex Pistols. He was a little git who needed a slap, that's what I remember most. Puffing myself up, I shouted after him, 'See you after school!'

That afternoon I went to the field at the back of the school when classes ended, but there was no one there. I didn't know what to think. Surely it wouldn't be that easy to see off these country lads? Then I met another kid on the way home who told me that I should have headed for the football pitch. Gearing myself up again for the confrontation, I started running towards the sports fields. The last thing I wanted was for him to think I had chickened out of turning up.

But when I came in sight of the football pitch, my pace suddenly slackened. My enemy was there alright, but he had what seemed like a thousand other kids with him. When they saw me, they pointed and shouted excitedly. Then the huge mass of them spread out and started moving towards me. I slowed to a walk and then stopped dead. I'll never forget that moment, I was scared stiff. But there was no going back. Taking a deep breath, I said to myself, 'Here you go, Ro,' and ran to face him in the middle of the throng. We eyed each other for a few seconds and then I flung my jacket on the ground and launched myself at him, getting digs in straight away.

Driven on by a mixture of fear and bravado, I was soon on top, punching the head off him, really killing him. The gangs of kids had moved back to form a circle around us, but just as I was about to claim victory, a mate of my opponent stepped forward to intervene. This was a guy from fifth year who would have been about sixteen years old, whereas I was in first year and aged twelve. It was a totally unequal contest, and it was mercifully short. He immediately put the boot in to me, kicking me in the stomach and I fell to the ground, all the wind knocked out of me.

That was the end of the battle as at that moment the teachers arrived panting on the scene and pulled us apart. I was told on the spot that I was suspended. Before I'd even got my breath back, I had been hauled inside and a letter had been written, explaining the situation to my parents. I'll never forget the journey home from school that day. It was the longest walk of my life. I was crying my eyes out, thinking about that letter in my shirt pocket and how my mother was going to react. I knew she would be furious. I could hear the words ringing in my head already, 'Ronan Keating! I thought I had taught you some manners!'

It was the thought of letting Mam down that was the biggest cause of my upset.

She knew by the look on my face coming in the door that something was up. I started to bawl my head off as I told how I had been picked on by the school bully, how everyone had ganged up on me and there had been a terrible row. 'I've been blamed and it wasn't my fault,' I wailed, not entirely honestly.

The tears worked. Mam made me some tea, sat me down and listened to my tale of woe and was sympathetic. It was only a temporary suspension and, after that row, I never had trouble from anyone in the school again. Maybe the determined way I had set about that little git had done the trick after all.

Mam opened a hair salon when we first moved to Dunshaughlin. Straight away she had all the young guys coming in looking for a shaved head. Using a 'razor number one', 'number two' and 'number three' was all new to Mam, but obviously she had to move with the times if she was going to do business. Up to then, she had been an old-fashioned hairdresser; setting about grannies and young lads alike with scissors and a comb. But now I became the guinea pig for her newfangled razor, and my brother Gerard offered to show Mam how to use it. Quite what made him think he was an expert, and my Mam believe it, is still a mystery to me. As soon as the whirring beast had touched my head, I knew he'd made a terrible mess of it. I already had a short haircut to begin with; now I had two bald patches that stood out a mile. I ended up going out in public around Dunshaughlin with two plasters stuck to the back of my crown until the hair grew back!

Obviously, the reason for my 'wounds' had to be kept a closely guarded secret around the village for the sake of my mother's business. I told everyone that I had been hit by a pole and it had caused two gashes to my head. Despite the weak subterfuge Mam's business did a roaring trade in the area because she was a great hairdresser. Whenever I got a new style, I'd advertise it in the school. 'Go to my Ma, she'll do it for you,' I'd tell the rest of the kids. Marie's Unisex Hair Salon was pitched above a butcher's shop in the village with access through a small ground floor door. It was a cosy little place. You made your way up stairs, where a sliding door welcomed you into the tiny salon, which was just big enough to contain one wash basin and three places for people to sit and have their hair styled. There was lino on the floor and out the back was a small kitchenette for making teas and coffees.

I used to help out in the salon when I was off school, sweeping up the hair. I washed a few old ladies' heads as well, always being careful to stick cotton wool in their ears to stop the water from getting in and making their hearing even worse.

I finished my secondary school education back in St Fintan's in Sutton, where my cousin Trevor was already a pupil. Compared with me, he was a fairly conscientious student. Trev lived very near the school and went home daily for his lunch. I was always hassling him, 'What are you doing, Trev, are you going home? I'm going with you.' It was a far better option than staying in school for lunch.

So we'd go to his house and every single day for two years his mother would give us a Superquinn burger and soup. These days I joke about that with Trev's mother, my aunt Irene. She's my mam's sister and we're very close. As well as being sisters, Mam and herself were best friends. They were identical in every way, the two of them, with the same mannerisms and humour and energy. Irene is like a mother to me now and she's now the one who worries about me the way Mam used to.

Some mornings I would travel from my home in Swords to Trev's house in Sutton so that we could walk to school together. There were times when I arrived, only to be told by Irene, 'Oh, Ronan, he's not well, so he's not going in today.' I'd gallantly offer to stay with him, and then head for the sitting room and plonk myself down in front of whatever was on the TV. Often there would be nothing but old films or horse racing, but anything was better than school. Trev would be upstairs in bed when I'd arrive, but it wouldn't be long before he'd join me downstairs.

Sometimes we just lazed around and listened to music. The day seemed to fly by and then I'd go home and my mam would be none the wiser.

'How was school today?'

'Fine.'

That was pretty shameless. On other occasions I'd pounce on the slightest excuse, a bit of a headache or a cold, to stay out of school and, shut away in the bedroom, I'd spend my time listening to music. I was never at school enough and when I was there, I was never on time. There always seemed to be something better to do. Even doing nothing was better! These days if I'm twenty seconds late I get annoyed.

In some respects I regret wasting my time at school. I would like to be more confident now with maths and know a little more geography, in particular. I've been to so many places around the world it would have been good to have learnt a bit about them at school. But, with the exception of English, I simply had no interest in it all. It would be very neat to say that all my lazy days at home spent listening to music acted as a different kind of education, But, come on, that's not really the case, is it? That I'm doing music now is very lucky and I wouldn't recommend all that bunking to anyone. If I hadn't been fortunate enough to travel and meet extraordinary people, I would know very little by now.

What I lacked in competitiveness and ambition in the classroom though, I made up for on the sports field. Long before music became my motivation in life, Gaelic football and athletics were my driving force. I lived for them. It was all about being a winner, being number one at something that I felt really passionate about.

I had to be the best at whatever I did, and if I wasn't I lost interest and moved on to something else. If I wasn't first then I wasn't happy. First is first … second didn't count for anything as far as I was concerned. In football, if I wasn't midfield then I didn't want to play. Call it petulance or call it ambition, that's the way I was put together.

As a kid I was a performer, a tryer. This stood me in good stead for the challenges of Gaelic football, where you need to be able to handle yourself in physical encounters. It also helped that I was always big for my age and fast too. I started off playing Gaelic football with Raheny GAA Club on the northside of Dublin when I was ten. Within a couple of years the family had moved to Dunshaughlin in County Meath. There I joined the local Gaelic football team and got a taste of the big time when we reached the Under-14 GAA Meath County Football Final.

For us boys that day was like the Wembley Cup Final. I'll never forget the buzz. I felt puffed up with pride and excitement – I was the midfield player, and had a starring role. As we made our way onto the pitch, each of us looked around to see where our families were amongst the spectators, and steeled ourselves for a great effort. We were all fired up and played out of our skins, but, in the end, our heroic efforts didn't match the form and skill of our opponents and, after the game had flowed backwards and forwards countless times, we finally got trounced. In time you learn that sometimes things don't go your way, whatever your efforts. But when you're only a kid it seems like the end of the world.

'Don't worry, Ro, there'll be other days,' said Dad.

'Yeah, right!' I growled, utterly gutted and kicked off in a sulk.

Because we moved home so much, I got the opportunity to play with different clubs. When we moved to the Hill of Tara in County Meath, I joined the local Skryne GAA Club and in 1992 I was caught up in a vital Under-15 match with them. Our opponents were my old club, Dunshaughlin, and it was a hot-blooded battle. From the outset it was clear that it was going to be a no-holds-barred contest. Once again, I was playing in the midfield and there were a lot of fairly physical tangles. Then, during one heated clash, a free kick was awarded in my favour and my opponent literally threw the ball into my face in anger. There was no way I was going to let my adolescent pride stand for that. I never turned the other cheek and would never let anyone get the better of me. 'Right,' I spat, 'You're not feckin' gettin' away with that.'

Without a moment's pause, I went over and loafed him one. He hit the ground like a ton of bricks. At this point my brain caught up with the rest of me, and I realised that the referee had been watching everything. He had no hesitation in sending me off the field. To make matters worse, the father of the guy I hit was a Garda and he was standing on the sideline beside my dad, who was obviously embarrassed, to say the least. Only seconds after the punch, things got really out of control. The guy's father came haring onto the pitch towards me, pointing and shouting. Still in a red mist, I started running directly at him, crying, 'Come on! Come on!' His expression changed in an instant from anger to alarm, when he saw a punch-drunk Keating bearing down on him and he turned and sprinted back to the crowd. Then some other fellow on the opposite side of the field started screaming and shouting at me, so I ran for him too. Eventually my father intervened, pulled me off the pitch, put me in the car and drove me home in disgrace. He was furious with me – and so were the Gaelic Football authorities. I was officially suspended from playing football for three whole months.

If someone wound me up during a match, I would always go for them big time, no bother. I was well behaved on the pitch until someone tried it on with me. If they crossed me or fouled me, then they'd know all about it.

Since I was big for my age, I was a member of the Skryne GAA Club's Under-15, Under-16 and Under-18 teams at the same time. One golden day I scored the winning goal for Skryne in the Under-16 Meath County semi-final against Duleek. At that moment I thought life couldn't get any better. I loved every minute I spent out on the football pitch. It was my early taste of the limelight, the first time I experienced that roar of a crowd, those blurred grinning faces cheering me on. I revelled in it. I'd hear the supporters shouting from the sideline, 'Go on Keating! Go on you good thing, Keating!' and I felt special. That's what kept me going.

At that point there was a very real prospect of a career in athletics, my other great sporting love. There was the chance of winning a scholarship to the States and I made the Irish team in my age group for the 200 metres, 400 metres and 800 metres. I managed to win quite a few races locally and was running against people who went on to become successful international competitors. As with my Gaelic football, Dad was always supportive and happy to drive me to athletic meetings however far away they were. On one occasion, though, in June 1990, there was an All-Ireland meeting in Waterford that gave us quite a scare.

It was my first outing with the Dunshaughlin Athletics Club and I was competing in the Under-13s. On the Saturday my dad drove me down to Waterford for the qualifying races. I put everything into it. Every bit of energy I had and I did well. I made it through to both the 200 metres and the 800 metres finals, which were to be held the following day. We drove back to Dunshaughlin that same night – a round trip of about 200 miles. The following morning we were up at the crack of dawn and on our way to Waterford again. During the races, cheered on like mad by my parents, I pushed myself hard and came out with a gold in the 200 metres and a bronze in the 800. The club, who had never won a national competition, were delighted, and I could tell my parents were bursting with pride. I was pleased, but seriously exhausted and on the homeward journey I began to feel sick. Dad stopped at a shop and bought me a bottle of water and after a while the horrible queasiness went away. But the following day I suddenly took ill with headaches and I started throwing up in the early hours of the morning.

'Mam!' I called, 'I'm ill. I don't feel well.'

She came into my room and felt my forehead. She looked worried sick.

'We'll have to take him to the hospital. I'm worried about that headache,' she said to Dad. It was two in the morning, but they weren't going to take any chances. They got dressed and rushed me by car to the local Blanchardstown Hospital. Mam and Dad hadn't said it in front of me, but they were terrified that it might be meningitis.

The doctors kept me in the hospital until the following Thursday and carried out a whole variety of tests, but they never discovered the cause of the problem. It could have been the stress of the travelling and the competitions. It was probably exhaustion! Whatever it was, I recovered and I was so happy when I left the hospital that Thursday. Dad tells me now how I was bouncing around the back seat of the car singing at the top of my voice 'I'm back on my feet again', my favourite song at the time from *Top of the Pops*.

I kept at the athletics for some years, and at one point there was the possibility of scouts coming over from Iona University, where my brother Gar was at the time, to check me out. But in my heart I knew that it wasn't what I really wanted and I started to care less and less. As soon as the total commitment was lost, so too was the willpower to do the daily training.

I was listening to all sorts of music at that stage. My brothers had exposed me to very different artists, from Squeeze to A-Ha, The Police to Cat Stevens. And as I got more and more into music, I gradually lost interest in sport.

The music came naturally to me in a way that the sport no longer did.

Every summer, without fail, Mam and Dad would take the whole gang off on a holiday around Ireland. Each year it would begin like an adventure and as the week unfolded there'd be no end of dramas and disasters. Large families always create their own special mayhem. We would set off as dawn was breaking, all over-excited, all squeezed like sardines into Dad's tiny car. For years he had a two-door, gold-coloured Ford Escort saloon, a real old one – not one of the biggest motors in the world. I doubt the designers expected it to have to carry seven. As I was the smallest and lightest, I would lie across Ciaran, Gerard, Gary and Linda in the back. Sometimes I would even be squeezed into the space just below the back window, which I loved because I had it all to myself. When the sun shone it was like an oven.

The journeys seemed to take forever. I have travelled to the other side of the world and it's never felt as long as one of those family trips. Inevitably we wouldn't be half an hour into the four-hour trip, and barely on the outskirts of Dublin city, when there'd be a chorus of, 'Are we nearly there yet?' from us kids. Cramped in the back, we rattled across Ireland, rowing all the way. 'He's sticking his elbow in me! He's pushing me!' we whined from the back seat. As the car bumped down the country roads, there were times when we were killing each other in the back, punching the heads off each other. Mam would turn around and warn, 'If you lot don't behave yourselves we'll turn around and go back home. There'll be no holiday.'

That would keep us quiet for at least five minutes. But there was a limit to how much real mischief we could create shut up in a car. It was a different story at the end of the journey when our natural gift for creating trouble could really shine.

True to form Mam was very particular about the bed and breakfast guesthouses we stayed in. She would go in to view the bedrooms before deciding whether or not to check in. The whole place had to be spick and span, impeccably hygienic and, of course, the standard of the decor was always of major importance. And if she saw a cat or a dog in the house, she'd be out of there as quick as lightning. Animals and my mother were never going to be a good combination.

On one trip, we arrived in Ballybunion, a quiet holiday resort town in County Kerry, and while Mam was off giving the rooms a thorough checking, Gary and myself waited downstairs in reception. Within moments, we were bored and fidgety, and as usual we were soon messing about and fighting. Gary, older and cooler, suddenly decided he was tired of me and made a great show of plonking himself into a wicker chair in the corner. The chair shot back, crashed into a table behind and knocked over a huge ornate vase. It went smashing to the ground.

Our hearts stopped. We stared horror-stricken at the shattered remains of what had looked like a fantastically expensive ornament. What could be the punishment for so terrible a crime? Visions of long prison stretches flashed through my mind. Gar, my dear brother, in a desperate bid to save his own skin, shouted in his loudest voice, 'Ro is after breaking the vase!'

'What are you talking about! I was here and you were over there!' I protested.

Before any more accusations could be thrown about, Mam and the landlady were back downsatirs. When Mam saw what had happened, I could tell straightaway that she was absolutely mortified. The landlady was all reassurance: 'Oh, don't worry about it. Don't worry about it.' But Mam was too embarrassed to be consoled. Unable to look the landlady in the face, she said through tight lips, 'We'll stay tonight and we'll be back in a couple of hours.' Of course, the poor woman never saw us again. On the way to the car, Gar was still insisting: 'It was Ro, Ma, nothing to do with me. It was Ro's fault.'

Little good it did him. We were both got a slap on the ear.

During a holiday in County Cavan we were staying in a bed and breakfast and Gary and myself were in our pyjamas, just about to go to bed. This was obviously the last chance of the day to cause trouble, and the plan on this occasion was for me to hide in a large wardrobe in the hall and jump out at Dad when he came past. Well, it seemed like a good idea at the time.

Once the plot was hatched, we were quickly into action. Gar helped me climb in and shut the doors, one of which had a heavy old mirror hanging on the inside. Gar was to wait and give me a signal for my surprise exit. It was smaller inside the wardrobe than it had looked from the outside and full of musty old jackets and shoes. There was silence for a few moments. I waited. Maybe Gar had wandered off leaving me behind. I tried to push open the doors to have a peek out. They were stuck. God! I couldn't get out. I got all short of breath as the darkness closed in. Help! Let me out! I started thrashing about, making the flimsy wardrobe rock and roll about. I hammered at the doors and shrieked and kicked. The next moment the whole lot came crashing down onto its front, trapping me inside.

Gary, who had all along been waiting outside with a studied look of innocence on his face, watched in horror as the big, wooden structure seemed to come tumbling forward in slow motion. When it hit the bedroom floor with a loud bang, he was terrified that I had been really badly hurt – and he'd get the blame. He had visions of my face being ripped to shreds from shards of glass from the heavy mirror, which he had heard smash. By this stage I was screeching and crying, desperate to get out. I thought I'd be trapped forever.

Gar eventually managed to push the wardrobe upright and I fell out of the doors sobbing. I lay there in a heap and heard Gar begin to snigger. What with all my crying and the ruined wardrobe and my panic about being buried alive, I was soon hiccupping with giggles and tears too.

Many of our family's summer holidays were spent in County Kerry, which is a really beautiful part of Ireland. We regularly went to Killarney, a popular holiday town famous for its lakes and dramatic scenery. But that wasn't the main attraction. Back in the days when Boyzone were just a twinkle in our parents' eyes, Joe Dolan was a major star on the international scene. He had a big UK chart hit in the sixties with a song called 'Make Me an Island' and he's still something of a legend in Ireland today. Mam was always a huge fan of Joe and, for as long as I can remember, he has had a summer residency there at the Killarney Glen Eagle Hotel. Hearing Joe sing was one of Mam and Dad's treats. Looking back I think they deserved a few.

I'm not sure we ever gave it a rest. We were standing outside the guesthouse one day, and my brother Gerard, who had just got a new camera, said to me, 'Ronan, go up and kick Dad on the shin and I'll take a photograph.' I was only four years old at the time, so really I had no sense and I did exactly as I was asked.

While Gerard waited, camera at the ready, I ran up and lashed out with my foot, landing a ferocious blow to Dad's shin. As he doubled over in agony, Gerard took aim and fired off a classic family photo. There's Dad, his face contorted with pain, rubbing his leg while trying to grab me. 'Come back here Ronan Keating! Come back!' he shouted.

'I will not,' I roared back, running as fast as I could.

We seemed to be intent on breaking each other's bones. And while we were playing golf in Killarney, I managed to give Dad a corker of a black eye with one of the clubs. Throughout the game, he had been warning us, 'Don't ever stand behind anyone when they're swinging a club.' Later, while I was taking a shot, I swung back, walloping him around the eye and almost splitting his face. He had an awful cut, but he knew better than to give me the chance to say he should have followed his own advice.

We always went riding in Killarney on deranged horses from the local stables. Gerard got up on one, one day, and it just took off. I was laughing my head off as both the horse and Gerard disappeared behind a tree. When the animal came out the other side there was no sign of Gerard. It turned out he was hanging on for his life down the other side of the saddle after being knocked off by the branches. It took us a while to spot him.

But Gerard had a bit of a way with horses. On another occasion, he and I were on a horse together, I was sitting in front and he had his feet in the stirrups. For once the horse seemed at least partly under control and we were bumping along quite happily. Then we came to a large log lying across the path. We spotted it at the same time. 'Gerard, we're not going to jump the log!' I shouted over my shoulder.

He said, 'We're going to jump the log!'

I said, 'Don't jump the log, Gerard!' But it was too late. As the horse took off into the air with a great leap, I lost my grip and went flying off, dragging Gerard with me. We both ended up in a ditch, with muck and water up to our necks, me saying to Gerard 'That's another mess that's your fault,' like a junior Laurel and Hardy.

Any Sunday on a Bank Holiday weekend Mam might announce, 'We're going to Knock.' Knock is a place of pilgrimage in County Mayo where the Blessed Virgin is said to have appeared. People go there to pray, to do penance for their sins, or in the hope of being cured of their ailments. The journey would take up to four hours each way and we'd return home the same day. In the cramped little car, it was an incredibly exhausting trip, particularly as the roads weren't as developed as they are today – a multi-lane motorway was something you only saw on American TV shows. We'd go to Knock, say a few prayers, fill bottles with holy water, turn round and come back again.

It seemed like the waste of a day to us kids at the time but now I realised how important it was to do these things together. That was exactly as Mam wanted it and I'm sure that's one of the reasons there is such a strong bond between the five of us today. Sunday was always a family day. You couldn't make the excuse that you wanted to play with your friends. It was into the car with everyone and off you went. 'Ah, Mam, can I stay home and play with my friends?' we'd ask.

'No!'

'Oh, go on!'

No! Get in that car right now!'

Once we were on the road, any plan could pop into Mam's head. 'Let's go to Meath and look at houses,' she'd suddenly pipe up. And off we'd go, trundling around the narrow country roads. So Gar and I would be reduced to bashing each other in the back seat with frustration. But at the end of the trip, they would find a little country pub where we'd stop for drinks and snacks and at last our parents would be allowed some peace and quiet.

The El Molino, a Country Club Hotel outside Drogheda, County Louth, was another favourite destination for our family on a Sunday afternoon. One of my memories of that venue is the large, artificial pond located just inside the main door. It was teeming with goldfish, which always fascinated us and we used to hang around watching them. But for someone as accident-prone as me, that pond was a disaster waiting to happen.

Sure enough, one evening I tripped and fell as I was running by the pond and went headfirst into the water on top of the fish, fully clothed. The rest of the gang thought that was hilarious, but I didn't know whether to laugh or to cry. What the smart owners of the club thought about this new arrival in their water feature is anyone's guess. No doubt Mam was embarrassed enough for everyone.

After our trips, on Sunday evenings we'd regularly visit Nanny Culleton in Raheny. She was a small woman with black curly hair and a big heart just like my mother. I feel sad for the fact that I never got to know her husband, Grandad Culleton because I was often told that I'm like him. Sometimes I'd say or do something and Mam would look at me and say with a smile, 'You're just like my father.' Gar and myself were keen visitors at Nanny's as we'd always get tea and biscuits and sweets. What's more, she'd give us fifty pence or a pound each before we'd leave, and for a day or two, before we got to the shops, we'd feel rich.

After visiting Grandma's we'd go down to the local sports club or the Old Shieling Hotel in Raheny. Mam's brothers and sisters would be there as well, so they'd have a drink while we hung out with all our cousins. We really were a close-knit group.

The hotel was a very old, rambling building with lots of corridors and little nooks and crannies. For young boys, it was the perfect place to go exploring.

'Ro, let's go down here!' Gar would say, and we'd be off.

Each time we'd find something new – a corridor behind a doorway or a flight of stairs climbing crookedly into a dusty attic. Needless to say, notices saying 'Private' or 'Staff Only' were blindly ignored. So many times we nearly got the whole family thrown out of the hotel when we were caught in rooms we shouldn't have been in. 'What are you boys up to there?' a loud voice startled us one evening as we were creeping about at the top of the building.

'Nothing, sir!' I answered, turning around to see a large man with a pot belly, glasses and a big red face staring down at us.

'We're just looking,' Gar added helpfully.

'How did you get in here?'

'D-d-d-don't know.'

'Up to no good, the pair of you. Now back to where you came from!'

We scurried down corridors and stairs until we found ourselves back in the lounge where the adults were enjoying their drinks. Then we tried our hardest to look like we'd been there all the time. That had been a close one.

Of course, I was just following Gar's lead! It's just that he always led me slap-bang into trouble. But I'm sure we found places in the Shieling that even the owners were unaware existed.

I also got a taste of life down on the farm when we went to Cavan to visit my dad's mother, Granny Keating. I never knew my grandfather on that side either, as he had died before I came along. But I saw a lot of Granny Keating and I loved those visits.

There was always a great welcome in her home for us kids.

Granny Keating was a small woman, just slightly taller than my other granny, and she had curly hair and wore glasses. She had a strong country accent and she was your perfect grandmother, with huge warmth and an endless love of kids.

Before we arrived she must have been baking for days. Going in the door you'd get the gorgeous smell of freshly-made cakes and tarts and the kettle was always on the boil.

It was a real novelty for us city kids being down on a farm and seeing all the animals close up. But I remember how we were always very wary of them, as we had no idea whether they were wild or tame.

One day Gar and myself were out in the fields when we spotted some the cows in the distance.

'Gar!' I said, 'I don't like the way they're looking at us.'

'What are you afraid of, Ro? I'm sure cows don't attack people.'

'Are you sure, Gar?' I was unconvinced. These beasts looked awfully big.

'Of course I'm sure, Ro.' Well, that was alright then. If my big brother says so…

Just then some of the cows made a sudden move in our direction. First one then the whole herd.

I stood rooted to the spot. I looked to Gar for help. As usual he led by example:

'Run Ro! Run for your life!' Gar screamed back at me, leaving a trail of dust – and his little brother – in his wake.

CHAPTER 3

THE REAL WORLD

I turned the key in the ignition and powered up the car. It was my first time behind the wheel of a car and my heart was pounding. As the engine started I felt a flood of adrenaline that seemed to turn my stomach upside down. Being a fourteen-year-old car fanatic, I had been just dying for the opportunity to have a go at driving and when it came I didn't think twice about it. Taking a deep breath I shifted into first gear, just as I had watched Dad do a thousand times, and gingerly put my foot on the accelerator. I heard the crunching of the gravel under the wheels as the motor moved forward and laughed and whooped with the kick of it.

But still I was terrified. 'What if the Garda see me and pull me over? What would Mam and Dad say?' Best not to think about it. It was far too late now to be having second thoughts about my actions. I was already motoring through the neighbourhood, past the shops and over the lights. It's a wonder I didn't attraction the attention of the police because I was driving so slowly. Thankfully, it all went like clockwork and after my little tour I returned the car safely to the spot where it had been parked.

'Wow! I did it. I actually drove a car,' I thought as I took the keys from the ignition, stepped out and closed the door behind me. No one ever knew about my little escapade that day.

I suppose there's a bit of a rebel in everyone when you come into your teens, and I was no exception. It's not that I caused any heartache for my parents, or was radically different to the person I am today. Good manners had been instilled in me by Mam, but I was wild in other ways. It helped that my mother and father didn't know half the antics I got up to.

When I was thirteen years old I decided it was about time I had a proper drink. We were living in Tara, County Meath, and our parents were away for the weekend. Unsurprisingly, it was Gar who came up with the idea of organising a party in the house for all his mates. When they arrived, they seemed to have brought the entire contents of the off-licence with them, and it soon turned into a wild affair. Cans and bottles littered the surfaces, and there were cigarette ends in pot plants and snogging couples in the garden.

I hung around eyeing the beer and sure enough, in the end, one of Gar's pals said, 'Here, Ro, have a can!'

'Yeah! Sure … thanks!' I said. Hey, this is great, I thought, I'm not being treated like some little kid. I'm in with the gang here.

It's not a night I'll forget. There I was slugging from my can of Heineken and dancing around in our front room, loud music blaring from the stereo. Eventually Gar's friends soon stopped being so generous with their cans, so I went in search of my own booze, having developed a bit of a taste for it. This was the moment when it all started to go wrong. After a bit of a search, I finally located a full bottle of Frangelico, a hazelnut liqueur (if you've never come across it, don't worry, you're not missing out, believe me).

'Yeah! This will do,' I thought, as I searched for a penknife to open it. Inconveniently, the manufacturer had made the bottle with a plastic dispenser at the top, which only allowed a certain amount to be poured at one time. I got a knife, pulled out the gadget and – gulp! – down it all went.

Everything was fine for a while. I found myself laughing at nothing in particular, talking to anyone and everyone, thinking I was the life and soul. But soon the party seemed to be taking place in the distance, the crowd began to swim in front of me and my head started to spin. As I felt my stomach rising up to my throat, I stumbled towards the loo and the next thing I had my head stuck into the toilet bowel, throwing up so much I thought I'd turn inside out.

I stumbled towards the bed, overcome with the worst sick feeling I'd ever experienced. Obviously I wasn't just drunk. I was dying. I seemed to have lost all control of my body. I threw up again, this time all over the bed and as I staggered around I pulled down some curtains while trying to stay on my feet. To be honest, I don't remember the half of it. Apparently at this point I went missing. Eventually even Gar noticed that his little brother had disappeared, and he searched the whole house. No Ro! Had anyone seen a very blond, very drunk boy dancing about? Then someone said, 'Yeah, some little guy went outside to throw up.'

Gar opened the front door to find me on the doorstep, in my underwear, huddled in a quilt, quietly continuing to be extremely sick.

'Oh Gar! I'm sick,' I muttered, as if he wouldn't have noticed.

'Jesus, Ro, you're a mess. Mam and Dad will kill us,' said Gar. I'm not sure whether he was more concerned about my well-being or his own skin.

I wasn't Gar's only problem. The house, my poor mother's pride and joy, looked a complete mess. As well as the damage to the curtains, someone had also broken the toilet (it could have been me as well for all I knew) and there was an unidentified flood in the bathroom. It was a mad scramble to get things back in shape before our Mam and Dad turned up. In the end, we got away with it, just about. But if anyone even offers me Frangelico they're likely to have an instant mess on their hands.

It was later in that same eventful year that I had my first experience of the forbidden delights of a nightclub, whilst I was on holiday in Killarney with Mam, Dad and Gar. Mam and Dad went out on their own one night and left me in the 'care' of Gar, who was then eighteen years old to my thirteen. Gar decided to go to a local disco and he said I could come along too, as I looked older than my age.

When we arrived at the venue, the stern-looking doormen in black suits scrutinised us and then said to Gar, 'You're alright. You can go ahead in. He can't, he's under age.'

I puffed up my chest and stood as straight as I could, trying to look more mature. 'Ah, lads, I'm old enough,' I protested.

'What's your date of birth?' one of the doormen snapped back at me, which is a standard bouncer trick, and one I should have been ready for.

For some strange reason the only date of birth I had in my head was my much elder brother, Ciaran's. 'The first of the twelfth, 1965,' I replied without hesitation. For a moment I thought I had the situation licked.

'So, you're older than I am!' The bigger of the two bouncers smirked.

I knew then I was on a loser and there was no way these guys were going to let me in. But then Gary, ever the big bro, intervened, promising, 'Look, he's with me, he's my brother, he'll be alright, I'll look after him.'

Reluctantly, they let me pass and I was on my way into a whole new world – the disco. The entire place was packed and seemed to shake with the music, as multi-coloured lights flashed about overhead. I loved feeling part of the crush of people, all drinking, laughing and dancing about. Gary was obviously able to drink legally, but I certainly wasn't. Still, it didn't stop me. I only had a couple of bottles of Corona, but that was quite enough to get me well on my way.

Everything was fine until the end of the night when I left the club, then my legs turned to jelly and something strange happened to my coordination. Gar looked at me with some concern, even though he was by now somewhat under the weather himself. 'Walk that line!' he demanded.

No matter how hard I tried, I couldn't manage to stay on the straight and narrow.

'Shit! Mam and Dad will kill me,' Gar sighed. 'Go over to that café across the road and get yourself some coffee.'

'Ri-ight Ga-Gaa-ar!'

Ten minutes later I arrived back. 'Ga-ar!' I stuttered.

'What?'

'There's no cof-fee!'

'Well go and get some tea for God's sake!'

So off I go again, rocking and swaying across the road. Five minutes later I arrived back.

'Ga-ar!'

'What, Ronan?'

'I don't like tea, Gar!'

He shook his head at me with frustration. 'Let's go,' he said, pointing the way forward, and then grabbing me as I lurched towards a lamp post. Even though he had been drinking a lot at the disco, the booze didn't seem to have affected him the way it hit me. The next morning was a different story. I woke up feeling fine, while Gar, in the bed opposite me, was dying with a hangover.

There was a baffled look on his face and his jaw dropped as he saw me bouncing around, full of the joys of life. I was a bit surprised myself by my healthy condition, considering the state I'd been in the night before. I clearly still wasn't all there, though. There was a Bible by the bed and I picked it up and began my best priest impression, reading it out very loud and serious in made-up Latin! I could always crack Gar up.

Some young people go through hell and back during adolescence, but I promise you I hardly have any bad memories at all. I got spots like everyone else, but they never bothered me. I wasn't self-conscious about them. I didn't get involved in big, heavy romances, as music and sport were my main interests, so I didn't have all that trauma. I was late away from the post in that area. The teen years were a good time for me, except for one thing – the slow shrinkage of our family. The break up of the Keating Seven, as my brothers Ciaran, Gerard and Gary, and sister, Linda, joined the exodus of young Irish who flocked to the States in search of work, was the only real sadness. There was massive unemployment in Ireland then and the country was experiencing what was described as the 'Brain Drain', bright young students who were leaving in their droves.

It didn't matter what they called it. It was a tough time for the family.

Ciaran was the first to go. People used to talk about the 'emigrant wake' and we had one of those for him, a 'going away' party with all the aunties, uncles and cousins invited. That day was probably one of the bleakest times in our house. I got the day off school (legally, for a change) and we all went to the airport to say goodbye. To me, going to the States then was like a journey to the other end of the world.

As Ciaran disappeared into the departures area of the airport, Mam could restrain herself no longer and burst into tears. It was deeply traumatic for her, watching the first member of the family fly the nest. We all went back to the house that day and felt as if there had been a bereavement in the family. There was a big, black cloud hanging over us all.

Of course, it was an exciting time for Ciaran, heading off to make his fortune. As soon as he arrived, he rang Mam. He was with our New York relations, who had offered to help him get started. 'It's brilliant here, Mam,' he told her. 'Don't worry about me. I'll be home to visit before you know it.' I don't think that made it any easier for Mam. Her kids were everything to her.

Ciaran is a real go-getter and he soon got himself sorted with a decent place to live in the Bronx and a good income. He held down two jobs, working as a mechanic by day and a bar-tender by night. He made a lot of money, threw himself into hectic New York life with a great gang of friends and loved every minute of it.

Linda was the next to leave for New York. She, too, must have felt that it was the only way to have a real chance in life. This was also devastating for us, in particular for Mam, as she and Linda were more like sisters than mother and daughter. Once in America, Linda started off serving in bars, but quickly moved into a managerial position. She is a fantastic business woman with great drive and she was head-hunted by lots of different firms out there. The next thing we knew, she had an exclusive restaurant in New York's financial district. Then she became a 'gun for hire', helping people to set up their own new companies.

I always looked forward to Ciaran and Linda coming home on holiday. Apart from anything else, they were rolling in the money and never shy about spending it on me. There were so many times on shopping trips in town when I persuaded Linda to buy that shirt or that jacket or those shoes I had my eye on in one of the city's shop windows.

'Ah go on, Linda, please, I'll look really cool in that!' I'd say.

'I'll have you spoilt, Ronan Keating,' she'd reply.

Then I'd sulk. I hated being told that I was spoilt.

Gerard, too, was to head out to the States. He had been the one in the family who really excelled at athletics and he got a scholarship to Iona College in New York out of it after being spotted by talent scouts. But just when he was gearing up to run in the Olympics, his sports career was cut short when he suffered a hairline fracture to his ankle. Undaunted, Ger delved into the books and rose to the top of his class in business studies.

One day he phoned home to say that he was working in the New York Stock Exchange, ironically as a 'runner'. Within only a few years he'd climbed the ladder to become a broker with Merrill Lynch and then Salomon Smith Barney. I imagined him as a character out of *Wall Street*, and thought of him and the others as fantastically successful and glamorous. How could I possibly compete with that?

It was bad enough when Ciaran, Linda and Gerard left, but then one day in that same year Gar dropped his own bombshell.

'Ro, I've just told Mam and Dad I want to go to the States. I've decided. There's nothing here for me.'

Not Gar! I thought. What am I going to do? I'm going to be on my own. I was stunned, somehow I'd never thought he'd go too. I tried not to show him I was close to tears.

I went with Mam and Dad to see him off at the airport soon after, and I will never forget the loneliness I felt that day. It was Gar! My best mate! How was I going to survive without him?

'What am I going to do, Gar? I'm the last one left,' I'd cried.

Gar tried to cheer me up. 'Ah, listen, before you know it I'll have you out on a holiday and we'll have the craic.' But it was a long journey back from the airport.

The house seemed so empty when we got home. The house that was so full of life was now silent and empty. Now I was the only child there.

Gary was the one in the family that everyone expected to become a rock star. He was always a lunatic.

'That one is terrible wild,' Mam would say.

'Ah, he'll be alright,' Dad would reassure her.

Gary broke all the rules. He was in trouble for staying out late. He got caught drinking. And he didn't seem to care what people thought of him. It was water off a duck's back. By the time I became a teenager, Gary had broken the ice and nothing

I did would have shocked Mam and Dad. But he went on to amaze everyone in the family. When he first went to New York, Gar became a golf caddie and made a lot of money. With those savings he put himself through college, first at Westchester and then at Iona, where he graduated with a marketing degree.

But with Gar gone, I was miserable for a long time. I will never forget one Christmas, in particular, when none of them made it home. It was just me and Mam and Dad sitting around the dinner table. It was one of our loveliest homes, and there was a Christmas tree in the corner of the dining room, with colourful lights flashing on and off and presents piled up underneath. But it just seemed so empty and depressing without all the gang of seven together.

Christmas had always been a happy time in our house. With so many of us, there was always plenty of presents and plenty of laughs. But this particular morning there was an empty, gloomy air about the place.

At lunchtime we got the phone calls from Ciaran, Linda, Gerard and Gar in the States. We were all wishing each other a happy Christmas and there was excitement and laughter for a while. But then they were gone. The house was all quiet again as Mam prepared the turkey dinner. I watched TV and didn't know what to do with myself. It was only when Mam served up the food and we sat around the table that she finally broke down and started to cry. Our first Christmas without all the family around the table. It was too much for her to bear.

Once Mam started crying it set me off too and I had to leave the house. I went down to my mate's to take my mind off it all.

I was never bitter with any of them for leaving as I understood even then why they had to go. They wanted to build a life, to earn money and make something of themselves. That just wasn't possible in Ireland at the time. You have to do what you have to do.

Soon it was time for me to get some sort of job myself. At the age of fourteen, while still at school, I found a part-time job in a shoe shop called Simon Hart's. I got on very well with the manager Niall O'Neill, and when he moved to Korky's, a sister shop, he took me with him.

I was delighted to get the transfer to Korky's because it was a much cooler store than Simon Hart's. I thought it looked like something out of London or New York. There was a wooden floor, wooden walls and metal shelves that displayed row upon row of funky shoes. At Simon Hart's I had had to wear a uniform, with shirt and tie, but Korky's was casual, which was far more to my liking. I'd always had a liking for fashion, but now it really took off. All the money I earned went on clothes. The very day I got paid, my every penny would be blown on a jacket or pair of shoes, and I'd have to get money off my mother to cover the bus fare and my lunch for the rest of the week. I loved looking good and was determined I wasn't going to disappear into the crowd as far as clothes were concerned. Even when I was around ten or eleven, I was fashion conscious. I was out shopping with Linda and Mam one day when I spotted a silver baseball jacket in GAP.

I said, 'Oh Linda, can I please have that jacket. I've got to have that jacket.'

It was about fifty pounds. Linda laughed, 'Would you get away out of that, Ro. Fifty pounds!'

'Oh please, Linda,' I cried. 'I'll pay you back.'

'Some chance of that!' she said.

Mam then intervened, 'Ah, go on Linda, get it for him.'

So Linda, like a fool, splashed out her fifty pounds on the jacket for me. I only had it a week when I got bored with it, so I pulled the buttons off and got my mother to take it back and exchange it for something else. A conniving little git, I was.

Working in Korky's was a real learning experience for me, and not just about selling shoes. I had to cope with all kinds of people who came through the door. I quickly wised up to the fact that it's a tough world out there and you need to have a thick skin when you're dealing with the public.

As a busy city store on one of Dublin's main shopping streets, Korky's was a prime target for shoplifters. They came in all forms: there were men, women, teenagers, old ladies and a lot of drug addicts. I saw druggies coming in wearing spectacles with no glass in them, trying to look studious so that they wouldn't get noticed robbing. But you could see a mile away that they were off their faces. A guy caught me by the arm one day and whispered in my ear, 'Here, listen, rob them shoes for me and I'll give you fifteen quid later on.'

I pulled away and told him what he could do with his idea!

People also came in begging for shoes. 'Here young fella, give us a pair of shoes. Sure no one will miss them.'

There was a lot of that kind of pressure from all sorts of characters and you had to accept that it was part of the deal, working in a shop in the centre of a very mixed city. But it taught me how to read people and judge whether or not they were straight or on the make.

In those years I saw more feet than were washed in Jerusalem, but I didn't hang around them. I dropped the shoes and walked away. I quickly learnt that you don't want to spend any more time around feet than is strictly necessary.

Being a fashion conscious teenager, I couldn't resist the shoes myself though. It helped that I got a twenty per cent discount and that Korky's also had a scheme whereby you could pay back the cost of the shoes by having it taken out of your wages. We tended not to remind them when they later forgot to deduct the money.

My fashion fetish got a boost when I did a free modelling assignment for the shop. Korky's were launching an advertising campaign and they decided to use me rather than hire a model. I have a feeling the decision to use me was mainly economic. But what the hell, the pictures were to appear in Ireland's national newspapers, the *Herald* and the *Star* and it made me feel pretty good. I couldn't wait to show my friends and family the pictures when they came out.

'Hey, Ronan, have you seen this?' Niall asked me one day as I was pushing some new shoes in the vague direction of a customer's feet.

He handed me a newspaper, pointing out an advert buried deep in the middle pages. It was something about auditions. Someone was putting together an Irish boy band. Niall was always aware that I was into music, and had gathered how much I enjoyed being in the limelight. All those football matches and races had given me a taste for it. I read the advert carefully and handed him back the paper. 'So what? Ireland is going to have its own Take That.'

'Ro, you should go for that, man, you're always singing,' he said.

I laughed and said, 'No, get out!' Me … auditioning for some Take That imitiation!

Niall insisted, 'I'm telling you Ro, you should have a go at it. Who knows what might happen?'

I went back to the customer who had been wearing the new pair of shoes around the store, standing in front of each one of the mirrors, trying to decide whether he liked them or not.

'They really look great on you,' I assured the nervous-looking guy who was still wavering.

'Do you think so?' he said. People were always so scared of looking stupid.

'Sure,' I said.

Finally he made up his mind and as I wrapped and boxed the shoes, I noticed the paper was sitting on the counter beside the cash register. When he'd gone I picked it up again and flicked through the pages until I found the advert.

I read it again. 'Ireland's answer to Take That?' It seemed unlikely, but not half as unlikely as some big music boss picking me out to sing. Still, I had to admit that was what I liked doing best …

I ripped out that section of the page, folded it up and stuck it in my back pocket.

In a way I'd been performing since I was three or four years of age. Gar and I used to regularly hold singing competitions at home. We'd both burst into song and then run up to Mam in a state of excitement and demand, 'Who is the best singer? Who is the best singer?' We'd do anything to be singled out, to get the most attention.

Mam would adopt the diplomatic approach, nod her head

and simply respond, 'You're both very good.' Of course, it was what the two of us wanted to hear. As I grew older I began playing around with songwriting but I didn't sing or perform in front of anyone. I always had a guitar in my room, even though I couldn't really play it, and I was always singing. Usually I had the stereo on so loud that I couldn't hear myself.

But then I took everyone by surprise one time while we were living in Dunshaughlin. All of a sudden, I picked up a guitar and started singing a song called 'Mary', which was then a big hit in Ireland for a local band called The 4 Of Us. I loved the song and I'd been practising away in my bedroom, day after day. When I finished I could see the look of amazement on their faces. 'Where did *that* come from!' Linda exclaimed. From then on, I was regularly coaxed up at family gatherings to sing a song. When we went around to each other's houses at Christmas, there'd always be a few drinks and people would start singing. They all knew by then that I was a bit of performer, so they'd say, 'Ronan, you sing.' My party piece was 'Father & Son', which had been a hit for Cat Stevens. It's a song that would turn up time and again during my career.

There was a history of music in the family as my uncle, Des Hopkins, who is married to Dad's sister Nuala, was in a band with his brother Billy. At one stage they were called Just Four and they played at all the family occasions and parties. Later, Des was in The Guinness Jazz Band in Ireland. He was the famous one in our family and I remember him being talked about quite a lot. Des and Nuala's son, Graham, also caught the bug and today he's a member of the Irish hard rock group, Therapy? Graham and myself were great friends when we were growing up and later he got into drumming when I started singing, so we had that in common as well. It would be fair to say that we ended up going off in different musical directions, though!

When Just Four performed at my brother Ciaran's wedding, Graham and his dad, Des, created a lot of excitement when they both played the drums at the same time. Graham took one drum stick, Des took the other and the two of them performed a mesmerising set. It was truly amazing to watch them that day. It was my first taste of watching real musicians hype up a crowd.

Dad and Mam could sing as well. Mam had a very good voice, but her repertoire only extended to a couple of songs, like 'Amazing Grace'. Some of her regular impromptu performances were in the clubhouse of Raheny GAA Club on a Sunday evening. I do believe that people used to come along just to hear her sing, as she had a beautiful, clear voice. Dad was always a fan of legendary country singer, the late Jim Reeves, and he'd sing some of his hits. It sounds a very Irish way to carry on, all of us breaking into song, but it was also about family, about being together and celebrating.

When I was around thirteen, coming on to fourteen, I knew I had a vibe about singing and that I wanted to sing, but I didn't know if I'd get away with it. I thought I looked cool … I had a Bryan Adams thing going on – the denim jacket … the fecked-up jeans (not much different from now! What goes around comes around) and I'd been practising singing into a microphone whatever songs were happening then, so I decided to give it a go.

I knew a bunch of guys at school who played music and they knew that I liked to sing. So we got together and started rehearsing and we found that we gelled well, apart from occasional spats that always happen when you put six teenagers in a room (particularly ones that aren't afraid to show off). We called our group, Nameste, which was the title of the twelfth track on a Beastie Boys album. There was Ian on drums, Stuey on bass, Gordon was on rhythm guitar, Adrian on lead guitar, John on sax and myself out front as the singer. We entered a few school-band competitions around the county, won a good bit of money, bought new gear and built it up from there. Between us, we were in to all kinds of different music. I'd never been snobbish or specialist about my music, just greedy.

I was singing everything – from Nirvana to Bryan Adams, as well as old rock 'n' roll classics. One of the biggest competitions we entered was down at Dorey's pub in Dunshaughlin. That was a big night. There was a thousand pounds up for grabs – 500 quid for the winner and 250 each for the two runners-up. All the groups and solo acts in the contest had their supporters and members of their family there and the atmosphere was electric and the booze flowed freely.

We performed 'Johnny B Goode', the old Chuck Berry number, and 'Ride On', a ballad by well-known Irish singer and songwriter Jimmy MacCarthy, and gave it our best shot. The audience, which was packed with our extended families, was right behind us, really getting into it. As soon as we finished, there was a massive uproar of applause from the audience. We just couldn't believe the reaction, and stood dazed for a second before breaking out in huge grins. But it was still a nail-biting experience waiting for the judges to come through with their verdict. You could feel the tension crackling around the smoky pub as they announced third place, then second place ... and we still weren't amongst the prizewinners. A hush fell over the entire lounge as the jury foreman reached the verdict on the winner ... Nameste! The place erupted. I'll never forget the moment. Even after the number ones, the huge concerts and all the success I later had, that night in a beery local pub is still one of my most memorable nights.

For the rest of the evening, we were on top of the world. We'd never had so much money and were determined to act the big stars. We splurged our winnings in a local night spot called the County Club, spraying around the dosh on booze for all our families and friends. I was supposed to keep the money to buy myself a new mic for the band, but that was far too sensible. Although Nameste didn't last that long we had a ball and a few other great nights. It was a shame I had to leave the band when we moved house again. But I'd really enjoyed myself. I felt I could get used to this ...

CHAPTER 4

THE DAY I JOINED A CULT

I pulled the tattered piece of newspaper from my back pocket and read it again.

Niall O'Neill had certainly planted the idea in my head. 'Ireland's answer to Take That!' I said for the fiftieth time. The more I said it, the more feasible it seemed.

I dropped the cutting on my bedside table and finished dressing, thinking about the huge success of Take That. They were everywhere in the media and had been selling massive amounts of records. Undisputed pop kings – for the moment.

I pulled the shirt over my head and reached for the cutting again. Where? When?

On the way to work that morning I thought about what I could do at the auditions. 'Father & Son', my party piece, it's got to be that one. OK Niall, I thought, yeah, why not? I'll give it a try. I've nothing to lose and it'll be a bit of fun.

That day in the store I announced my intentions, 'Hey, Niall, I'm going to go.'

'Where?' said Niall.

'Oh, y'know, the Irish Take That.'

Mark Maher, one of the other store assistants, who was around my age, piped up, 'I'm thinking about going too!'

'Remember me when you're famous, guys,' Niall laughed.

'Yeah! Yeah!' What a joker.

On the day of the auditions, Niall had a surprise for me. The modelling picture I did for Korky's was in the *Herald*.

'There you go, Ronan, fame at last,' he said showing me the paper. I looked at it and laughed. But I still thought it was a pretty cool picture. Perfect timing, too. An omen, maybe, but no... no future in getting your hopes up.

It was a chilly November afternoon in 1993 as Mark and I raced along the city streets to Litton Lane. I stopped to pick up my own copy of the *Herald* from one of the news vendors.

'What are we like, Ronan?'

'What do you mean, Mark?'

'I'm sure this is a waste of time. We don't stand a chance.'

'Ah, c'mon, Mark, it'll be a bit of fun. Let's have a laugh.'

I wouldn't admit it, but every now and then I had to take a deep breath from the nerves. Mark is right, I thought, what am I doing? But there was no going back now. We were soon at Litton Lane but could immediately see there were only a handful of people about. 'This is going to be a disaster,' I thought. 'Really embarrassing. Look at the state of them!' Not one of the fellas there looked like a star.

Then a young guy came out of the studio and announced, 'There's nothing on here. It's the wrong address in the paper. Yer man in the studio there says those auditions are down at the Ormond Centre.'

Straightaway, the little gang of us raced around to the Ormond. As we turned the corner, we could see it was a different story there. There must have been three hundred lads there before us. The queue was like an army of ants stretching back from the doorway.

'Ah, I'm not into this, ' Mark shrugged. 'I can't be bothered.'

'Ah, c'mon Mark, you're here now. Hang around and give it a try.' I, of course, just wanted some moral support.

'Nah, this is too much for me. You go ahead. Good luck.' Mark turned and I watched him striding away. For a split second I thought, 'Maybe he's right.' But I was there. I was all buzzed up. I had to give it a try.

I got chatting to some of the other guys while I waited in the queue and it helped to pass the time.

'I'm already in a pop band … just here for the laugh, y'know man!' one of them said to me.

'Yeah, right!' I thought.

Every one of the three hundred boys in the queue tried as hard as they could to look as if they didn't really care either way. Who were they kidding! Standing around, taking time off work, skiving school to freeze their arses off! The line was a real pack of Liquorice All Sorts. There were all kinds – guys with tattoos and ear rings, bald blokes, fellas with long hair. Some were in track suits, others had come really dressed up to the nines. I hurriedly compared my own gear – a casual bomber-type jacket and T-shirt-style top over baggy jeans, set off by a pair of funky brown boots from Korky's. I had tightly-cropped hair under a tartan cap. I relaxed a little. I didn't think I came off too badly.

At last we were herded inside and I watched several of the other guys going through their paces. I could see that many of them were dying with the nerves. I knew how they were feeling. My whole body was jigging with anxiety. Some of the acts were terrible. 'Eh, sorry, can I do it again?' said one after fluffing a chorus. But there were some very good singers as well and I felt any confidence I might have had draining away by the minute.

While waiting my turn, I'd found out which of the people

sitting in judgement was Louis Walsh, the pop manager who was putting the band together. Until then, I had no idea what he looked like or who he was except that the advert had been placed by him. He certainly didn't have the appearance of a big pop guru, which I'd imagined would involve flash clothes and plenty of jewellery and attitude. Instead, he was casually dressed in a jacket and jeans and seemed to laugh a lot.

And then it was me. 'Hi, my name is Ronan,' I said, trying, and failing, to sound relaxed.

'Hi, Ronan,' said Louis.

I had my copy of the *Herald* under my arm. 'I just brought this along to show you the kind of stuff I do.'

Flicking as casually as I could to the page with Korky's advert, I handed it over to Louis. 'I'm a model,' I lied straight-faced.

'Great! Great! Looks good,' said Louis, smiling. 'But can you sing?'

'Yeah, I used to be in a band.'

'What kind of band?'

'A sort of rock band.'

'A rock band?' Louis didn't look impressed. 'This is a pop group, Ronan.'

'Oh, I'm a big pop fan. George Michael is my favourite singer.'

'OK, Ronan, what are you going to perform?'

'"Father & Son".'

'The Cat Stevens song. Great!'

The power was gone from my legs and my feet were like concrete blocks as I stood there all alone on the stage and sang unaccompanied. I had done this song nearly a hundred times at family gatherings, but this was completely different. I closed my eyes and concentrated on the words and the singing. Once I heard the sound coming out of my mouth I felt stronger. Most important of all, I kept going.

'OK, Ronan, we just want you to show us some dancing,' Louis said, when I'd finished. Now this was something that my experience with Nameste had not prepared me for. A bit of flailing about had been all that was required. They put on a backing track of Right Said Fred's 'I'm Too Sexy' and with a sinking heart I started to shuffle, then bop, around. At first all I could think was that everyone watching must be saying to themselves 'What a tosser!' But then after a little while I forgot, I was back in my front room, arseing around, enjoying myself. Still, I thank God that particular performance was never captured on video.

But Louis didn't seem to notice or mind. 'OK, Ronan, that's fine. Come back next week. Here's the details,' Louis said.

'Jeeezus!' I said to myself. 'He wants me back. Cool!'

Louis later told me that he thought my performance of 'Father & Son' had been 'really amazing' and that by the time I'd finished the song he'd decided I was in the band. Of course, I didn't know that at the time and lived on tenterhooks for the next three weeks, racing between school and Korky's, always singing under my breath. Occasionally I'd allow myself to daydream about Number One singles, beautiful women and BMWs, but not too often. That would have been tempting fate.

Seven days after the first audition, I was back again, and Louis Walsh had everyone sing and dance once more. This time I chose George Michael's 'Careless Whisper', a good song for my range and I'd even managed to smarten up my dancing. To my complete delight I made it through to the final ten.

I still kept the auditions secret from my family. Unless I was successful, I didn't want them to know about it. So my poor mother didn't know what to think when I kept disappearing for whole days on end. A natural worrier, she soon had me in some sinister cult. Her Ronan in the grip of some terrible maniac. Then she saw some of the media coverage of the auditions and put two and two together. 'Ah, so that's what you're doing,' she said to me one day.

At the final audition, all ten of us young lads were confident that we were going to make it. Each hopeful had one final chance to make an impression. And those waiting had a last chance to size up the competition. There was plenty of chat, with everyone announcing how good they were. We all had big heads on us. A bunch of fools, that's what we were. 'Oh, I can sing anything,' I said at one point. But when it came to the moment that Louis was about to announce the line up of the band, the bravado drained away and the tension took hold.

We sat in a small room, ten nervous, paling young guys, waiting for the judgement. Finally Louis came back in. 'OK guys,' he said and there was hush in an instant. 'It's Shane Lynch, Keith Duffy, Stephen Gately, Ronan Keating, Richard Rock and Mark Walton.'

'Yee-yes! Yee-yes! I'm in!' I punched the air.

I was fifteen years old and I thought my life was made.

The image people probably have of Boyzone is that we were designed, manufactured and marketed in a very slick and easy fashion. The reality is a million miles away. If someone made a TV drama that featured the story of Boyzone, the critics would say it was too far-fetched to be true.

The fact that we eventually made it to the dizzy heights of the pop industry is nothing short of a miracle. They say that ignorance is bliss and that was certainly true in our case. Had we known just how hard you must work to make it, and how much luck you need to have on the way, we might have had a more chastened attitude.

After the decision me and my five new bandmates hugged each other as if we'd won the lottery. Then I hurried home to Swords, the Dublin northside suburb where we were living at the time. When I told Mam and Dad that I had been chosen for Boyzone their response was muted. It was no big deal to them because I had already been in a band and sure, what was Boyzone to them, only another little band that they saw as my pastime. 'Would you not be better concentrating on your sport instead of this music malarkey,' Dad quipped. But there was no time to even think about it. Boyzone had begun and we were to be 'launched' straightaway. My old life had gone in an instant.

Our first outing into the heady world of media exposure was a complete disaster. It was the sort of debut very few bands would have survived. The auditions had attracted some coverage in Dublin and Louis was determined to ride the wave for all it was worth. The very next day, he had us booked onto the country's biggest TV chat show, *The Late Late Show*. It was to be the official unveiling of 'Ireland's answer to Take That'.

The thing was, we'd had no time to get to know each other. Stephen was the only one I'd talked to much. He had wandered into the shop a few times around the auditions and we'd chatted. And as for having prepared a set … What's that then? Still buzzing from the previous day, we just rushed on to the stage full of enthusiasm, like kids at a party, and blagged our way through the questions. God, we were terrible! The show's host, Gay Byrne, asked us to strut our stuff and we all did silly dance routines, some of which you couldn't even describe as a routine! We didn't even sing!

We were so bad it's now legendary.

The result was predictable. The next day we were savaged by the critics and everyone in Ireland had us written off as doomed to failure. And I wouldn't blame them because we really were laughable. The clip of that brief appearance on *The Late Late Show* has come back to haunt us time and time again on TV around the world. When I look at it and see myself as a skinny little guy in denims acting the fool, I cringe with embarrassment.

Now I can look back and laugh at that first appearance because we went on to become successful. If we had flopped, I know I would remember it all with horror. It only takes one bad show to ruin a band's career. But to make such eejits of yourselves on your first outing! At the time, though, none of this registered. We didn't know or didn't care that we'd looked pathetic. As far as we were concerned we had to be stars just to have appeared on the show. In our eyes we were now the top cats on the Irish showbiz scene. We'd been on telly. We were Pop Stars.

The *Late Late* appearance was on a Friday night and the next morning I went in to work at Korky's. I was strolling along the street and all that was going through my mind was the thought, 'I'm famous. I'm famous!' I looked at other people, waiting for their reaction. 'Hey, do you recognise me?' I wanted to say. 'It was me on the TV last night! You must recognise me!' What was I like?! I was desperate for someone to say, 'Can I have your autograph?' What an eejit! The only people who acknowledged me were those who already knew me from working on the street.

The following Monday morning it was school as usual and there was plenty of slagging from my classmates.

'Oh yeah, here he is, the big star.'

'Lads! Roll out the red carpet there for Ronan!'

'Is that your limo parked outside the school gates?'

It was big-time abuse, but I didn't mind. I consoled myself that they were only jealous.

Now that the band had members there was the little matter of putting together a show. For four weeks we met to rehearse frequently in a Dublin city centre dance studio. But we were up the creek without a paddle; we were all over the place, with no direction or order.

It was all quite comical. Louis left us to our own devices, and we didn't have any original material to rehearse, so we'd just turn up and try to perform other people's songs. We were just getting used to singing together. There was nobody there to guide us or to take control of the mayhem. The only people who seemed to know what they were doing were Stephen and Shane, as they were good dancers, and so they became our choreographers. Half the time we would finish up after twenty minutes and head off to the pub. That was pretty much our normal rehearsal in the early months. Looking back it was only when we recorded 'Love Me For A Reason' that we started behaving like a serious pop band.

It was in those early weeks that we began to gel with each other. We were competitive, and we were sounding each other out, but more than anything we were excited about being in a band with a manager with big plans. We were all equally convinced that we couldn't fail to make it. We all agreed we were going to conquer the world. There was a lot of friendly banter as we all got to know each other's jokes, expressions and ways of doing things. We all loved cars, and had long discussions about what we'd buy with all our pop-star millions. Although there was no rivalry between the band members, I do remember standing back from the others during one of those early rehearsals and looking at them thinking, 'These are all really cool looking guys. They look like they should be in a band and I don't.' Keith and Shane, in particular, really looked like proper pop stars. Keith was all tanned up and he worked out so he was really muscular. 'I'm in rapid shape!' he'd say.

Shane was tall, good looking and wore really cool clothes and Stephen had that cute look that girls liked. I thought to myself, 'They all look great. And look at me! A little white boy who's never had a sun tan in his life.'

But just being in such a happening band was enough. In my head, I was already a star. In no time at all, I started behaving like one. After an early evening rehearsal, the whole group decided to go to a trendy bar called Café En Seine. Needless, to say, we came up against a stone wall when we were confronted by their security staff.

'Sorry, you're not allowed in,' said your man on duty.

'Do you know who we are?' I asked indignantly.

'No,' said your man.

'We're Louis Walsh's lads!' I informed him, as if that was the magic password.

Nothing registered. He just reiterated, 'Sorry lads, you can't come in.'

By this stage the other guys in the group had slunk back in embarrassment. I looked around at their mortified expressions. 'Ronan, what are you talking about?' they asked.

'I don't believe I've just done that!' I said, feeling like such a tosser.

As we did those first rehearsals, Louis would pop in to watch us carefully, his mind whirring with plans. He decided that Richard and Mark weren't knitting together with us as a team, sometimes the dynamics work and sometimes they don't. A band has to be a tight little team. So after just two months it was all change. It was obviously a huge disappointment for the two lads after they had come so far and my heart went out to them. Richard, a tall, skinny dark-haired guy is the son of a well known Irish singer called Dickie Rock. So, I'm sure he was hoping to follow in his father's footsteps. Mark, who was also tall, but blond, later admitted in the media that he just wasn't ready for this kind of life and didn't have the commitment.

Mikey Graham, who had originally got through to the final audition, was then drafted in. I had really felt for Mick at those auditions, seeing his disappointment when he hadn't made the original line up. He had looked really cool in a red bandanna and he had had a sort of Sean Penn vibe about him.

Louis had his boy band members in place, he had a buzz about town and already we even had our own critics. Now he needed some pictures. But everything had to be done on borrowed money. So Louis went in to the AIB bank on Dublin's Baggot Street and took out a loan for our first photo shoot. The man in the bank looked at Louis as if he had two heads when he learned what it was for – to photograph a pop band! Nevertheless, it made a difference from a new kitchen or a credit card debt, and Louis was always pretty persuasive, so the cash advance was approved.

Having spent twenty years working as a showbiz promoter, agent and manager in Ireland, Louis knew all the right people. He hired a really good Dublin photographer called Kip Carroll, of Lad Lane Studios, to do our first shoot. We got a selection of smart frilly shirts from Irish fashion designer Michael Lyon and Kip gave us three or four different images. We thought the pictures were amazing. It was extraordinary what some new outfits and hair-styles did for us. We looked like a totally polished pop act … not like the green horns that we actually were.

Armed with the pictures, Louis set up a meeting with Paul Keogh, who was head honcho at the PolyGram record company in Ireland. He did say he was interested in signing us up, but he was still cautious and refused to fully commit to the project.

Louis also sent the photo portfolio to everyone in the UK music industry, hoping for a reaction. One of the people who took the bait was a big-gun pop manager called Tom Watkins, who had been involved in the management of Bros and the Pet Shop Boys, and was currently managing East 17. Watkins rang Louis and said how great we looked and that he was interested in getting involved on the management side.

Louis was leaping around in excitement at this development. Boyzone were just minnows in the music industry, while Watkins wielded considerable power and influence, and could open doors for the group in the UK. It would be a brilliant coup to get him on board. A meeting was arranged with Watkins in Dublin's Shelbourne Hotel and Louis organised a limousine to pick him up at Dublin Airport. We were determined to give him the whole star treatment.

Watkins arrived in to the Shelbourne looking every inch the power lord. A large man, he was dressed in black, the unofficial uniform of the music industry. The meeting started with great expressions of enthusiasm on all sides, but it quickly emerged that Watkins was only interested in taking over Boyzone altogether. Louis was desperate to have him involved, but there was no way he was walking away from the project he had only just started. He offered Watkins a large percentage of the action. Watkins wasn't interested. He wanted total control or nothing, so the deal fell through.

There was no big bust up, it was just a normal business meeting that failed to produce an agreement and we all parted on friendly terms. Later, when Watkins' group, East 17, came to Dublin to perform at the Point Depot, we were invited to the show and their party afterwards. Cheekily, we had people handing out Boyzone pictures at their concert to promote our own group. Some of the East 17 fans handed them back. 'Nah! They're rubbish,' they said.

Louis didn't let the setback with Watkins slow him down. He continued to work on Paul Keogh at Polygram and managed to secure a distribution deal. But there was still no record contract, and everything the band did was on borrowed money. I think that Louis must have been close to quitting at times, as he saw his final reserves of cash and credit disappearing with no deal to show for it.

The only option was to take the offer of a distribution deal with Polygram and make a record ourselves. After hundreds of listening hours Louis selected 'Working My Way Back To You' an old disco classic by American group the Detroit Spinners, and started another trawl through his address book looking for a backer. At the same time he got a copy of the UK music yearbook and tried every producer in the business. During that period Louis never seemed to relax. He was on a mission, and he was *always* on the phone. At first nobody wanted to know about a boy band from Ireland with no record deal, but eventually, a guy called Ian Levine said he'd do the track. The snag was we'd have to pay him ten thousand pounds cash up front. It was money we simply didn't have.

We had hit a brick wall. It seemed the cost of getting a boy band started was just too high. But then, in a last ditch attempt to find a loan, Louis approached a friend, Dublin nightclub owner John Reynolds. John is a very astute businessman and he recognised that the Boyzone project had potential. After half an hour of persuasion from Louis, he agreed to put up the cash. Louis was so thrilled, he instantly offered John a half-share of the management. That turned out to be the best ten grand John has ever invested in his business career! Apart from his financial backing, John's association with Boyzone also gave us some extra profile and glamour, because his uncle, Albert Reynolds, was then the Taoiseach (Prime Minister) of the country.

It was a pivotal moment for Boyzone. Without John's timely backing we might have remained wannabes for ever. Now, with a recording in London in the offing, anything was possible.

With everything at last in place for our first single, I felt I had some decisions to make. Rehearsals and meetings with the band meant I was getting getting busier and busier. And the longer we went on the more I realised I had stumbled on the one thing I could imagine doing for ever – singing, meeting people and making things happen. I was fully committed to it. Although I had only four months to go, I made up my mind to leave school.

Breaking the news at home wasn't easy. 'Mam,' I said, 'I'm going to quit school because things are going really well in the band.'

'Oh Ronan,' she said, her face falling, 'Would you not be better to have an education as well, in case anything went wrong?'

I took a deep breath. How to make her understand that this felt more right than anything before? 'I don't have the interest in school and this is really working out, Mam. It's really what I want.'

She was quiet for a while but then said, 'Well, Ronan, it's your decision. If that's what you want.'

I started to reply but she stopped me and said, 'But, promise me one thing, Ronan, if it fails you're to go back to school and finish your education.'

'I will, Mam, I promise.'

And that was it. Once I had broken the ice and told Mam what I wanted to do, she then supported me all the way. But both my parents were obviously concerned that this whole Boyzone thing might fall flat on its face and I'd be left with nothing. But I knew it all in those days. I had no idea of the risk I was taking. Music is an industry littered with the corpses of would-be stars.

CHAPTER 5

LONDON CALLING

If Louis had flown me to the moon, I couldn't have been more excited than on our trip to London. It was my first time out of Ireland and we were on our way to record our first single. 'This is the business lads, we're finally jet-setters,' I announced once we were in the air.

'This is rapid,' Keith agreed.

'Ah, get a grip, lads!' Shane was keeping his cool.

But for once I couldn't contain my excitement. In no time at all, we were descending again and I began pestering the others. 'Can I sit at the window? I have to see what London looks like from the sky!' I thought I might never have another chance. Little did I know the journey between London and Dublin would be an almost daily grind over the next six years.

'Here, change with me, I can't be arsed,' offered Shane.

Louis just sat there laughing at us. But you could see that he was enjoying the moment as well. For us youngsters, all the now over-familiar hassles of the airport were new and exciting and taxiing through London we were like kids on a school trip, everywhere marvelling at the landmarks, the noise and pace of it all and, most of all, the flash cars.

I didn't admit it, but I was scared stiff as well. London was just so big. By comparison, Dublin seemed like a village. We were all a little overawed. The buildings seemed bigger, the streets noisier.

Eventually, we found Ian Levine's Tropicana recording studio. I'd never even been in a studio before and had no idea what to expect. We leapt out of the taxi only to be told that we couldn't start work yet. A little deflated, we found we had another couple of days to explore London. The gang of us spent the time wandering and window shopping in the West End.

Levine had already recorded the backing track to 'Working My Way Back To You' by the time we eventually got in the studio. He showed us round, explained how the recording process worked and then said he wanted to try each of us in turn on the vocal. 'You sing!' he said. 'Now you sing! Now you!' After we'd all done our bit he took Louis aside and had a private chat with him. It was decided that Mikey and Stephen would do the vocals on that first recording.

Just as we were finishing up I had a word with Louis and asked him what Levine had said to him. He told me the producer had said 'You know, that little blond guy can't sing.' He was referring to me. I was furious. 'I am going to prove this guy wrong,' I told myself. It was a turning point. From that moment on I was determined to ensure that nobody in the business was ever going to talk about me like that again.

The Tropicana sessions over, we stayed on in London for a few days, hanging out and meeting people from record companies. We were having a ball, staying in a hotel, involved in serious music business, and getting to mooch around London too. But because it was our first time away from our families and friends, we were constantly on the phone to Ireland. We didn't have mobiles. In those days they were the size of a brick and just for rich businessmen. We were skint at the time, so we were using the telephones in our bedrooms.

Everything was fine until it came to checking out of the hotel. Louis had taken care of the accommodation and the breakfasts and he had gone ahead to do some business. We had arranged to meet him later. But as we were preparing to leave our telephone bill arrived. 'Eighty bleedin' quid!' Keith announced.

'What are we going to do?' Stephen asked, looking very worried.

I was very concerned as well. 'If we don't pay they'll probably get the police. Louis won't know where we are … we have to think of something fast.'

In the end, we could only see one way out – do a runner. 'Right lads, here's the plan,' said Keith.

We were on the fourth floor of the hotel and we couldn't make our getaway through the foyer with all the luggage as we would have been spotted. So we arranged that Shane, Keith and Mikey would slip outside and wait under the bedroom window. Me and Steve would then throw our bags down to them.

It was daylight at the time and the three boys looked really suspicious down on the street, particularly as there was a Barclays Bank in the background. Four floors up, Steve and I could hear these Irish accents shouting, 'Are ya right!'

We decided to throw down our own bags first, as we reckoned the other guys would run off and leave us behind if they got their own. I can't imagine what people on the street must have thought as they saw the bags coming hurling out of the hotel window. They probably thought we were robbing the place and chucking the bags of loot to our accomplices.

Steve and I then slipped down and out through reception, probably looking like two escaped convicts with the worried heads on us. We scurried across the lobby, completely paranoid.

Once we got out the door we belted it round the block and met the other lads in McDonald's at the end of Oxford Street. We only had enough money between us for six chicken McNuggets, one for each of us and then one to fight over. Suddenly we heard a police siren blaring outside on the street. We looked at each other for a split second before high-tailing down to the loo to hide out. They must be on to us!

After ten minutes we started feeling foolish and ventured back out on to the street to wait sheepishly for Louis to arrive to take us back to the airport for the trip home. Some jet-setters!

But the wagon had started to roll. London was just the start of what was needed to get a single out. Now we had to do some more songs for the B-side of the single and we would need a video. Recording studios! Video shoots! My Mam couldn't believe it.

But back home in Dublin rehearsing and still working at Korky's, Ian Levine's comments were niggling at me. 'I can sing! I can sing!' I assured myself. I had it in my mind that I wanted to record 'Father & Son', so I approached Louis and asked him if he could arrange for me to do it.

'Of course I will,' he told me.

Louis set me up with a guy called Paul Barrett at the STS recording studios in Dublin's Temple Bar and borrowed the five hundred pounds it cost to record the song. I was delighted with the opportunity to record 'Father & Son', but I was really frightened going into the studio, particularly as I was on my own. Paul was great; he talked me through the process and put me completely at my ease. It turned out to be a very good vocal.

'That's good, Ronan, you should be proud of yourself,' said Paul.

'I am,' I thought and a certain other producer went through my mind.

Everyone liked my version of 'Father & Son', so it ended up on the B-side, along with a twelve-minute version of 'Working My Way Back To You'. When the single was released, 'Father & Son' got just as much airplay as the A-side, so I was thrilled.

There was great excitement when it came to filming the video for 'Working My Way Back To You'. Each one of us had a film star inside trying to get out and we loved the cameras and lights. Every new stage was fresh and exciting. The video was shot in a dance studio called Digges Lane. We danced around like a gang of eejits for the day as they filmed us. We all had clothes on loan from a sports store.

As far as we were concerned the video was brilliant but looking at it now, you can see it was done on a shoestring. It's not the world's most impressive video. We had around four thousand pounds to spend on it. Later Boyzone videos would cost close to £150,000.

But the video was the easy part. Next came the real challenge. Making people like us. We had to get out on the road, build a fan base, and support the single when it came out. At that time, there was no home-grown pop industry in Ireland. We had produced some of the best rock acts in the world – U2,

The Cranberries, Sinead O'Connor – but pop didn't command any respect. Boyzone felt the backlash as soon as we hit the live scene. We were immediately ridiculed because we didn't play instruments. It was like taking on Mount Everest.

In the ten months around the release of that first single we travelled the length and breadth of Ireland and played literally hundreds of shows. We always had one gig, sometimes two a day, and we generally made four hundred pounds per performance. After the expenses were deducted, we ended up with sixty pounds each, which seemed enough at first, but after a few knackering months seemed distinctly less.

The strange thing is that that period of Boyzone was the most fun. Five boys, one van, a few songs and a couple of dance moves, and we were having the time of our lives. It was gruelling work, and we spent long hours travelling to gigs, but it was all new to us and we laughed our way through it. We used to call some gigs The Doorstep Tour because the stage was literally the size of a doorstep! Typically, we'd be travelling to a remote area of the country and the nightclub would be an extension of someone's house. We'd be given the front room of the home to change in, or sometimes the toilet, and we'd be tripping over each other, flinging trainers off and muddling up our outfits. We could have been behind the scenes at a school play except for the fact that our audiences were mostly hostile, and the venues were usually smaller than a school hall. If we hadn't been so naive, I'm not sure that we would have had the resilience to keep going. At one show in a club up the north of the country only five people turned up. Five people!

The owner invited the five of us upstairs and he said, 'Lads,

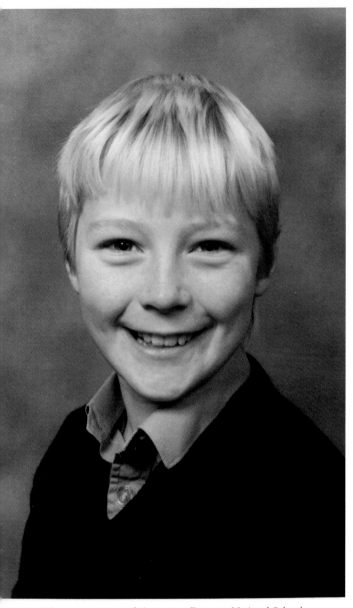

The not-so-star pupil. Age seven, Dunsany National School

'I stood out a mile from the rest of them. All gangly legs and messy snow white hair.' The whole family on holiday in Kilarney (Mam is standing on the right, at the back)

Gary, Gerard and me, looking enthusiastic about my first day at school, 1981

Gary and I on the day of my first communion, 1983

My confirmation at Bayside
Community Church, 1987

Stepping out in my first year at
Dunshaughlin school fashion show, 1988

'If I wasn't first then I wasn't happy.'
The regional finals of
the 200 metres, 1991

On holiday in New York,
bound to reunite the Keating
Seven, 1993

'I was regularly coaxed up at family gatherings to sing a song.'
Celebrating in a New York bar, 1993

Me, Dad and Gary in New York, 1993

'*Shane was tall, good looking and wore really cool clothes and Stephen
had that cute look that girls like. I thought to myself, "They all look great. And look
at me! A little white boy who's never had a suntan in his life".*'
Boyzone: the beginning

'Something strange was happening in Swords… I'd get up in the morning, peep out the window and the driveway would be full of young girls.'
At home, age 16

Left to our own devices. Boyzone down the pub

Singing 'Oh Carol' on tour in the UK in 1995, a string of hit singles,
the Smash Hits tour and a long apprenticeship behind us

'Success seemed to happen in a dream.' 1995

'Stylists had a difficult time with Boyzone during those days.' 1995

'We had no shame. We wore funny coloured shirts and jumped off chairs. I can't count the number of times I answered questions about my favourite colour…'

At home in Swords writing the lyrics to 'Coming Home', 1995

*'In the summer of 1996 we travelled the length and breadth of the
UK and ireland, and more than 250,000 people came out to see Boyzone.'*

© Ray Burmiston/Idols

'The British fans seemed very different to the girls back home.' Fans waiting outside our hotel on the 1996 UK tour

There was never much privacy on tour... Belgium 1996

The less glamorous side of touring – unpacked cases and cluttered rooms. UK Tour 1996

Home for Christmas. Swords, Dublin 1996

Making contact with the real world, 1995-7

'More than anything we are travellers. Most of my time in the last six years has been spent travelling on a plane or in a car, or waiting in airports, in venues or in TV studios.'

Summer tour, 1997

listen, I'll give you the agreed fee if you don't go on, or I'll pay you extra if you do.'

We thought, well, fair play, we're here for the fans (which was stretching it at the time), he wants the show to go on, we won't ask why, so we'll do it and take the extra cash. But it was ridiculous. There were as many people on the stage that night as there were in the audience. As we performed, Keith kept himself refreshed by drinking Babycham, which was being handed to him by one of the punters on the dancefloor. The ten of us had quite a night!

We usually performed in the middle of a disco, so there'd be disco music before us and disco music after us and, more often than not, the clubbers would have preferred it if there had been no Boyzone messing up their night. To be honest, the flack we took during some of those early performances was justified, as we were a pretty raw bunch. We were busking it big time. We were miming to really crap demos that weren't even properly produced. We didn't have enough songs, so we used to do 'Working My Way Back To You' twice, including the twelve-minute version from the B-side, which we always performed at the end of the set.

We only had two live mics, the other three were dummies, so we had to coordinate the dance routines in such a way that we could pass the mic to each other, so that the person doing the next link would have something to sing into. It was hilarious.

As summer approached we started going to gigs held in marquees and we'd have to get kitted out in a field, slipping around in the mud. We were always particularly apprehensive about those outdoor shows because the crowds were very unpredictable. Sometimes it was like being thrown to the lions at feeding time. All kinds of missiles were hurled or flicked at us during the performance. Everything from cigarette butts to cans of beer bounced off our heads. While we were performing at the Rose Of Tralee festival in county Kerry, I got my lip split open after a coin came spinning out of the crowd, hitting me on the mouth. But we laughed at those incidents. Maybe I should call this book, *A Sense of Humour is Essential for Survival in Pop*.

Guys in the audience seldom liked us and there was always the threat that their aggression might actually become physical. This is exactly what happened at one of our first gigs in a country nightclub. A gang of blokes stormed the stage and started throwing punches. Keith, our big, burly knight in shining armour, picked me up under one arm and Stephen under the other and charged across the dance floor, fleeing the battlefield. Of course, once we were safely in the van, we found it all hysterically funny.

Even though I was the youngest in the band, Louis appointed me to the role of the fee collector at shows. Keith, who had muscles on his muscles at the time because he was doing weight training, used to stand behind me in case anyone started getting heavy about it.

There were times when we made a three to four-hour journey to do a gig and afterwards there would be a hassle about getting paid. We'd face a whole series of excuses and moans, 'Oh, we had a small crowd, what can you do for us?' Or they'd complain that we didn't have a band, or that we didn't perform for long enough … anything to get out of handing over the cash. This happened often and it was always a real kick in the gut to us because we were so skint ourselves at the time.

I was still working in Korky's and Niall and the staff there were fantastic to me. I often had to leave early on a Saturday afternoon to do a gig somewhere distant in Ireland that night and I never had any problem getting the time off. They'd pay me for a full day of work as well. They also gave Boyzone free shoes! I still go there today to kit out myself or Yvonne or Jack.

Mikey and Shane were still earning a living as mechanics and Louis got jobs for Keith and Stephen, working as assistants in Makullas clothes shop in Dublin's Suffolk Street. All the time, Louis was still struggling to get us a proper contract with PolyGram. Meanwhile we were barely scraping by.

'This is not what I thought fame was all about,' I said to Keith one day. We'd had a bad few days of crappy venues, long drives and mouthy audiences.

'Yeah,' he agreed, 'I thought it was going to be big flash cars and nice hotels.'

Some moments, though, made it all worthwhile. I thought I knew I was a star the day I held our first CD in my hand. I'd just got my early copy of 'Working My Way Back To You'. I just stood there staring at the artwork. It was the five of us looking up at a camera with the Boyzone logo in the middle. Our CD! 'This is it,' I said to myself, 'I've finally arrived.' Little did I know!

As the single slowly made its way to the record shops, we were building up the mileage on the transit van. We never actually got to stay in a hotel when we did those early gigs. Instead we'd drive home through the night, arriving back to our houses just before dawn. We played Take That and other boy bands and would stock the van up with beer for the journey home. It was like being on a constant stag do. As tiredness and the beer got the better of us, we'd crack jokes and generally slag each other before degenerating into mindless, endless conversations that made no sense whatsoever. We were the travelling party-van and we'd do anything to break the monotony of the long-haul journeys.

It was an apprenticeship. We were learning how to perform, about life on the road and how to survive an audience! It was a traditional training for a band. Gradually our hard work began to pay off. Every time we played a town, we established a fan base. And we could see it growing all the time.

While we were getting a lot of press, what with the release of the single, Boyzone weren't actually doing interviews. It was Louis who was dealing with the Irish journalists and getting us publicity. Louis didn't want us to talk to the press in the early days because I guess he thought that we were incapable of saying anything remotely interesting or intelligent. In fairness, I was only sixteen years of age, so what did I know about the music business? That quickly changed. We all found our voices and we all had something to say before you knew it.

Something strange was also happening in Swords. My mother thought the world had gone a bit mad as girls had started to hang around outside our family house. I'd get up in the morning, peep out the window, and the driveway would be full of young wans. 'Hi'ya Ronan!' and they'd wave and giggle.

'Morning girls!' I'd wave back. It beat watching out for the postman.

I was getting used to female attention by this stage, as it had been a gradual phenomenon. A group of girls had started to follow the band around and Louis used to tell them where to find us when we were rehearsing in the city. We'd come out to find them outside the studio.

At first it was a strange sensation having these girls following us around and asking us for our autographs. I found it really weird. I was always a late starter with the girls at school, because I'd always been so taken up with sport and training, but I had to admit it was cool to suddenly find them interested in me. Louis used to say, 'Without the fans, guys, you are nothing. Be nice to everyone on the way up because you're going to meet them all on the way down.'

It started off with a couple of girls, then it was half a dozen, then a dozen. Before we knew it there were fifty or sixty girls around us every time we did something in town. And then they started hanging around our homes.

Although, at the start, I was mortified having them outside the house, I got used to it and came to like it. It was reassuring to have the fans there. As long as you could still see them, you still had a career.

I don't know what our neighbours must have thought, though. They'd never seen the likes of it before. But they all knew through the media that I was in a band, so I suppose they thought, 'That's pop stars for ya! And we have one on our bloody doorstep!'

But the girls were great. There was never any screaming or singing or anything like that. They were all very well behaved and it was very civilised. Some of the fans would hang around outside my house for hours and hours waiting for me to come back.

Mam used to feel sorry for them. 'Ah, come on in girls and have a cup of tea,' she'd say. And in they'd troop. She even let them take photographs of my (specially tidied) bedroom!

As the buzz grew among young girls in the city, people

started talking about Boyzone mania. Whenever we had a gig at the weekend, the white Transit van would pick us up outside the Royal Dublin Hotel on O'Connell Street. We'd all arrive on the public bus to be collected for the trip. Soon the girls discovered our regular rendezvous at the Royal Dublin and eventually we'd find ourselves running the gauntlet of up to a hundred fans on our way to the van.

But nothing compared to the first time we heard 'Working My Way Back To You' being played on the radio. As it happened, we were all together. It was March 1994, and the single had just been released. Paul Keogh of PolyGram was driving us down the country to do promotion in Wexford and the song came on 2FM radio in his Jeep. It was the Tony Fenton show and we pulled over to the hard shoulder to listen to it. I remember opening the door of the Jeep and Steve and myself jumped out and sat on a cut stone grey wall, listening to the song.

I said to Steve, 'Can you believe it, our song is on the radio. That's *our* song!'

Then we listened intently for the DJ's comments afterwards. 'That's Ireland's new pop sensations Boyzone with their debut single, "Working My Way Back To You",' he said, 'a cool version of the old Detroit Spinners hit, destined for Number One.'

'Yeeeaaahh!' We roared, sending half a dozen sheep running scared.

I was glued to the radio at home in Swords a couple of days later when the charts were being played on the radio. It was Larry Gogan on 2FM and it was a Saturday. I was sitting at home with a cup of tea in my hand and the radio turned up full blast.

Sure enough, Larry announced, 'And straight in at Number

Three, Ireland's very own answer to Take That and streets ahead they are too … Boyzone!'

'Yes! Yes! Yes! Yes!' I punched the air. I was a legend in my own living room.

CHAPTER 6

NOW WE ARE MOTORING

Ever since the day I'd taken my dad's car for a spin around the block, I'd fantasised about having my own motor parked in the driveway. I couldn't grow up fast enough to realise that dream. Nothing could compete with that kick you get from putting the keys in the ignition of your own machine, cranking up the engine and roaring off into the sunset.

I didn't have two beans to rub together when I went out and bought my first set of wheels, but for the princely sum of fifty pounds I managed to get hold of an old Opel Astra. Needless to say, it was a bit of an old banger!

Shortly afterwards, I went down to my local bank, the AIB in Swords, County Dublin, and spun them a yarn about having joined a very successful band, even though Boyzone was just in its infancy at the time. I was obviously very plausible because, to my surprise, they gave me a loan of four grand. The story of my life – splashing out the cash, even before I earned it.

With that money, I bought a 1987 white Opel Astra hatchback (OK, I liked Opel Astras!) and in the early days of Boyzone I could be seen whizzing out to RTE (the Irish television and radio network headquarters), with some of the other lads to do interviews. With the exception of Stephen, we were all into cars. We were all in love with our little vehicles. Shane, in particular, was a fanatic. He had a big old Ford Granada and he drove us around a lot.

Once we had wheels, whenever we had a gig north of Dublin, all the lads would drive to my house and Mick Devine, a really nice guy who runs a very successful chauffeur business in the city, would collect us there. He would take a couple of the Boyz, while the rest of us followed in our own motors.

Mam may have initially been sceptical about how long Boyzone would last, but there was no way we were going to fade away through lack of feeding. The afternoon before a gig would find her in the kitchen cooking sausages and making piles of sandwiches for all the gang, which would be loaded into the cars before we set off. Once she was happy we wouldn't starve, her next concern was all of us lads out on the road. Let's face it, none of us had been driving for long (well, officially anyway). Mam would be much happier, though, once she had equipped the cars with miraculous holy medals to keep us safe.

After the show, we would roar back to the estate in the early hours. I must have had very understanding neighbours. Shane would be revving up his engine at three or four in the morning outside our house in Swords. It was like a Grand Prix. My dad would stick his head out the window and roar, 'Shane Lynch, stop making that racket! Do you hear me, Shane Lynch! Be quiet with that car!' Shane would do it purposely, for the fun of winding up my father.

Boyzone's progress in those days could be gauged by the standard of our motors. The first time I got some decent money, I splashed out on a 1987 BMW. And from that day to this, it's been a series of cars. As the saying goes, the difference between the man and the boy is the size of the toy.

Boyzone's career was also beginning to pick up speed. We were still touring the country in the white Transit van, playing church halls and discos, when Louis broke the news about a 'mega gig'. Soccer fever had gripped the Irish nation in the summer of 1994 when the Republic of Ireland squad staged a valiant bid for top honours in the World Cup over in America. Jack Charlton, who had achieved royalty status in Ireland after taking our team further than any other manager had done before, had been our great hope once again. The team did produce enough thrills and spills to entertain the 'Great Green Army' of supporters, but, sadly, they found the ultimate prize to be out of their reach.

But, the Irish love a party, and the boys were treated like heroes upon their return from the States. Dublin city almost came to a stand-still as fans made their way to a big reception in the Phoenix Park, where the team arrived in a fleet of helicopters.

And there to provide the entertainment for the 80,000 people who flocked to the open air party would be ... Boyzone!

As the big day approached, the nerves began to build. Playing in front of 80,000 people was a mind-blowing prospect and one we had never anticipated at such an early stage in our career. After all, we had only been performing for a couple of months and, we were still at the very raw stage.

Going on stage in front of so many people scared the hell out of us that day. Looking at the faces of the punters in the first four rows was no help either. It was obvious that they were there to see the footballers, not a bunch of kids bouncing around the stage in orange jumpsuits! I was so nervous on stage I forgot the dance moves. It was only a very short performance and it seemed to be over in a flash. As soon as we got off the stage we wanted to turn around and get back up there again. But to be part of that special day in Ireland was a signal that, hey, this was really working.

More importantly, the success in Ireland of 'Working My Way Back To You' had finally persuaded Paul Keogh of PolyGram to sign us up for an album. When Louis announced the news he could hardly restrain himself. He had worked so hard to get this breakthrough, and there had been many times when he had been knocked back. For him there was a sense of relief more than anything else. So much money had been borrowed against the possibility of us getting a proper record contract. For the lads, too, it was the break we had been hoping for and working so hard towards. We were pleased, but also slightly overawed. The group was now really serious business. We were determined not to let down those who had put so much faith in us. It was no longer just our own careers on the line.

The signing of the album contract was a serious business as well. Everyone was warning me not to sign my life away. 'Make sure you don't get ripped off. That music industry is full of sharks,' a friend of the family warned.

Because I was only sixteen at the time, I was too young to sign the contract myself. I had to get my parents' consent and they had to go down to the PolyGram offices in Dublin's Aungier Street to sign on my behalf. I don't know who was the more emotional, me or my Mam. I was trying to remain as cool as possible – hey! I sign recording contracts every day, you know – but when I saw the look my Mam gave me as she signed, a grin took over my face and refused to let go for ages and ages. She was so proud of me. All four of my elder siblings had established themselves and were doing well. Now her youngest was on his way. Mam was delighted.

Before the ink on the contact was even dry, Louis had hired a UK producer called Ray Hedges, who had worked with Take That. It was time to get some songs in the can. He sent him over a number of suggestions, including the Osmonds' 'Love Me For A Reason' and the Monkees' classic 'Daydream Believer'.

The Osmonds' cover was a group decision. Sometimes Louis would travel with us and he'd play us tapes of songs he thought might be suitable for Boyzone. He'd put 'Love Me For A Reason' on and we all said, 'Yeah, love that one. Let's do that one'. Also Ray thought it was a good choice for the next single and this time Stephen and I were chosen to do the vocals. Louis saw us as the Gary Barlow and Mark Owen respectively of Boyzone, or so he said. So it was just the two of us who made the trip to Ray's studio outside London.

I was thrilled to be on a lead vocal this time. Not that I had a burning ambition to be the front man or the lead singer. Going into the group initially, all I thought was, 'I'm joining a boy band, something is going to come out of this.' I didn't care what it was, I just wanted to be in a group and whatever came with it was fine by me. I knew I would be out there in the limelight and that's what I wanted. Although I had been the lead singer in Nameste, my early band, Boyzone was completely different. This was pure pop, there were five of us singing and dancing and there were no instruments. It was more of a group thing, rather than a singer fronting a band. So I wasn't thinking about being a leader. I also knew that Mikey had been in several bands and he was talking about having written loads of songs, plus Stephen stood out as a singer, so I knew that Boyzone wasn't centred around me.

Ray was a cool guy, tall and skinny with a good sense of humour. The studio was called The Mothership and it was part of his house, which was a big advantage as, although it was fairly flashy and high-tech, it had a homely feel to it. Ray was a good guy to be around, and he made Steve and myself feel comfortable. He wasn't the big, high-powered, know-all producer guy talking down to us. It was all very relaxed, and I thought he got good performances from us.

It was one back over on Ian Levine when the Irish public agreed with me and put the song at the top of the charts. It was autumn 1994. Our first Number One! Perhaps more of those sullen crowds out in rural Ireland had liked us more than we thought!

Louis was delighted, but acutely aware that the Irish market was small-fry compared with getting a hit in the UK. But we met a brick wall trying to get 'Love Me For A Reason' released outside of Ireland. PolyGram had put it out at home, but we were an Irish signing and Polydor in the UK didn't want to know. We were just an Irish boy band trying to be Take That. They passed on the record.

Everyone knows how difficult it is for a British band to break in the States. I suppose we've learnt that ourselves with Boyzone. But for us the situation was the same after the Irish release of that single. We'd had a huge hit at home, but the UK, just across the water, seemed a million miles away. The UK exports hit music all over Europe, but the traffic is almost all one-way. British record companies weren't much more likely to pick up an Irish hit group than they were an act who had topped the charts in France or Germany. The Boyzone wagon seemed to have got stuck in a bottleneck.

While we were in Dublin jealously watching Take That continue their fantastic success in the UK, Michelle Hockley was sitting down in her home in West London to listen to a record she had been sent by a friend. Michelle was in charge of setting up the *Smash Hits* event, a major pop tour around Britain. It was to be headlined by several of the leading chart acts of the day, but she also wanted some newcomers. Our guardian angel was working overtime: the record was 'Love Me For A Reason' and she loved it.

She contacted Louis. He was an easy guy to find, everyone in Ireland seems to have his number. Michelle told Louis that she loved the single and she felt that we had real potential. Would we be interested in joining the roadshow? Louis took about a tenth of a second to say 'Yes'.

Boyzone were in a sombre mood when Louis told us he wanted to have a meeting. Why would no UK record label touch us? What were we doing wrong? There was no sign of a smile on Louis' face as he asked for our attention. I hope this isn't bad news, I thought.

'Guys, I have something to tell you!'

We all looked at Louis' deadpan expression.

'You're going on the *Smash Hits* Roadshow!'

'Feck off!'

'Yeah!'

'C'mon Lou, no messin', are you serious?'

'Yeah!'

Then Lou rolled around the room laughing.

At that moment we realised, 'Oh my God, it's finally the big time!'

We didn't need telling about the *Smash Hits* tour. This was our ticket into the real pop world, going on tour with all the acts we'd been reading about over the years in *Smash Hits* and the other teen mags. We knew, too, that we'd be up for the Best New Act on the road award. If we won that, we'd get on to the cover of *Smash Hits,* which would mean maximum exposure for Boyzone and our single, 'Love Me For A Reason'.

Apart from our brief appearance at the football party, we had been doing really small gigs up to then. Now we were going to be performing to an average of 10,000 people every night. In some cases, it was 25,000! What's more it was the UK. It was our big chance to make it in the international market. Everyone connected with Boyzone was completely fired up.

That night we all went out to celebrate and got hammered drunk. 'Lads!' I spluttered. 'I just wanna say, we've done it! We're showing everyone who said we couldn't do it that we can!'

As we celebrated we had high hopes. Surely we now had a chance of a UK release for the single? We certainly never envisaged the explosion that would follow over the next few months. We had no idea that The *Smash Hits* tour would unleash a whirlwind that has swept us along for the last six years.

I don't know what would have happened to Boyzone if it wasn't for Michelle.

We knew that there was a lot at stake as we rehearsed and rehearsed again in preparation for the tour. It was all pretty daunting. We knew that we were completely unknown in Britain. We would be just one of a massive bill of young entertainers, and it was going to be difficult to make an impact.

Each night people voted for the all-important Best New Act award. Every show we would have to be our very best.

We hurtled around the UK in the *Smash Hits* coach. It was a mad, mad scene, like a bunch of kids on a school outing, but with alcohol and attitude. We were all up at the front drinking while we careered along motorways, slagging the hell out of each other and having a laugh. I hit it off big time with Sean Maguire, the English soap star who had just launched a pop career. Sean had Irish connections and his grandad still lived in Cavan, where my dad comes from.

There were also others on the bus, including a group of girls who were as mad as brushes. They'd be swigging from a bottle of vodka, hurling abuse at everybody … throwing plates at people … lunatics! Forget about Oasis, these girls were the real rock 'n' rollers! It was like being in a confined space with Courtney Love clones.

We were also travelling in the company of a male duo called Real 2 Real and one of them, who was known as The Mad Stuntman, was a persistent wind-up merchant, slagging everybody on the bus and taking the piss.

I said to Shane, 'Let's get this one!'

'Yeah, how?'

'Don't worry, I'll think of something.'

One day we seized our chance. I grabbed a bucket of water and threw it over his head … and then ran for my life. That was the level of the carry on when we hit the *Smash Hits* tour, complete childishness!

At each town we went out and met as many fans as we could. We signed all the autographs and posed for all the pictures with the girls. We did everything that was asked of us and we loved every minute of it. It was an incredible buzz having all those young British girls chanting our name.

We were dying with nerves every night before the show. But once we got on stage we had a laugh and were just basically ourselves. We didn't try to be Take That or anyone else. We also flaunted our Irish identities and the fact that we were five young guys from the northside of Dublin city just out for a good time.

And it worked. The fans took a real shine to us.

During those couple of weeks away, when not on the road, the five of us lived together in London, in a rented four-storey town house near Waterloo station. We were well used to each other by then. Obviously we had particular friendships but we'd all become great mates.

Stephen and myself were the two who had bonded straight away. Shane and Keith had already been mates, so they were very close and Mikey tended to hang out with them as well after he joined.

At first I thought Stephen was very shy, but it quickly became clear that he was really very streetwise. He was much more savvy than he led people to believe, and I could sense that he was very ambitious and was working hard to achieve a dream. Keith was the big, loud joker, always up for the craic, always entertaining us with his stories of his nights out partying. Shane was a mad car fanatic, so the only conversation we ever got out of him was cars, cars, cars. That was fine by me because I love cars as well, but poor old Stephen was bored silly by all that. Mikey always seemed like he was locked deep in his own thoughts. He was a good guy to be around, but he kept to himself most of the time.

But having a house all to ourselves – five wild young lads away from home – was courting trouble. We were like children the first day we arrived, fighting over the beds. 'I'm having this room!'

'Ah, this is a better room than mine!

'Feck off, I'm not moving.'

Mikey and Keith, who was by now known by his nickname Duster (on account of an incident involving a teacher and a blackboard duster!), ended up in one bedroom. Shane was in the top room and Stephen and myself shared the third one.

We were each given an allowance for our meals, which worked out at fifteen pounds per day, and we got it in a lump sum. The first day we went out and bought a few groceries between us. I still had about two hundred pounds left in my pocket, as I had taken all my cash with me. Bad move.

Stephen and I found ourselves in Piccadilly, so we took ourselves off to Planet Hollywood for a snack. On the way back to the house I saw a jacket in a shop window for two hundred and fifty pounds. It was an orange one with cream sleeves. Nice!

'I have got to have that jacket!' I said to Stephen. So I borrowed fifty quid off him, went in and arrived back out wearing it.

When we arrived at the house, Duster asked, 'Where did you get that?'

'Bought it.'

'And what are you going to live on for the rest of the week?'

'Ah, don't worry about it, I look great.'

That was me, always putting fashion first. Spend the money now and somehow still live afterwards.

As it turned out, I ended up doing all the cooking in the

house for the lads during the rest of the week, so that I could eat!

The house in Waterloo was really up-market, or so it looked to us. 'Jaysus, this is very flash!' Duster announced the first day we arrived. It was like a showhouse when we moved in, but by the time we left it looked like a dump. If they'd put five wild animals in the house for three weeks they wouldn't have made such a mess. On reflection, they did put five wild animals into it for three weeks.

'Ronan, you do the washing up.'

'Feck off, what do you think I am, your mother!'

'Ah sure leave it, we'll be gone in a couple of weeks.'

There was empty food cans and take away trays all over the living area. Food was stuck to the seat covers and the carpets. Beer cans were in every room. One day there was some horseplay going on. Shane had hit me and I chased him, but in the struggle in his room I smashed his bedroom window. I just bashed off it and the glass shattered.

'Oh shit!'

'Don't worry, we'll be gone before it's discovered.' That was our answer to everything.

There was a phone in the house, so we used that to ring our families and all our friends back home. It didn't have a coin box, so the calls were endless. I still don't know who picked up the phone tab for that, because it never came our way.

As the tour came to a close, the big event got nearer and nearer. During my school days, the *Smash Hits* Poll Winners Party was always a big Sunday afternoon live TV spectacular, which I never missed, particularly as everyone would be talking about it in the playground the following day. I remember seeing Take That and all the other big pop acts performing on it and scooping awards.

Eventually the Sunday of the party arrived. We wandered through the crowd, completely star-struck, unable to believe we were actually there. Everywhere I looked there was a star on my shoulder. Several of the Take That guys were wandering around backstage. East 17 were over in another corner. It was a huge buzz.

When the Best Newcomers award was announced and Boyzone were called up on to the stage to collect it, it was like winning an All Ireland Football Final. That still rates as one of the most exciting moments of our lives. To be on that show was exciting enough, but to win it as well! We were picking up a prize that had been previously won by Take That and E17. Duster said into the mic on stage, 'Everybody at home – we made it!' It was like, we're over here in the UK with all these happening young bands and we've pulled off something that's never been achieved before. No Irish pop band had done it before us. And we wanted Ireland to be proud of us.

Suddenly, the pop industry sat up and started to take notice of Boyzone. *Smash Hits* put us on the cover of their magazine, with the headline: 'The Six Days That Made Them Famous'. That title was pretty accurate as far as the UK was concerned. Even though we had been serving our apprenticeship on exhaustive tours of Ireland, it was virtually overnight stardom in Britain. The *Smash Hits* event had made us. Gazing at the cover of that particular issue, with Boyzone staring back at me, I thought, 'Yee-yes! Superstar!'

As a teenager, *Smash Hits* was part of my regular read. It was always crammed with stories and gossip on all the pop stars and

I lapped it all up. Now I was a pop star myself in *Smash Hits*. Unreal!

As far as we were concerned, we were going back home in a blaze of glory after a great victory. I hate to admit it, but we were on a real star trip on the return flight. I cringe at the thought of it.

First off we started telling everyone we'd been away for six months, rather than three weeks, and then, like a bunch of eejits, we started singing 'Coming Home Now' on the plane. At this point, I would like to apologise to anyone who was on that flight. One of us was going, 'Bah! bah! Bah!' and Stephen was going, 'We're going home now …' It was priceless, the innocence of it. We were kids. We didn't have a clue.

Upon our return, we had an appearance on the *Late Late Show*, where we had first been introduced to the Irish nation the day after Boyzone was formed. This time we seemed to have got it into our heads that we were superstars. Gay Bryne may be the talk show king of Ireland, but we acted as if we were doing him a favour by appearing on the show!

What did we look like! A bunch of rejects, that's what! We had been to a fashion show in Birmingham the day before we came home and we got a load of promotional gear. It was all baggy clothes. We thought we were super cool that night as we strutted out into the studio after being introduced by Gay.

And, boy, were we oozing attitude! We were like, 'Alright Gay! How's it goin'? Alright man!'

People must have looked at us and thought, 'Who do these eejits think they are?' We were pop stars in our heads before we had any real success. Like a bunch of spoilt brats.

But then we *were* kids. I was still only sixteen years old.

CHAPTER 7

WHEN ALL IS SAID AND DONE

Like most things in showbusiness, not everything was as it seemed. It was Christmas of 1994, which was a surreal period in my life. Boyzone was finally a happening group. There was a huge buzz around us. We were Number Two in the UK charts and we had our very first concert coming up at the Point Depot, Ireland's premier concert venue. I couldn't have asked for a better Christmas present.

But the December Boyzone Christmas Party hadn't sold out, so we had to pull the curtains across half of the venue to make it look good. But it didn't matter to us. It was still The Point. Everyone from U2 to Tom Jones had performed there. When you got there in Ireland it was a sure sign that you had made it to the big time.

'Alright, Duster?'

'Yeah, Ro! Can you believe this, man, The Point!'

We were hanging out in the maze of little dressing rooms in a building adjoining the venue itself. As a kid going to the Point to see shows, I had always imagined that backstage was a really special, magical place. The reality, of course, was totally different. It was just a warren of small, plain changing rooms, each one with a basic chair, table and mirror. At the back there was a canteen with a pool table.

There was chaos backstage at that concert because Louis had allowed hundreds of people in for the meet and greet. We didn't care. It was all new to us and we were just so excited to be the biggest stars in town that night. The whole of Ireland could have come back and said hello and we'd have made them welcome. We were just kids and full of energy.

Despite the fact that it was our first big concert in front of a home audience, the pre-show nerves were no worse than usual. We were more excited than anything else. Before going out, we were giving each other hugs and kisses and wishing each other the best.

'Can you believe this!' Duster announced again as we weaved around big trunks behind the stage.

We emerged to the roar of the crowd: 'Boyzone! Boyzone! Boyzone!' It's good to hear it anywhere, but Dublin will always be extra special.

But anyone who had been to see the Take That concert at The Point must have been bitterly disappointed with Boyzone's stage set that night. Take That had come in with a million pound production because they were at the peak of their career and they could afford to splash out on a fantastic backdrop with spectacular lights and special effects. We, on the other hand, had a black stage, no set, and just our own performance to rely on. Fortunately, the experience of playing all those little venues around Ireland, as well as the *Smash Hits* shows, had given us the confidence and training to produce a professional vocal performance on the night. There were no embarrassing hiccups, no fluffed dance routines and it turned out to be a slick set. The crowd loved it and it was a proud night for our families who were sitting out among the fans.

It was the *Smash Hits* tour that had made things happen so fast in the autumn of 1994. From then on, the goal posts kept on moving. Polydor, the UK branch of our Irish label, had come on board with all their machinery behind us, and 'Love Me For A Reason' had been released at last in the UK for Christmas.

The band had been buzzing as we rehearsed for our first appearance on *Top of the Pops*. The studio looked much smaller than I'd imagined, but we could scarcely believe we were actually there. Like all kids, the show was a must-see every week for me. I never missed it. I remember sitting mesmerised in front of the telly whenever George Michael was on. Now here I was in the famous BBC studios treading the same boards, hanging out in the same dressing rooms. Cool!

The single almost caused a major sensation. We were only kept off the prestigious number one spot in the UK charts by East 17, whose single, 'Stay Another Day', took the honour. But getting to number two was conquering the world, as far I was concerned. God bless my innocence. Little did I know that the real work was only starting.

After Christmas there was no time to sit back and enjoy our little bit of success. We had to buckle down to our all important debut album, *Said And Done*. Louis decided that Stephen and myself should work with Ray Hedges, co-writing the songs. Mikey, Keith and Shane would also drop in and out. I felt very nervous and insecure going into that first songwriting session with Ray. I had never written properly in a studio before that.

'Don't worry, Ronan, it won't take you long to get into the groove,' Ray reassured me.

Stephen and myself were green horns where songwriting was concerned. Even though Ray was easy to get along with, I was afraid to say anything. I was eager to write, but I didn't have much confidence. I might have been able to sing and dance in front of 80,000 people, but this had the potential for real humiliation.

But Ray eventually coaxed it out of us. It was he who taught me how to write. He would get us to throw out lines and we'd take those and build on them. Soon I'd see a song coming together with lyrics and melodies. It was a magical experience. A whole new avenue had been opened up to me. We ended up getting credited with a whole batch of songs on the album including, 'Coming Home Now', 'Together', 'When All Is Said And Done', 'So Good', 'Key To My Life' and 'Believe In Me'.

It was only at this point, when I co-wrote and sang on so many songs on that album, that I thought, 'Things are changing here. Things are looking good.' And even though Stephen was on just as many, I was still very pleased with myself. I never thought I'd be on half of them.

That summer we took on Ireland with a vengeance by performing all over the 32 counties, with Virgin-Cola coming on board as our sponsors. It was the biggest nation-wide tour the island had ever seen. We did 36 shows in 30 days, matinees included. It was a massive, ground-breaking event, covering arenas, nightclubs, the whole spectrum. The five of us piled into a Snoopy Bus for 30 days and worked our backsides off. We were living off energy, ambition and cola.

Everywhere we went, every town and city we played in, helped to swell our fan base.

Now all we had to do was repeat that around the world.

1995 was a rollercoaster for Boyzone. There wasn't a day to take a breather during that major year in the early history of the group, as we struggled to keep up with the never-ending demands of a breaking pop act.

It was a difficult period for all the individuals in the band, trying to get a handle on this really bizarre lifestyle. We were constantly tired from the late night and early morning. You never get enough sleep in this business. We hardly ever saw our families or friends any more, and that part of it was particularly hard to deal with. There was a lot of loneliness, a lot of heartache and many, many tears. But it's something you just have to come to terms with and in time you do. You create your own world. You learn who to talk to, to make yourself feel better, and how to deal with separation.

Sometimes our family had to come to us. Our first live performance after the recording of 'Love Me For A Reason' was in a little venue called Togher's in the County Kildare town of Naas, about twenty miles outside Dublin. Our families and some friends were travelling in convoys, about sixty people in all. So it was a proud moment for us. However, the small club was thick with dry ice during the set so we didn't realise until later that, apart from a half-dozen fans, our families made up the entire audience.

It was probably a good thing that the Number One hits didn't come straight away in the UK, because it kept us hungry. That target remained elusive, always out there to be worked for.

It meant we could see it was still necessary to do that early morning radio interview, that extra TV breakfast show or that magazine photo shoot, crammed as they were in to a schedule that already seemed humanly impossible.

After our Number Two with 'Love Me For A Reason', we came close to the top spot again with a string of singles put out over the next fourteen months. 'Key To My Life', released in May 1995 got to Number Three; 'So Good', two months later, with me singing lead vocal, reached Number Four; 'Father & Son', a huge favourite at our live shows, got to Number Two in November; and 'Coming Home Now' came out at the beginning of the following year, peaking at Number Three. It wasn't until we released our version of the Bee Gees song 'Words' that we finally clinched the big prize. I'm glad that we had to wait and that we had to work hard for it because it made us appreciate success when it did come. It also steeled us against the setbacks that would inevitably happen in the future. As a result of that early experience, we never took anything for granted throughout the rest of our career.

We took on everything that was asked of us during 1995. Some successes seemed to happen in a dream. In August we released our first album, *Said And Done*. It immediately sailed into the Number One position in Ireland and the UK. We were in shock. A Number One album! But we were a pop band, we were no U2! What had we done to deserve this? We might have talked the talk, but inside we were seriously surprised. Along the way, there were a million magazines to talk to and we did all the silly stuff that people requested for interviews and photo shoots. We had no shame. We wore funny coloured shirts and jumped off chairs. I can't count the number of times I answered questions about my favourite colour or what I did first thing when I got up in morning, or, daftest of all, 'If you were a biscuit, what biscuit would you be?' The silliest things they make you do in the early days! But you do them because you want to be on the magazine covers. It was all new in the beginning and we were willing to do it. Looking back, I can't believe I went along with half of it.

Stylists had a difficult time with Boyzone during those days. We had our own ideas, not all of them good ones, as you will see from early pictures of our stage clothes. Some of the gear was hideous. The zips ... The red leather ...

We had different stylists along the way, but we usually lost them because we wouldn't wear the clothes they tried to tog us out in. 'Feck off! I'm not wearing that!' We were so headstrong. Stylists can be very sensitive, so they just ran.

Other times we had to tow the company line. There was a lot at stake for everyone involved. Life in a boy band is like being in an army. That's not far off the mark. It requires huge discipline. But what matters in showbusiness is what is seen, and, I admit, out of the public eye we were far from model boy-band material during those first couple of years.

I know the impression was out there that butter wouldn't melt in my mouth or that I was 'Mr Responsible'. But in actual fact I was just a normal young guy like everyone else, doing things that young guys do for fun. We just didn't publicise it in the media. Bands like Oasis were bragging about how much they drank or whatever. Why go on about it? We weren't into drugs, but we did enjoy a good booze up. To put it mildly.

If the truth be known, we could have drunk any rock band under the table.

But I'm glad that we had our wild days because it is part of growing up and developing. As a lot of the fans could see, we were normal young fellas. There were numerous times when they saw me half-cut in the corner of a hotel, trying to play the piano and singing out of tune.

At the end of our first tour in Germany, we were all partying back at the hotel. There were about fifty or sixty fans in a circle around us, some guy was playing the piano and we all started singing songs. As the night went on the bottle of Jack Daniels just got lower and lower. The people who really knew Boyzone were aware of what we were like – the fans used to give me gifts of Jack Daniels. We never tried to hide it, but neither did we go out of our way to promote it. In the end it is down to the media – they decide you are a certain thing and then stick with the stereotype.

Our schedule nowadays is a lot more controlled, but in those early times it was really full on, total madness half of the time. We couldn't let any opportunity to promote Boyzone pass us by. Things were constantly going wrong, one of us was always missing a flight and I was always losing my luggage. Occasionally we lost each other as the schedules collapsed and one of us would be in totally the wrong city.

We seemed to spend half our time at the airport. Some of those TV shows we had to do in Europe were a real pain in the ass. If you were at home in Ireland, you'd have to fly out at six o'clock in the morning to get to Germany. Then you'd drive for two hours to get to the studio where you'd rehearse once and then find you have to wait five or six hours until the next rehearsal.

There was always extra pressure on Steve and myself to be there because we had emerged as the lead vocalists. Just getting there was the main thing. In fact, once one of us turned up, it would be acceptable. And if everyone was there for the TV show on the night that was just grand.

We knew we had cracked the big time in the UK when fans started holding all-night vigils outside the hotels we stayed in. We were on our first major UK arena tour in the autumn of '95, having just finished the marathon series of Irish shows that summer, before embarking on a short tour of Germany in the winter. Alongside the drudgery, the early mornings and late nights, there were some great, unrepeatable moments.

One of the highlights of that UK tour was an appearance at the Royal Albert Hall on 5 October 1995. It was a major achievement for Boyzone and one that hit the headlines in Ireland. Our families rang to say even Irish rock critic Eamon Carr had said this was a big moment. He wrote in the *Evening Herald* newspaper: 'Today the heavyweights of the classical music world pack up their violins, oboes and batons and move out of the Royal Albert Hall. They must make way for five working-class lads from Dublin. Tonight the Royal Albert Hall, one of the most prestigious venues in the world, belongs to Boyzone.'

That night was fantastic. Boyzone mania lifted the roof of the Royal Albert Hall. The British fans were loud and wild and seemed very different to the girls back home. They were older and they seemed wealthier. A lot of them had cars and they followed us from city to city. We began to spot the same faces outside hotels as we ran for our coach.

They seemed to know every movement we made. I think they had our itinerary before we even got it. They all had mobile phones and they networked, passing information between fans around Europe. For a while, we couldn't understand how fans knew when we'd be arriving into European airports. Then we discovered that one of their sources was working in an airline and she was handing out information from the details on the computer.

I never got into the groupie thing. For me, I was happy for the girls to chant my name, for it to be an unreal fantasy. I didn't really want it to get real. It never could have been, anyway. You'd always be Ronan from Boyzone, never Ro from the Wilson Estate, and I just wasn't interested in rock-star style flings. But we were always very accessible to the girls. We didn't have fifty security guards with us pushing the fans away. Instead we had a great guy called Barrie Knight. A big black guy, he looks tough on the outside but has a soft centre. He can control fans single-handedly in the nicest possible way. To be honest, he's there as much for the fans as for Boyzone. Unless there's a controlled situation, the fans can end up getting hurt.

Barrie would say, 'Girls, you know the rules!' And there'd be instant order. He was like a ringmaster cracking a whip at the circus lions. The girls respected Barrie because he treated them with respect.

The fans got to meet us up close. We tried to keep it as normal as possible and not a star-fan thing. We always loved to have a chat, but we also needed our own space. Barrie was there to make sure that we got that.

Sometimes he had a job on his hands. Wherever we went, the fans would book rooms in the hotels we stayed in. Their aim was always to end up on floors near our rooms. You'd get gangs of them in the same room, kicking up a racket throughout the night.

Barrie would go down banging on their doors, 'Shut up now or I'll have you put out!'

It was a tough year. We knew that the success of our debut album had meant that we weren't going to disappear overnight, but the work-rate never slackened. That year also saw our first visit to Asia for three weeks. In the middle of everything else that was thrown at us, we were to head off on our first really long-haul trip away from home.

Looking back, I don't know how we got through that year. By the time we finished our final show in The Point at the end of December, we were all basket cases. I don't think any of us could have taken any more at that point. I was worn out.

Fortunately, holidays had been finally planned into the itinerary and we all went off in different directions to recharge the batteries. I had no hesitation about where to go. I had made some money and I wanted to spend it. As ever, it was burning a hole in my pocket. I headed out to Linda and Gary in New York.

I really lived it up in the States. I bought anything I could. Linda and Gar had no idea of the success that Boyzone had become until their little brother arrived out to them with a big wad of dollars in his back pocket. They had spent a fortune on me on visits back to Ireland and now it was payback time. Linda laughed at me at I determinedly shopped from one end of Fifth Avenue to the other. After a couple of days Gar suggested going skiing, so I went off to a store and splashed out on all the gear. We had a brilliant time on the slopes. I found it hilarious crashing into great snow piles completely out of control. On the second day, we found ourselves trapped after a serious snowfall. But the Keating luck didn't desert us – we were trapped in a pub, and were forced to drink ourselves silly.

It was a total release valve for me going out there. With Linda and Gar, I didn't have to live the Boyzone thing all the time. No one knew who I was, which, although a bit of a shock at first, gave me complete freedom. It put into perspective the frantic previous eighteen months. At times the treadmill of the pop business had pushed us beyond our limits.

I wasn't considering quitting, but I was surprised how great it was to forget about the band for a while.

CHAPTER 8

FASTEN YOUR SEATBELTS

Bangkok is crazy. It's like jumping on a space ship and going to Mars. Only worse.

We are racing through the narrow streets in tuk-tuks, motorbike taxis with a little cart for the passengers.

'Faster! Faster!' Shane Lynch shouts at his driver. The motorbike engines sound like high-pitched screams. Up ahead, Mikey is in the lead, just. He swivels round to shout and gesticulate.

The city around soaks up the noise and throws it back at volume ten. It's my first day in Asia and I am in a state of shock. I can't believe the smells and the dirt. Going out on the streets the humidity seemed to sap my energy in an instant. We grabbed the taxis as soon as we could. Being on the pavement was like being caught up in some panic-driven evacuation. The crowds were so dense that you could easily get lost in them.

We're approaching the river, weaving through thick traffic and choking on warm, oily fumes. By the side of the road, there seem to be open sewers, clogged with rubbish being picked over by mangy dogs. There are people on all sides, everyone seems to be rushing and shouting. We stop by the river and shakily climb out of the tuk-tuks. The high spirits of the race have drained away. The others look as freaked out by this place as I am. The river looks disgusting – it has a rotten, sickly smell and unidentified objects float in its brown, greasy waters. To our amazement, there are people here, living in makeshift shacks by the banks. We see clothes and children being washed in the river. I think of all the horrible diseases they must be exposing themselves to. Over their heads, set back from the river, loom the towers and turrets of brightly coloured temples and palaces. It's a million miles from the northside of Dublin.

'Race back to the hotel?' suggests Mikey.

I was only a kid just out of school. I didn't know anything. On that first trip to Bangkok I was shell shocked by the strange locals, the weird culture and the food. 'Just get me through these three weeks,' I thought. A week later we read how a tourist had lost a leg in a tuk-tuks crash. There's nothing for it during our free time but to hide out in our hotel rooms and count the days to when we can go home. I flick through magazines or read the hotel brochure for the umpteenth time, looking forward to when I can ring Dublin again. Mam is always full of reassurance and support, but right now home seems further away than ever. At least when I was in the UK and Europe I knew that I was only one or two hours' flying time to Dublin.

After three days the homesickness becomes unbearable. I sit in my hotel bedroom and cry my eyes out. I'm lonely and I don't want to be here. Turning on the telly to distract myself, all I find is foreign channels. Flicking it off and throwing the remote control on to the bed, I sob to myself. Now I understand why rock 'n' roll bands throw TVs out of hotel windows.

Pacing around the room at four o'clock in the morning, still awake from the jet-lag and feeling sorry for myself, I'm thinking, 'Is this what I'm going to have to live with for the rest of my life? Can I really do this?'

On our fifth day, the five of us are sitting in Mikey's room and he is strumming a guitar. We start throwing around lines and end up writing a silly song called, 'Five Nights In Bangkok'. It went something like, 'Five nights in Bangkok/we haven't got a clue. Five nights in Bangkok/we don't know what to do.' Luckily, that one never saw the light of day.

But by the end of the three weeks, our mood had improved. We were coming to like the food and the lifestyle. The people, whom we'd thought totally crazy when we first arrived, were actually very gentle, kind and sweet.

Eight months later we were back in South East Asia with a more positive attitude. This time we knew how to enjoy the culture and the people and that was probably one of the best trips we ever had to foreign parts. We went out drinking, hanging out in clubs and bars, having a laugh, making the most of it and appreciating the opportunity to be there. This time we were trying out the local cuisine and experimenting that little bit more.

Even in those early days, the Asian fans made us feel like superstars. Touching down at airports, it was like the scenes of Beatlemania we had seen on old footage. When our plane hit the tarmac we'd find thousands of female fans waiting to give us a hero's reception. It was chaotic, but exhilarating.

The Asian fans go really wild, because they only get their bands in once a year or maybe twice, if they're lucky. So they make the most of it when you do visit. They are with you all the time. It's really full on – they even slept outside our hotels.

As time went on and we got to grips with that part of the world, we learned how to wind down and let off steam there. Indonesia is an amazing place and we were in Surabaya doing a daytime TV show. Afterwards we all went on the rant for the night. We borrowed a rattley old windowless van – a complete banger! – and drove around town. Keith Duffy, Shane Lynch and myself were standing on the back of it as it careered through the crowded streets. People were shouting, 'Weeahhh! Heeahh!', at us and we were roaring back. This was about two o'clock in the morning. It's a wonder we didn't get arrested.

We went on to Singapore to do a big TV show there. It was one of those situations where we arrived forty-four hours before the event. The hanging around could be incredibly boring, but we always sparked off something to break the tedium. 'Mr Security' Barrie Knight started singing, 'Swing low, sweet chariot …' and off we went.

Taking Barrie's lead, the Boyzone entourage launched into a couple of hours of Gospel singing. Before we knew it, the time had come around to do the actual show. We had been stuck down in the basement and we made our way up to the TV studio, singing all the way. We got into the lifts, which were in darkness, and we continued the big Gospel sing-in. And as the whole mass of us made the final entry on to the set, we were still in full flight on the vocal acrobatics, with Stephen Gately out front in his high voice. That was our way of giving ourselves a day off. I can see the other side of it, where rock bands who don't have any imagination might do something outrageous to stop the boredom. But we always had our own take on it all.

Living out of a suitcase became a way of life for us, and packing those damn cases was our eternal nightmare. I developed a routine ... fill them up and sit on them! On our initial trips away we brought everything with us except the kitchen sink. Out of all the lads, I am the worst. I carry so much crap. Half the clothes, CDs, books and gadgets I carried around never got taken out of the suitcase. Instead I would wear the same things and spend a fortune on hotel laundry.

Covering all eventualities, clothes-wise, was also a juggling trick. Hopping from country to country brought its own problems. How many different climatic changes were we going to experience? In one place they'd be monsoon weather, the next location would be a desert, and then it would be straight on to somewhere freezing. All in one trip.

It's not as glamorous as it might sound. Inevitably I'd end up shivering in a damp T-shirt in a cold airport before emerging to a tropical heat wave. It was often more than my more body could cope with and the result was that I had a constant streaming cold whilst on tour.

After our second visit to the Far East, when we were all a little older and more open-minded, the forthcoming tour of the UK seemed less daunting than before. In the summer of 1996 we travelled the length and breadth of the country, and more than 250,000 came out to see Boyzone. It was a great opportunity to try out the new songs we'd written for our second album, *A Different Beat*, which was to be released that October.

And there was Wembley.

On 13 July 1996, we played the first of four shows at the Wembley Arena. It may not be the biggest venue in the world, but you know you've made it when you get there. Wembley has that extra special magic about it. I remember Matt Goss of Bros saying to me one time, 'Wembley is sacred. Savour every moment of it.'

On the way to the Arena it felt like the first time we did a concert at The Point Depot in Dublin. This was the big time. We got the bus to stop outside the venue so that we could savour the moment of seeing the Boyzone name, massive bold black letters against a dazzling yellow background, emblazoned on the front of the building.

It took Duster to sum up the moment, 'Jaysus, lads, it's a long way from Toghers in Naas.'

Backstage is the same at every venue the world over. You pass empty massive trunks that hold the stage gear as you weave through the area to the dressing rooms. There's always a room called 'catering' where the food is dished out. And the dressing rooms are never as luxurious as you imagined.

After getting there and doing the sound check for the performance later in the evening, we had a few hours to kill. So we were fooling around backstage to pass the time. Our agent Louis Parker, who always looked like a real rock 'n' roll head in his T-shirt, jeans and hair hanging down around his shoulders, had provided a couple of motorised scooters out the back for us, as he knew the kids we were and how we liked to fool around.

So I went out to mess around on one and a massive scream went up. Hordes of fans were gathered at the railings hoping to catch a glimpse of the acts on the bill. The scooters were great little machines and I hopped on one and started showing off in front of all the fans. I was booting all around the outdoor area when I decided to pull up the handlebars and do a wheelie by lifting the front wheel in the air and whizzing around on the back one.

Problem was, the scooters don't work like that and I was propelled up into the air. There's only one place you're going to go after that and I hit the ground with a massive thud, landing on my coccyx. I let out a roar with the pain, but I think my ego was more hurt than anything else.

Barrie Knight came running over.

'Are you OK, Ro?'

He looked really concerned, after all, there was a big show to do in a couple of hours.

'Yeah,' I muttered, 'but I think I just smashed up me arse!'

Barrie picked me up off the ground and I hobbled around for a few minutes while I recovered. 'I'm OK, Barrie,' I said eventually, as I meekly crawled back into the venue dying from the embarrassment.

That first Wembley concert was also a special night for our families. We felt really proud flying them all over to be there for the big moment. We wanted to show them their sons had 'done good'. But I think that knowing our mams and dads and brothers or sisters were out there probably made us even more nervous on the night in case we let them down in some way during the performance.

Our first duty of the night, like the routine at most gigs, was the 'meet and greet', where fans who have won competitions as part of the promotion for concerts are brought backstage to meet us, get autographs and have souvenir photos taken with each member of the band.

Next we always had a little Boyzone quiet moment alone in

the dressing room, to collect our thoughts and bond as a group before going on stage. I remember saying to the lads before we went out, 'It's just another venue, it's just another show, you got to look at it like that.'

As the lights went down at Wembley that night, I heard the roar of the 15,000 fans who had come to see us, and I was shaking with a mixture of excitement and nerves. 'This is it,' I thought, 'Wembley!'

There's darkness and smoke on stage and when the lights go up we're there and it's straight into 'Together'. From that moment on I made sure I enjoyed that special time on stage. I knew I would be back at Wembley the following night and later that same month, but that particular show was the one that counted.

Wherever we went, the venues and the crowds got bigger and bigger. It was Boyzone mania. If we thought the fans were crazy on our first trips out East, when we toured South East Asia, the Middle East and India in 1997, it was bedlam.

This time when we arrive in the Philippines we are met by the National Guard and the Chief of Police. There are unbelievable scenes awaiting us as we step off the plane. We run from plane to car to hotel, always in a little bubble, separated by glass from the crowds and the screaming. Next we fly to Taiwan, where we're overtaken by the news of the death of Princess Diana. Her image in newspapers and magazines would follow us round our tour. The following nights in Seoul and Kuala Lumpur, we stand a minute in silent tribute and the crowd hushes from a din to a murmur.

At each stop, we seemed to collect more and more luggage.

The tour was sponsored by Swatch and they gave each of us a big Swatch watch, a massive thing, more like a clock. It was a nightmare to lug about. And at each city I shopped all the time. Soon I had so many clothes that they won't fit into the case. As we descended to land at Surabaya in Indonesia, rather leave them behind, I put on some of the bulky ones. As we emerged into the sweltering heat, I was wearing a leather jacket, a denim jacket and a puffer sleeveless jacket over them. I also had on a cowboy hat and a thick pair of jeans. There were about ten thousand fans waiting at the airport. It was complete and utter madness and chaos. Keith and Shane went out first, Mikey followed and then Stephen and myself. I had the big Swatch clock under one arm and hand luggage under the other one.

In no time, we were all pounced on by the fans. I disappeared out of sight after being helplessly propelled along and swept into the body of the crowd. In the frenzy that followed, I was sent crashing to the ground, with thousands of bodies all around me. I was lying on the floor, hanging on for dear life to the Swatch watch and the luggage under my arms. Above me there were what seemed like thousands of arms and legs and faces. All hysterical, all shouting and sobbing.

Suddenly I felt an arm pick me up. It was Barrie Knight, and he dragged me through the battle zone. Along the way I lost my bag and my Swatch watch. They just disappeared into the heaving mass of people.

We managed to fight our way out of the terminal and I could see a Mercedes car with the engine running. The door was open and Stephen was lying in the back. Barrie chucked me in on top of him, closed the door and roared at the driver, 'Go! Go! Go!' The car zoomed off with me shouting, 'Where's me

Swatch? Where's me bag?'

Boyzone always had a fantastic team looking after us. There was a great sense of security, that everything would be taken care of and there was nothing for us to worry about apart from our own job. This incident was no exception. Eventually both my ridiculous Swatch and my hand luggage arrived safely at the hotel where we were staying. How they got them back I'll never know. That's professionals for you.

Of course, Sod's Law then came into play. I arrived back in London at the end of the tour, only to discover that the airline had lost my luggage. Among that missing baggage was the giant Swatch I had minded with such care on the tour!

After two more stops, we flew to Bahrain where we were to perform in the grounds of the Prince's Palace. Our itinerary also included a public signing session for the fans. The people there are very religious and they're normally very placid. But at this event you could sense tension in the air. There was a ring of local security, with their arms entwined, trying to hold back the army of people surging forward. It was a situation that threatened to explode in our face at any moment. Our own security was conscious of this, so plans were quickly put in place to get us out.

Our cars were already waiting for us around the back, and Barrie told us, 'When I give you the signal, go!' At this point it was getting a little scary because there were so many people and we were really exposed.

Eventually, Barrie gave us the signal and Stephen and Shane were the first to shoot off. I was following close behind, but in the line of the escape route there was an awkwardly placed chair. Shane jumped it, but I was so close behind him that I didn't see it until the last moment. I tried to jump, but too late. My foot clipped the chair back and I ended up face down on the ground. There were fans swarming all around, but I managed to regain my balance, only to be sent flying again by Duster who came charging from behind and walloped into me.

Down I went again, sprawled across the floor, with some little old lady underneath me. Where on earth did she come from? Keith and myself both managed to get up and start running across the marble floor. We were sliding around the place trying to find our way out, screeching around corners. It was just like a Scoobie Doo cartoon! All the time the fans were in hot pursuit. Just behind me, Keith tripped and fell again and, as he went down, he grabbed the belt of my trousers. At this stage he was laughing so much he couldn't find his feet. I was trying to pick up speed, but Duster was still hanging off the back of me. It looked for a moment like he was water skiing. Eventually, we found our way through two exit doors and Barrie was roaring, 'Get in the van! Get in the van! Go! Go! Go!'

My last sight was of Barrie being pinned against a glass door holding back the swarm of fans. It's a totally different world over there. Some of the live concerts we did were nerve racking because we feared for the safety of fans. The security sometimes left a lot to be desired. It wasn't like the shows we did back home and in Europe, where safety standards at concerts meant that you didn't have to worry about the people out front. In places like South East Asia and India it was a different story. I used to get freaked out when I'd see kids being crushed at the front of the stage. I'd stop the show until it was sorted. That scary scene was repeated time and again on those trips.

India, our last stop, was the highlight of the tour for me. It's the other side of the world and nine thousand people want to hear our songs. They know who Ronan Keating is and who Shane Lynch and Boyzone are! Wow! I think. Fantastic. But here the local stewards and security were armed with big canes and they'd start thrashing the kids to keep them in order. They'd literally be beating the young girls back into place and this seemed to be an accepted practice because the fans would smile through it. We couldn't stand by and condone that kind of treatment, though, so we used to get our own security guys to advise the local crew on how to manage that side of the event.

Travelling through those countries also opened my eyes to the other side of life that exists out there. I witnessed, at first hand, the heartbreaking poverty that many people in that part of the world are coping with, day in and day out. There we were, living the life of pampered pop stars, while they were dealing with the daily grind of just existing. While we were focused on record sales and chart positions, their main preoccupation was finding the next meal for their starving kids. It made us feel so helpless, because what can you do?

So many in India have nothing. We'd go into catering on our tour there and all kinds of delicious food would await us, a sumptuous spread. But on the other side of the wall, people were starving. Barrie used to take loads of the food and bring it outside to them. The whole scale of the poverty trap in places like India and the Philippines is just mindblowing. In Manila as we were driving along a street, there was a little kid running along beside us begging for money. We had all been given fruit hampers by the management of the hotel where we were staying and we'd taken them with us from the bedrooms. I gave the little kid a bunch of grapes and, suddenly, it was like a swarm of locusts descending on us. Kids came from nowhere and we gave them out all the fruit. Money was nothing, all they wanted was the food.

I watched one child being instantly surrounded by three other little guys after Shane had given him a mango. Then they all ran off together to a woman sitting beside a pillar on the side of the street and they gave her the fruit. The lady was obviously their mother and cut it up and shared it out. That's the way they were living.

On that 1997 tour we were accompanied by a little bald guy called BP Fallon, or Beeps as he is known to his friends. Beeps is one of those guys who seems to have been around forever. In his various incarnations as a publicist, DJ, writer, photographer and general 'vibe master', BP has been associated with everyone from Marc Bolan and T. Rex to John Lennon and U2. Recently he's been around a lot on the Dublin scene. I suppose it was inevitable that he would eventually find his way into the Boyzone camp.

Beeps wanted to do a book on Boyzone – he had already written a tome about U2, and filled it with his own photographs, after accompanying them on their Zoo TV tour as a DJ – so we agreed that he could tag along.

The fact that he had been around the music business for so long, and had such a wealth of stories to tell, really fascinated me, so we became good friends on that trip. In fact, I don't think my sanity would have remained intact during those weeks if it hadn't been for Beeps, because I was feeling really down on that tour. By that stage, I had been away from home for about four or five months. We'd gone straight on to the Asian tour from another tour and there seemed to be no end to the work. I'd phone my Mam all the time, but it just wasn't the same as having some time at home.

Having Beeps around proved to be a great distraction. He made me laugh. Imagine the Rowan Atkinson character, Mr Bean … well, some of the things that happened to Beeps reminded me of him.

It has to be said that he wasn't everyone's favourite person on the trip. Our tour manager Mark Plunkett wasn't impressed, because poor old Mark now had six kids to mind rather than five, even though BP is a fifty-something.

Beeps was constantly losing his luggage and he was always held up at customs. It just went on and on, one incident after another. We laughed, but Mark had the job of keeping the show running smoothly and BP was throwing a spanner in the works. So he was constantly in trouble with Mark.

When we were in Jakarta, BP accidentally ran into a glass door. He hit the floor harder than he hit the glass – boom! – and bounced backwards. I'll never forget it. He was carted off to casualty and ended up getting six stitches in a gaping head wound. Was Mark sympathetic? Was he heck! 'That bloody BP,' he muttered.

There was another BP incident one night and I missed all the action because I had to stay behind in bed, due to the fact that I was suffering from a wild fever. I was really ill. All the gang went down to the nightclub in the hotel, leaving me in my sick bed. That night there was a police raid on the club and everyone was ordered up against the wall. It was really heavy stuff, they told me the following day.

'We want your passport! We want your passport!' the police officers demanded.

Mark Plunkett was looking after our passports and they checked all those and that was OK.

But BP had his own passport and he refused to hand it over to the police. 'I'm not giving you my passport,' Beeps insisted.

'Give me your passport or we will arrest you!' the police officer warned.

'I'm not giving you my passport,' a defiant Beeps told him.

Bad move. Your man was arresting BP.

'Mark! Mark! Please tell him not to arrest me! Mark! Mark!' BP pleaded.

I can only guess what was going through Mark's head. The situation was eventually resolved after BP relented and handed over his passport for inspection.

There was a memorable morning – and night – with BP in Bahrain on that trip. We were all suffering from poxy jet lag, waking up at five and six every morning. So, rather than stay in the hotel room, we'd give each other a call. One morning Beeps and myself strolled out on to the beach and the picture postcard scene that awaited us was like heaven on earth.

It was a beautiful morning. Next to the beach there was a man-made lagoon with birds floating above it. Further out the dark ocean stretched to the horizon. An old gentleman was raking the sand and the peace and serenity of the moment was wonderful. It was a lovely memory to take from that trip. There is a brilliant picture in BP's book from that morning. It shows me, a lone figure with my back to the camera, strolling along that magnificent deserted beach in the early dawn, clad in a sarong.

By the time evening came, much later in the day, we were all sitting on the same beach, but with a drink in our hands. Beeps was there and Stephen was there. It was a really peaceful night, the moon was glistening on the water and I could see the reflection of the stars in it.

BP started talking about Marc Bolan (of the Seventies rock group T. Rex) and how they had been best friends. It was really moving, the things he was saying. That night twenty years ago, Marc had died tragically in a car crash. Then Beeps, who had become very sentimental at this stage, started saying how he could feel Marc's spirit there on the beach at that moment and I, who'd never even met Marc Bolan, was getting all emotional too …

Boyzone have had a lot of laughs with BP along the way and not just on that trip. He came over to London another time to do a newspaper story on us when we made an appearance at Harrods to open their sale.

You arrive at Harrods in a horse and carriage as part of the promotion and Mark had said to Beeps, 'BP, you are not getting into that carriage!'

So Boyzone decided we'd have a bit of fun by winding up Mark, saying, 'BP, get into the horse and carriage.'

'Will I? Will I? Mark won't let me, he won't let me!' BP exclaimed, all bright-eyed like a little child.

We insisted, 'Ah c'mon, get in, get in.' It was like Mrs Doyle in *Father Ted*, 'Ah, ye will!, ye will!, ye will!, ye will!, ye will!'

Needless to say, Beeps couldn't resist getting into the horse and carriage, but he hid down between our legs so that Mark wouldn't see him. We arrived at Harrods, the door of the carriage opened and out fell BP as the press photographers were going click! click! click! I later saw an aerial photograph taken while we were in the carriage and you can see Beep's little white baldy head sticking up from between all our legs.

Inside Harrods Beeps was strolling around with us as we made our way to meet the owner, Mohammed Al Fayed, and, behind his back, Barrie Knight and the rest of us were picking up pieces of silver – salt cellars and knives and forks – and sticking them in Beeps' bag. Then we enlisted the cooperation of Harrods' head of security to complete the wind up. So, fair play to him, the guy goes over and he says to BP, 'Hello, Mr Fallon, excuse me, sir, can we check your bag please?'

Beeps looks startled and he asks, 'What do you want to check my bag for?'

'I'd just like to check your bag as we have a report that some items have gone missing.'

BP was raging, 'I don't steal! I don't know anything about that! This is hideous! Oh, check my bloody bag!'

So the guy opens BP's bag and starts taking out all the silverware. I'll never forget the look on Beep's face. He was stuttering and stammering, 'They're not bloody mine! I didn't take those. I'd never do that! Ronan! Ronan, tell them I didn't take those. Barrie … Barrie is a good man, he will tell you …'

By this stage, we were in tears. We were crying. Then the penny dropped with Beeps and he roars, 'Them bastards did this to me! They did it to me!'

But BP is one of those people who always sees the good side in life, he will always get the best out of something. And because he is steeped in the history of the music business, I would listen to him and I have learned a lot from him. He's a good friend.

Mick Jagger once said that he had been in the music business for over twenty years, but the amount of performing he did in that period only added up to two of those. It's the same with me. As well as being singers, we are sales people. You have to get out there and push yourself, sell your single, your album and your concerts. Probably ninety per cent of what we do is marketing; that's the way the business works, whether we like it or not. And I have no problem with that, as long as it means I have the time to do what's most important, my music.

More than anything, though, we are travellers. Most of my time in the last six years has been spent travelling on a plane or in a car, or waiting in airports, in venues or in TV studios. That is what singers and bands spend a huge chunk of their time doing. From the moment *Smash Hits* ignited Boyzone's fuse, my feet barely touched the ground. Doing the round of press, radio and TV interviews, showcase gigs, roadshows and all kinds of public appearances became my way of life. I found that I had less and less time at home and phone calls to Mam were often my only contact with home for months. We spoke nearly every day, me calling from a different city in yet another identical hotel room, imagining her at the end of the phone. I knew just where she'd be sitting and she'd tell me what had happened that day, and what Gar or Linda had been up to, and it was like a lifeline to the real world.

CHAPTER 9

MARIE KEATING

I was nineteen and I thought I had the world at my feet. It was autumn 1996 and Boyzone had broken records and travelled the world. What I had achieved at that point was the stuff of every young guy's dreams. I had fame, money, cars. We'd just completed our sell-our tour of the UK and had put the finishing touches to the album *A Different Beat*, which was due out soon. We were pleased with it and were hoping it would follow the success of our first and that we'd have a second Number One album under our belt. We were optimistic, too, that 'Words' would finally win us the coveted Number One single on its release at the beginning of October. It was going to be our Christmas.

As they say, people make plans and God smiles.

My fairy tale world came crashing down around my ears on 26 September 1996. One phone call changed everything. It was from my brother, Ciaran. It was clear from his tone of voice that there was something terribly wrong.

'Ro,' he said quietly, 'Mam has cancer.'

My mind just seemed to close down. I couldn't believe what I was hearing. We had all known that there was something wrong with Mam, as she had been going to hospital for check ups. She'd also seemed very worried, but we were so used to her thinking she was ill, that we didn't panic. Mam was always a hypochondriac. She thought she had everything under the sun. 'Oh Jesus! I have Alzheimer's, I can't remember where I left the keys,' she'd say.

Honest to God, there was something different wrong with her every day. 'Oh Jesus! I have this or I have that.' We laughed. That was just her way and we ignored it. This time we had to take it a bit more seriously because the hospital were doing tests, but out of habit we said, 'Ah, Mam, you're alright, for God's sake, you're imagining it.'

But for once she was right and we were very wrong. They found a tumour in her breast and there then followed an agonising few days while we waited to find out if it was malignant or benign. We still couldn't really believe it. Of course she would be alright. Then came the blow, it was the real deal. She had cancer. Breast cancer.

Within days they'd scheduled a mastectomy and follow-up chemotherapy. It was a horrendous ordeal for Mam and very hard for all of us to deal with. I was on the road with Boyzone at the time, and I think part of me ignored what I knew was going on, or refused to believe it. I just continued with what I was doing. It's not an uncommon reaction. People don't want to believe the truth. But soon it was unavoidable. The exhausting chemotherapy took its toll on Mam and she lost her hair. She looked like a shadow of her old self.

Everyone in the family reacted in their own way. To an extent it depended on each person's own relationship with Mam. She and I were so close it was really hard for her to talk to me about it, and for me to talk to her and face up to the illness. It was as if something had come between us. As soon as I'd get home I'd be gone out straight away with my mates, down to the pub. I just couldn't handle it.

As the agony wore on, I looked around for something that I could actually do to help. Mam had always wanted to visit New York, so I arranged for her to go there on a month's holiday. I couldn't believe it when she agreed to the trip but she got on a plane on her own and went out to my sister Linda. It was her first time away without my dad. Mam and Linda had a ball, seeing all the shows on Broadway, going up the Empire State Building, walking in Central Park. Mam loved it and it was just the tonic she needed at the time.

Mam was devoted to a saint called Padre Pio and I also arranged for her go to his place of worship in San Giovanni Rotondo, Italy, accompanied by Keith's mum. Pio, Mam was never slow to tell us, had become the first stigmatised priest in the history of the Catholic Church when five wounds appeared on his body. She had great faith in him.

Our own prayers were answered when the doctors gave her the all clear in August, 1997. I was in Belgium when I got the call from Linda.

'Ro, she's going to be alright!'

I couldn't believe it. It was the best news I'd ever received in my life. I ran out of the hotel room to tell the rest of the group. Everyone was so pleased for me. There were major celebrations that night.

But the miracle was short-lived. At the beginning of December, she started feeling really bad again and complained of a terrible pain in her back. 'Don't worry, Mam,' I said. 'I'll organise a specialist for you and you'll be grand.'

So she went to the chiropractor, but the pain persisted and tests revealed the worst. The cancer had spread into her spine.

Maybe if it had been caught in time, we were told, it could have been cured. But in Mam's case, there was nothing the doctors could do.

But you just don't give up. Even with Mam in hospital, we were still living in hope. I was on the road with Boyzone, convincing myself everything would be OK again. I thought if I didn't imagine the worst, it wouldn't happen.

I'll never forget that Christmas Eve and Mam coming home from hospital. We were all waiting outside the house for the car to come up the road. For the first time in years, all Mam's five children were there. When she arrived she was in a wheelchair.

We had been told that Mam would regain the use of her legs, but that turned out to be wishful thinking on the part of the doctors. Whatever we were hoping for that Christmas, the wheelchair was always there as evidence of Mam's frailty. It was impossible to ignore her illness, as some of us might have wanted. Mam hated us seeing her like that; she didn't want us to feel that the cancer had made her something else. She wanted to be the Mam of old.

For as long as I can remember, one of Mam's traditions on Christmas morning was to give each member of her family a selection box of chocolates. No matter what other gift she had bought you, it would always be accompanied by a selection box. That particular Christmas morning, she sat there in her wheelchair and she said, 'Listen, I'm sorry, I couldn't get you any gifts.'

She looked devastated that being in hospital had meant she couldn't get us our presents as usual. It seemed to affect her more than anything else. But she had managed to get Linda to buy selection boxes for us, and as she handed them out sitting in her wheelchair, the family stood around, overcome by emotion. I avoided catching anyone's eye, knowing that it would be impossible to hold back the tears. Instead I focussed on Mam and tried to prevent the swirling feelings of anger, despair and, above all, love, from overpowering me.

That last Christmas was an emotional time for the whole family. I remember it as a very special time, heartbreaking but wonderful. The last time the family would be together.

Mam went back to hospital afterwards and I went back on the road with Boyzone again. We all did what we had to do. We still thought that everything would be fine, as Mam had such spirit. For her to leave us was unimaginable.

In the end, though, there was nothing any of us could do. Her family, her doctors and even my brave Mam herself were powerless against the disease.

My next chance to get home was a month later. Mam was so sick. Linda and I were holding the fort at home, one of family always with her in the hospital. It was the first of February and Linda had wanted to stay with Mam in the hospital, but that day she was having none of it.

'You go home and get your sleep,' Mam told her. Linda promised to be back at eight o'clock the next morning.

When she returned to the house, Linda set her alarm and asked me to do the same, saying, 'Wake me up because I'll never wake up.' Linda could sleep on a bed of nails.

At six o'clock the next morning, 2 February 1998, Linda got what is known as the 'dead knock'. She suddenly woke up, thinking she had heard a rap on her bedroom door. She sat bolt upright in the bed, whispering 'Oh, Jesus!' She knew there was no one at the door.

She remembers thinking to herself, 'What am I going to do? If I answer the door will she still be alive? If I don't answer the door will she still be alive?' She padded softly to the door, found that there was no one there, then panicked. She rushed into my bedroom saying, 'Ronan, I'm up, I'm gone. I'm on my way to the hospital!'

I woke up with a start. I had been in the middle of a dream in which Mam was sitting on a chair dressed in gold, with Linda and myself either side of her. Mam had looked at us and said, 'It's OK, I'm happy now. Please let me go.'

In her panic, Linda crashed into a car when she arrived at the hospital. She jumped out of her own vehicle and ran into the building leaving the driver of the other car swearing after her. Linda flew to the hospital and burst through the hospital doors, scrutinising the faces of all the nurses for a sign that Mam was OK. She was thinking, 'Just let me know it's alright, that Mam is still alive.'

Linda came hurtling into Mam's room to find her very conscious and very awake. Mam looked at her as if to ask, 'What are you doing here so early?'

Linda took a few deep breaths and managed a smile. Then she fetched Mam a cup of tea and a muffin, and sat with her awahile. Then Mam asked Linda to go out and buy her a new pair of slippers. Linda knew that Mam already had some slippers, but she did as she was told. When she was gone, Mam called a nurse to her and began, softly, to tell her about her five wonderful children … and then she passed away.

Obviously she had known her time was near.

Linda had the slippers in her hand when she got the call on her mobile phone. She threw them to the floor and ran. I had also received the call that Mam had 'taken a turn' and as I drove like a maniac through the streets I came up behind a hearse with about 20 cars behind it. Afterwards I thought how that was an omen, but at the time all I wanted to do was get past those bloody cars as quickly as I could. I was blowing the horn and I wasn't stopping for anybody.

When I got to the hospital, I spotted Linda's car abandoned by the side of the road, with the driver's door wide open and the key still in the ignition.

As I raced up the corridor, a nurse stopped me just yards from my mother's room. 'Ronan, wait,' she said, 'Your mother passed away fifteen minutes ago.'

They say that when you're involved in a crash, everything seems to happen in slow motion. That was my experience at that moment. I remember watching my hand as it reached for the handle on the door. It seemed to take an eternity to turn the handle. I vividly remember seeing every detail of my hand, every line, every crack and every nail on my fingers.

I saw Linda and Ciaran sitting there with Mam when I entered the room. She looked so at peace. No longer in pain. Mam had refused to take morphine because she'd been afraid that it would affect her mind. She wanted to be fully alert right up to the end. She was such a strong woman. I was crying inside for somebody to take away my pain … and my anger.

Even though she'd been very ill, Mam had never directly said that she was dying. She'd always insisted everything would be alright. She hadn't wanted to say goodbye, because that would have been too final for her and too upsetting for us. But two weeks before she passed away, she took my hand and said, 'Ronan, listen, whatever happens to me, I want you to continue doing what you do. Don't ever stop because this is what you are best at and it's something you can do for the rest of your life.'

Having my Mam say that to me was a real comfort. We both got very emotional and bawled our eyes out. We both knew what she meant, even though it wasn't said.

It was the same with Linda, she never said, 'You know I'm dying.' But the night before her passing, she told Linda where she wanted to be buried and how she wanted the funeral service to be in a country church. She also told Linda that she should go back to America and get on with her own life. That was Mam, always thinking of her children, even at the very end.

The funeral was a private family affair and I'm very grateful to the media for respecting that on the day. One of the first people we saw when we arrived at the church was Joe Dolan, the singer who'd drawn Mam to the County Kerry holiday resort of Killarney every summer, with her family in tow. We were all touched to see Joe there that morning and each one of us went up to him and shook his hand. Mam had got to know Joe and they had talked about my life and plans with Boyzone. That would have meant so much to Mam, for him to be there.

Cancer was always a disease that affected other people, other families. I'd hear of people dying of cancer, but, to be honest, it didn't really cost me a thought. It was just like news of an accident or a murder on the radio or TV, you might listen to the details, but they don't really register unless you know the people involved.

So I never really had an awareness of cancer or of the way it can destroy a life and devastate a family. Until the day it came to my own door.

In the immediate aftermath of Mam's death, when all the family was gathered together in the home, we came up with the idea of setting up a cancer charity in her name, which has now become the Marie Keating Cancer Awareness Fund.

It was probably our way of dealing with our loss. You need an emotional outlet, something to help you come to terms with a death, Our way of coping was to latch on to this charity and try to prevent the same thing happening to another family.

Two weeks after the funeral, I went on to *The Late Late Show* in Ireland and talked to the presenter Gay Byrne about our plans. I asked to get on that show, to start the ball rolling straightaway. I wanted to hit people with what we were doing immediately. I knew my first TV chat show appearance after Mam's death would make a big impact, as people would be interested in my reaction and how I was coping. So I used that moment to tell people, 'I'm back and I want to make money for cancer research.'

It's all about awareness and once the public heard about the fund it snowballed from there. The media got behind it. They wanted to know what was going on and what was involved.

But going on to *The Late Late Show* that night was probably one of the hardest things I ever had to do. It was a very emotional experience for me. I remember Mam's words going through my mind as I went into the studio that night. When Mam was around she would always ring me before major things to wish me the best, 'Good luck, Ronan, be careful what you are saying.' Those sentiments will always go through my mind, regardless of what I do. They will always be with me.

Later, I went on TV in the UK with Angela Rippon to let people there know what was going on, too. Basically, I'll do anything to prevent other people having to go through the ordeal we experienced. That's why we do it as a family. If we feel we can help another person, then we're making something good come out of a tragedy, which helps us in turn.

The Marie Keating Cancer Awareness Fund is not about keeping our mother's memory alive, because she will always be there in our hearts and in our minds. Always. We're just dealing with the loss, and passing on what we've learnt. We also felt that by helping others, we were carrying on Mam's spirit. She was such a kind-hearted person. I remember when Louis was managing an Irish pop group called The Carter Twins. They were two young Dublin guys who were orphans. My brother Ciaran was their tour manager at the time and my mother didn't think twice about taking them under her wing, driving out to the airport to pick them from a trip and taking them back to our house for a meal. That was the nature of my mam.

Setting up this charity also gave me the opportunity to use my celebrity status for something worthwhile. We decided that through the charity we would launch mobile units and put them on the road around Ireland so that people could go and have regular checks. Cancer can be cured if it's caught in time.

My sister, Linda, has been the driving force behind the Marie Keating Cancer Awareness Fund, and has done numerous TV interviews to promote the charity. On one occasion she met a lady who told Linda that having listened to her on television one evening she'd examined herself when she'd gone to bed that night and discovered a lump on her breast. She'd immediately gone to her doctor who set her for a biopsy, and it turned out that she had a malignant tumour. It was so small that they had been able to remove it.

'Linda, you saved my life,' said the woman.

So there is one life saved, one woman spared all that pain and suffering, and, if we never did anything else, our campaign has been worth it for that alone.

The public in Ireland have been so generous to us. They have undertaken all kinds of fund-raising activities for the cause. A group of guys in County Tipperary agreed to dye their hair blond provided that people donated money towards the charity. They raised a staggering £20,000 and called themselves 'The Bleached Blonds.' It's great when these events can be fun as well.

Even people who had cancer themselves and were going through chemotherapy took part in events like mini-marathons to support the fund. They say the more hope you give yourself and the more you concentrate on getting better, the greater your chances of recovering. Cancer can be beaten. Unfortunately, it was too late for Mam, but we know plenty of people who have lived through cancer. It's very inspiring to see people fighting the illness with a positive attitude.

One of the people who has given the Marie Keating Cancer Awareness Fund a tremendous boost is a young woman called Willo Ward, who is now a very good friend of ours. She produced a book called *Anything But Balls*, a series of interviews with soccer stars, and donated the profits to the fund. The legendary George Best joined me at an official signing session for the book in the Eason's book store in Dublin, and it went on to raise a staggering £60,000.

My work keeps me out of Ireland for long stretches, but Linda and the rest of the family tried to get along to as many of the fundraising events around the country as was humanly possible. They have met some wonderful people as a result of it.

In July 1999, I was invited to perform at a concert in aid of breast cancer relief at London's Hyde Park. I sang, 'This Is Your Song', which was inspired by Mam and one I wrote myself.

No words can describe how much I miss my mam. We were so close, best buddies. I was the youngest and we had a special bond. No matter where I was in the world, I called her every day. She was constantly worrying about me, 'Are you eating properly? Are you getting enough sleep?' normal things like that. It was a wonderful mother and son relationship. One of the consoling things I hang on to is the fact that she got to see a lot of the success I achieved through Boyzone. I know how proud she was of me, as she was of everyone in the family.

I am also so glad that I was in a position to buy a dream home for her before she died. Set in lovely countryside at Ardclough near Celbridge in County Kildare, it was filled with happiness while she was there. Mam sat in the window one day and looked out over the land and she remarked to her sister, my aunt Angela, 'I've never been happier.' That meant the world to me when I heard that.

But, at the same time, every time I earn money now it kills me that I can't spend it on her. I want to take her into the top stores, like Brown Thomas in Dublin, sit her down and organise personal shopping for her, get her whatever she wants. I want to fly her around the world first class. I want to give her it all. That is one pleasure I've been robbed of. But my mother will never leave my heart.

She will always be a beautiful memory to me.

CHAPTER 10

BIRTHDAY BLUES

It was a couple of weeks after Mam's death and I was looking out over the rainswept fields around our home at Ardclough. What with everything that had happened I hadn't even thought about the fact that it was my birthday on 3 March.

I was on the verge of my twenty-first, a real landmark, and I was thinking, if only things were different, what a party we would all have, how Mam would have enjoyed it.

Why couldn't it be just like my eighteenth birthday, which was such a great night for me? I was still on a high from the success of 'Love Me For A Reason', the group had just taken off and I was the happiest eighteen-year-old in the land. My mam and dad had organised a surprise do for me at the local Lord Mayor pub in Swords and it was so good to be home with the family, doing what we really love to do ... partying.

'Coffee, Ronan?' Linda asked, as she came into the room, breaking the silence and rousing me from my memories.

I turned away from the window and stared through her, my mind still in another place.

'Are you OK?' she asked, the change in tone indicating her concern.

'Yeah, sorry, I'm just thinking about my twenty-first. What am I going to do, Linda? I can't be dealing with a party.'

Linda sighed. 'Well, Ro, it is a bit soon...'

'Yeah, I know,' I interrupted.

'Do you want that coffee?' she enquired again, changing the subject.

I sat by the fire in the sitting room, watching the logs spark in the grate. I love real fires, and my memories drifted back to my childhood in Bayside, where Mam had always had one burning in the open fireplace in the winter. To me, fires meant cosiness, warmth and security. It's a welcome feeling to walk into a house where the fire is lit, to kick off your shoes and settle down in front of it. Mam's cosy fire. It's funny what you take with you through life from your childhood.

'There you go, Ronan,' Linda said, handing me a steaming mug of coffee. 'Y'know,' she added, 'isn't it strange how your birthday actually falls just a day over the month?'

I hadn't realised, but I knew what Linda meant. In the Catholic Church it's customary not to celebrate for a month after suffering a bereavement. It was odd that my birthday was a month and one day after Mam's passing.

We looked at each other and our eyes welled up with tears. We both felt as if Mam was saying, 'It's OK, Ronan, go for it! Have your party and enjoy every moment.'

The more we talked about it, the more emotional we became. Then we sat in silence for a while. Eventually the cloud lifted from me and I said, 'Y'know, Linda, this is quite cool! This is what Mam would have wanted, let's do it.'

Linda perked up. 'Yeah, you're right Ronan,' she reassured me. 'Let's have a bloody party. Life is too short.' And from that moment the twenty-first birthday party became something new to focus on, a welcome distraction from the pain of our loss.

If there's another era I could have chosen to have lived through, it would be the 1950s. Movies have given me a fascination for that period. I love motorcycles and I love the whole scene – leather jackets, jeans and turn-ups. I belong somewhere in there. That's where I live in my head. If I had a time machine, that's where I'd go.

Seeing as the chances of that happening were pretty slim, I decided to recreate that era, at least for a night. I took the theme of the movie, *Grease*, as the dress code for the twenty-first bash at the Red Box club in Dublin, which, like the Chocolate Bar, is owned by Boyzone's co-manager John.

Of course, with Louis Walsh also playing a major role in the organising of my birthday, it rapidly became a showbusiness event and another opportunity to keep Boyzone in the public spotlight. Ireland's national pop station, 2FM radio, decided to devote an entire afternoon show to it, through my friend DJ Tony Fenton. I had grown up listening to Tony on Irish radio. He had a programme called *The Hotline* and it always featured the latest chart hits. I was a big fan. Tony gave Boyzone great support when we released our first single, as did his colleague Larry Gogan, the king of the Irish jocks.

On the day of my birthday Tony and his producer came up to Ardclough and did the broadcast from our house. Once the word got out, the quiet rural setting was soon under siege from girl fans. We had a great time, though, and it was good to have the house that Mam loved so much full of life once more.

The show was broadcast from my bedroom, and soon listeners could hear the sound of champagne corks as Tony and I got into the swing of things. The star prize of the afternoon was the duvet from my bed. I'd chosen some of the birthday cards that had been sent to me by my fans through Tony's programme, and the whole bunch was put in our washing machine downstairs. We gave it a spin and picked one out. 'Ronan Keating, another year older, another year wiser, another year sexier and more gorgeous to me,' said the message. It was from fourteen-year-old Maria Nolan from Arklow, County Wicklow. We phoned her up on the spot and told her she'd won my duvet. 'Oh, Ronan,' she gasped. 'I'm going it put it on my bed and I'm going to sleep with it every night.'

It was a great afternoon, loads of people phoned in to wish me happy birthday. There was a card from U2 and I spoke to the band's drummer Larry Mullen on the phone. Irish snooker ace Ken Doherty, who's from my home town, phoned in to send me best wishes. Tony and I had a real laugh.

Tony, like myself, has a passion for motorbikes. In fact, he made me green with envy one day when he announced he was the proud owner of a Harley Davidson, my dream machine.

As soon as the big bucks started coming in from Boyzone, I went out and treated myself to a Harley. Money is there to be enjoyed, as I always say. Tony, in fact, had been encouraging me to get one, and I was so excited when it came in that I rang him and said, 'I got my Harley today!' At the first opportunity, we set off together down the country and it was just the best sensation. There is nothing to beat having that power between your legs and an open road ahead of you. I have always fantasised about travelling across the States on a motorbike. Who knows, maybe some day!

Before the radio show ended on that afternoon of my birthday, I asked Tony to play a special record for me. It was the

R Kelly hit, 'I Believe I Can Fly', one of my mam's favourite songs, which now means so much to me and my family.

Gary came in to the kitchen afterwards and I could see by his expression that something was up.

'What's the matter Gar?' I asked.

'The bloody dog is after eating the birthday cake,' he blurted out.

A local showbiz journalist had arrived down that day with a birthday cake, which was a gift from his newspaper. I could sense his embarrassment as he went through the rigmarole of presenting it to me. The things some guys have to do for a living!

I was like an excited kid as I dressed up for the party that night. I put on a a leather jacket and jeans and gelled my hair into a huge quiff. In the build-up to the event, I had thought how it would be really cool to ride the Harley into the belly of the club where the party was taking place. John Reynolds had said that that wouldn't be a problem.

I must admit, I enjoyed that moment. It was a real movie-style entrance, the doors opening, the roar of the Harley and then zooming in to the waiting crowd. The cavernous, stone interior of the Red Box was buzzing with a party vibe, and I was greeted with the blinding flashes of press photographers. (Especially when they saw I had a beautiful blonde on the back of the bike …)

My Harley wasn't the only machine that came through the doors that night. Behind me with Keith and the lads was my fantasy car, a magnificent 1966 Ford Mustang, a green-coloured classic beauty. It was a birthday pressie from the other guys in

Boyzone! My young nephews, Ciaran's little sons, Conall and Ruairi, fell in love with it too, and spent the night playing there. I can only guess where they travelled in their imaginations.

With my passion for classic cars, getting the Mustang was like having all my Christmases at once. But it wasn't the only treasured gift I received. Boyzone's record company, Polydor, also presented me with a precious microphone, which had belonged to the legendary Elvis Presley!

What a party! There were a lot of Irish celebrities there from the fashion, radio and TV scenes, including the family favourite, Mam's beloved singer, Joe Dolan. The music was loud, the drink flowed, and all my friends and family were there. Various people had conspired to spring a sort of *This Is Your Life* on me, which was a complete surprise. There was even an old video showing me playing Gaelic football in Dunshaughlin, complete with action commentary. I wouldn't have minded only it wasn't one of my better performances.

The trip down memory lane was compered by Keith Duffy, who by this stage had slipped away to change out of his Teddy Boy outfit and re-emerged dressed as a woman (not bad looking either!), wearing a blonde wig, a slinky gold lamé dress and a black feather boa. Along with his female accomplice, the inimitable BP Fallon, they gossiped liked two auld ones about my antics as a child, trying their best to embarrass me.

During the party, a photographer from one of the newspapers caught me by the arm and said, 'Ronan, would you mind a shot with the soccer guys?'

'Sure, no problem,' I told him. Soccer guys, what soccer guys?

I was taken to the bar upstairs where there was a group of

very fit-looking blokes.

'How'ya lads!' I said.

A black guy shook hands with me and said, 'Happy birthday, Ronan.' The cameras were flashing and it wasn't until I saw the papers the next day that I learned his name. It was John Barnes. I am an eejit sometimes.

Newcastle United were in town and Louis had arranged for them to attend the party, obviously to give it added prestige in the media. I'd played Gaelic football, but I'd never got hooked on soccer, so I just didn't recognise the guys from the Newcastle United team.

There was also another chap in that photo with me who seemed to be attracting a lot of attention, although I didn't know him from Adam. I found out later what all the fuss had been about. I was pretty pleased when someone pointed out the guy I was standing next to in the picture was Alan Shearer!

Festivities aside, my twenty-first was obviously a very emotional night for all of us in the family. It was the first time that dad, Ciaran, Linda, Gerard, Gary and myself had been out together at an event since Mam's passing. I remember making a little speech that night and saying, 'I wish my mother could have been here tonight … more than anything in the world!' But it was a night to celebrate and not one for wallowing in self-pity. With all the formalities out of the way, and having enjoyed twenty-one kisses from all the beautiful women in the club, I urged the crowd: 'Let's get pissed!' And that's exactly what we did!

The party at Red Box in March was a great chance to let off steam during those months after Mam's passing. There weren't to be many others.

Boyzone were as busy as ever. *A Different Beat* had, as we'd hoped, made the number one slot and had produced five hit singles, including two number ones, for 'Words' and the title track. By now we had a new album ready, *Where We Belong*, and the first single from it, 'All That I Need' was due out on 20 April. I'd done the lead vocals for the ballad, and was pleased with my performance. Before that, Stephen and I were due to head out to Tokyo to help promote the launch of the *Mr Bean* movie there. We'd done a song for the movie – 'Picture Of You', which had been a Number Two hit single for us in the UK back in July of the previous year.

To begin with I didn't object to the frantic schedule, and threw myself back into work. It was my way of trying to deal with the pain, of coping with the fact that Mam wasn't around.

Looking back, I can see now that I was racing around the place, pretending that nothing had happened. Fooling myself. At moments I would and think, 'I'll give Mam a call.' Then I would remember and cry out, 'Oh God!' I tried to get home from abroad as much as I could. But I had many painful nights alone in hotel rooms.

There were a million things to be done every day with Boyzone and by taking those on I wasn't dealing with my bereavement. They were a distraction from the horrendous upheaval in my personal life. The other lads in Boyzone were great. They were there for me. They tried to keep things going as normal as possible, and yet they were there if I needed to talk. But I was trying to shut it out.

The problem was, there wasn't anything anyone could say or do to make things better. The only way things were going to be made better was to have Mam back.

No matter what I did, the pain wouldn't go away. It was always there with me at night and still there when I woke in the morning. At any time of day or night, all the memories of my days with Mam would come rushing back. Her image was constantly in my mind.

My friend Jack Daniels got me through those nights. I wanted to knock myself out, to get to sleep and forget about it. Eventually I had to face up to the fact that Mam was gone. And I realised I couldn't keep on working until I had sorted it out in my head.

The whole thing came to a head when Boyzone were doing a day of interviews with the European media at a London hotel for our new single, 'All That I Need'.

Every media person who came through the door asked me about Mam's death, taking me through the whole ordeal time and time again.

'What's it like to lose your mother?'

'Can you sum her up in one word?'

'Do you miss her?'

As the questions kept coming the flashbulbs kept popping in my face, I was getting more and more emotional and choked up trying to answer the questions. Eventually, I just couldn't handle it any more. I stood up, saying to the lads, 'I'm out of here. I can't do this.'

Within moments I was out of the glare of the lights, resting, hands on knees, trying to regain control of my emotions. There were more interviews to be done, but I just pulled them. I went to our tour manager Mark Plunkett and said, 'Look, Mark, will you sort this out. I'm not able to take any more of these questions. I need a break.'

It was just the day before we were due to perform on *Top of the Pops*. It was an important appearance, as it could help decide the chart position of the new single. If it got to the Top Five, it would be our eleventh single to do so, breaking Kylie Minogue's record. Just a few months earlier, I would have been totally focussed on the performance and on the success of Boyzone. But at that moment I couldn't have cared less. I was worn out. I had to get away from it all.

The rest of Boyzone knew I was in an emotional state when I called them together to explain. 'Look lads, I can't do this,' I told them, 'I need a break, even for just a couple of days.' They understood what I was going through. As I looked around at their expressions of kindness and concern, I couldn't stop the tears.

Needless to say, my sudden departure from the group on the eve of *Top of the Pops* led to all kinds of media speculation. One newspaper even claimed that I had cracked up and suffered a breakdown, that a doctor had been called and that I had needed medication to calm me. That was nonsense. I just needed to be able to sort myself out away from the glare of publicity.

I got on a plane that day and went home. A week later, I headed off on holiday. This time, though, there was someone special to share the travelling with me.

CHAPTER 11

GIRL NEXT DOOR

The little blonde girl with pig-tails in her hair caught my eye. She was leaning against the wall outside the village shop in jodhpurs and the whole horsey gear.

I was sitting in the front of my dad's truck waiting for him to come out with an order. 'Bloody fizzy drinks,' I thought. 'If I never see another can I'll be happy.'

It was the summer of 1990 and at this time Dad's business was delivering soft drinks to shops around the country and I was his helper during the school holidays. The inside of the cabin of the truck was like an oven. A gang of my mates had gone to the beach in Portmarnock on the northside of Dublin that day and had asked me to come along.

'Lads, don't do this to me,' I'd said. 'I want to be there, but I'm on the truck.'

This is such a boring job, I thought. I don't know how Dad does it. But, of course, he was driving, so there was some satisfaction in that.

That cute little girl in the pigtails was glancing at me again. She smiled, showing off the braces on her teeth. Lots of my mates had girlfriends at the time, even though they were only thirteen like me, but I wasn't bothered. I was mad into sport and nothing else.

Eventually Dad arrived out. 'Ronan, get us two boxes out of

the back there, good lad!'

'Yeah, Dad.'

On the way into the shop, the girl smiled at me again. 'Hi!' I said, trying to look as laid back as you can when carrying two crates of fizzy orange.

When I came back out she was chatting to Dad. 'She's a nice young wan,' he said to me with a sly grin, as the truck pulled away from the shop.

The following week I had ended up in hospital, suffering from headaches and nausea and missed going out in the van again. Dad arrived home one evening and announced, 'That good lookin' little blondie was askin' for you today, Ronan.'

My face went beetroot.

But I never went back to that particular shop again. The next week I was still in ill, and then I was back at school and Dad had lost his summer holiday sidekick.

I'd almost forgotten about that little wan.

Boyzone's co-manager John Reynolds ran one of the coolest hangouts in town. The Chocolate Bar, the POD nightclub and the Red Box live music venue were all part of the same complex. Whenever I was back in Ireland and on the rant, I'd go to the Chocolate Bar and the POD to meet my friends.

A lot of bigshots from the entertainment, media and fashion worlds were part of the clientele. Dublin is a small place, and I soon got to know many of the regular crowd and always looked forward to getting down there for a laugh. One of the earliest times I was at the Chocolate Bar, a model friend of mine wandered over and introduced me to Yvonne Connolly. I'd seen her around and knew she was one of Ireland's most successful models. We got talking and she struck me as cool and very relaxed. We seemed to make each other laugh and since we had a lot of mates in common we soon became really good friends.

One evening in the summer of 1997, a gang of us, including Yvonne, were driving towards her house. As we passed a shop near her home, I told everyone, 'I used to deliver drinks to that shop!'

Yvonne turned and stared at me. She seemed amazed. 'You're joking!' she said.

'No, honestly, I used to help my dad on the truck and that was one of the shops he called to.'

'I don't believe you!' she said.

'What's wrong with that! What do you mean?' I asked, bewildered by her reaction.

There was silence.

'I met you years ago,' Yvonne said eventually.

'Where?'

'Back at that shop!'

'No way!'

As we talked, Yvonne remembered the day she had seen me on the truck. 'That was you, Ronan!' she said.

'Yeah, it was.'

'Jesus, isn't that amazing!'

The little girl in pigtails. Of course.

As the next two months passed, I began to see Yvonne in a different way. At first I found that I was extra disappointed if she wasn't one of the group out on a certain night. Then I tried to make sure that she was. Then I started thinking about her all the time. We were still great mates, but I'd realised my feelings were much stronger than that. I had fallen in love. She was glamorous, beautiful, wonderful to talk to (and had this fantastic laugh) but she was also a very laid back and confident person. She always has a calm air about her and is the best person to have around in a crisis. Whatever happens Yvonne gets on with life in a quiet way, without any drama.

One night we were with our gang in the POD, the drinks flowing. As was becoming a habit, I had manoeuvred myself to sit next to Yvonne. I watched her laughing and talking and thought to myself that this was getting daft. I was going to have to tell her that I'd fallen in love with her. But how?

As the night went on, I resolved that I was going to make my move before I left the club that night. No excuses. If I didn't do it tonight it was never going to happen.

A seemingly endless stream of Jack Daniels and coke disappeared down my throat as I built up my Dutch courage. While my confidence grew, I felt my control over the situation slip away. Eventually, with the booze singing in my head and the nightclub blaring away all around, I suddenly turned to Yvonne and blurted out, 'There's someone here I am in love with.'

She stared at me straight-faced.

There was nothing for it. I'd come this far. 'It's you,' I said.

There was a pause, and time seemed to stretch out, seconds becoming minutes, minutes becoming hours. As I waited for her reaction. I thought my chest was going to burst from the pummelling of my heart. All my Dutch courage seemed now to have assembled in the pit of my stomach and started dancing. Yvonne seemed dazed, but looked at me very directly, as if she was trying to take me all in for the first time. Then, very slowly, a smile began to spread across her beautiful face. She glanced down, then looked back up into my eyes, and said simply 'I feel the same way.'

In that moment, my life took on a whole new meaning. We smiled at each other, gently at first, and then the grins seemed to take over our faces. Holding hands, we talked and talked for hours that night. I was besotted, head over heels in love, the best feeling imaginable. I wanted to shout it from the rooftops. I felt so lucky.

Part of the reason why our relationship became so strong, so quickly, is that we were friends first. Before there was any emotional involvement we were first and foremost great mates. It has provided a solid foundation for us as a couple. Yvonne is the first woman I've ever loved. I'm so glad, too, that she came into my life before Mam died. They met and got on very well. Mam said she thought Yvonne was a lovely girl, which meant a lot to me.

After Mam's death, Yvonne was my rock. I don't know how I would have survived if she hadn't been there for me. She couldn't take away the pain, but she went through it with me and supported me all the way. I don't know if it can be explained, but when the right person, your soulmate, comes along you instinctively know it. Sometimes people let it pass by and sometimes they grab on to it. I'm glad I grabbed on to it. It was the best thing I ever did.

Up to the time of my birthday, I hadn't gone totally public on the relationship. Although I hadn't made any effort to hide it, I was letting it seep out slowly into the public domain rather than making a huge song and dance about it. As a successful model with Assets, one of the top agencies in Ireland, Yvonne was well known in her own right. It was obviously a good media story, but because we hadn't made an official announcement about the state of our relationship, the press had been fairly reserved in the way they'd handled it.

There had been speculation in the newspapers that Yvonne was my new girlfriend. She had been seen by my side at Mam's funeral, supporting me through that ordeal. I had hinted that there was 'someone special' in my life when I appeared on *The Late Late Show* to do the interview after Mam died. But we had never been pictured together.

Wivvy began staying over at Ardclough when I was home and, as we talked through the plans for my twenty-first, I suggested that she arrive with me in style on the back of the Harley. Yvonne laughed. I'm sure she thought, 'Boys and their toys!' But the Harley did seem like a great idea to her.

'You know,' I added, 'Louis has invited the press, so we're going to end up splashed all over the papers. How do you feel about that?'

She just smiled. 'That's not a big deal, Ro, let's do it.'

So my twenty-first party was also a public announcement about me and Yvonne. Although the last thing I wanted were newspaper headlines that might upset Yvonne, I had no problem letting the world know that I had found true love. I was thinking, 'I really don't care. I love this girl. I'm not hiding it.'

When the papers arrived at the house at Ardclough the next day, there was a huge sense of relief. The reports of 'the girl in Ronan's life' hadn't been sensationalised. Although the pictures of the two of us were prominently displayed, the stories focused on the overall party, rather than homing in on the relationship and making a big deal out of it.

Thankfully, the fans couldn't have been more supportive, as I would discover from the reaction we both experienced in the weeks ahead. Yvonne was obviously the one out and about on the streets of Dublin, so she was getting it more so than me. 'Hi, Yvonne, we're glad you're making Ronan happy,' said one of a group of girls she met on Grafton Street.

At the time, Boyzone had a weekly column in the Irish *Sunday World* and the letters that flooded in to it were all supportive as well. One girl wrote, 'Ronan I'm so glad that you have found somebody to make you happy. Everyone deserves happiness. Best of luck to you and Yvonne.' I found that really touching.

It didn't take me long to realise that Yvonne was the woman I wanted to spend the rest of my life with. It was early April in 1998 and we were in the bedroom of the house in Ardclough when I popped the question.

We had been joking and having a laugh and suddenly, in the traditional way, I got down on one knee in front of Yvonne, looked up into her eyes and asked, 'Will you marry me?'

She burst out laughing and said, 'Would ya feck off!'

My face fell and she suddenly realised that I was serious. 'Yes! Yes! Yes!' she laughed.

A couple of weeks later came the realisation that I needed to take a break from Boyzone. Yvonne and myself immediately booked a holiday and flew to the tiny Caribbean island of Nevis. It was there, on 30 April, that we became man and wife, an event that stunned everyone, including the members of the band. I hadn't even told Keith, my closest friend in Boyzone.

But my marriage wasn't, as people concluded, a snap decision. Even before the break from the band, Yvonne and I had set our wedding date. It had been planned for a month later in Florida, where we had arranged to holiday with my friend from Dublin, Glin Donnelly and his girlfriend Elaine. We had confided in Glin and Elaine, but no one else was aware of our plans.

Nevis was beautiful, with palm trees, white beaches and a wild, tropical forest. It was the real paradise island. Soon after arriving I said to Yvonne, 'Why not get married now, while we're here?'

The moment just seemed right. Yvonne agreed. 'I'll see if it can be done,' I said and immediately made enquiries.

From then on, everything just fell into place. It turned out to be quite easy to get hitched on Nevis. The major requirement was that we had to have been on the island for three days before the ceremony could be performed. So we went along to the registry office, filled in the forms, handed in our passports and it was all stations go.

My brother Gar was in college in New York at the time and I contacted him. 'Gar, I'm getting married.'

'Whaat!'

'Listen, I want you to be there. I want you to be my best man.'

'When did I ever miss a party, Ro!'

Gar arrived in the night before the wedding after a seven-hour flight from New York. He'd just grabbed some clothes and left. I was so relieved that he could make it. We had shared so much growing up that he had to be a part of this experience.

When we first arrived on Nevis the weather had been fantastic. The sun beamed down and it was almost too hot. I was gutted when I woke up on the morning of the wedding to find dark clouds overhead. It was just like Irish weather. At around nine o'clock we met Gary for breakfast. 'Gar,' I said, 'it's going to rain on my wedding. I don't believe this.'

'Have a bit of faith,' he replied. 'Mam won't let it be overcast. She will look after us.'

The wedding wasn't happening until four o'clock that afternoon, so I thought maybe he'd be right. When we had finished eating, I said goodbye to Yvonne. It was a semi-traditional thing – not seeing the bride before the wedding. Gar and myself headed off for a round of golf, while Yvonne had an appointment to pamper herself, to get the hair and the nails done, to have a facial and all that kind of business.

My golf wasn't too hot and I had to admit to Gar, 'My nerves are killing me.' I'd have been less nervous if I'd been due that afternoon at a Boyzone concert in front of a hundred thousand people.

'I know just the job for that,' said Gar. And off we went to the nineteenth hole. A few hours later and there was still no sign of the clouds disappearing.

'Gar, this is not looking good.'

By a quarter to four, we were dressed and ready to go and meet Yvonne. I was wearing a black sleeveless shirt and black trousers. Watched by slightly bemused but smiling holidaymakers in shorts and bikinis, we made our formal way to the rendezvous point near the beach. Within moments Yvonne appeared. She was just dressed in white linen trousers and a T-shirt but she looked so beautiful. We all exchanged nervous smiles.

As we headed out onto the beach, we kicked off our sandals and could feel the cool sand beneath our feet. At that moment the sun came out, lighting up the beach and the sea, and it was glorious. Gar and I exchanged glances. 'Oh ye of little faith,' Gar quipped under his breath. 'Mam's letting you know that she's here.'

'You're right, Gar.' I genuinely believed that it was a little sign from Mam that she was blessing our wedding. I felt as if she was witnessing the whole thing.

From there on in everything went like a dream. The service was performed by an old gentleman called Judge Byrone, who was eighty-three years old. Before we exchanged rings, he read several beautiful passages from the Bible. It was a simple, yet very moving ceremony.

The moment when Yvonne said yes to taking me as her husband was extraordinary. My heart seemed to leap, and I felt a great surge of love, gratitude and happiness. There wasn't one niggling doubt that I had made the right decision. As we exchanged vows, tiny waves from the Caribbean Sea tossed up on the beach behind us, providing the perfect sound effects to our personal, perfect wedding.

We finished off the evening with a lovely, laid-back dinner … and had an early night.

From the moment we decided to get married, after a whirlwind romance, I was the one who wanted to keep the plans under wraps. Apart from avoiding the media, I didn't need to hear people's opinions or have them offering advice. I knew I was doing the right thing.

After the wedding, our varied honeymoon started. We went

on to New York for a few days with Gar and then we stopped over in Ireland to tell our families the good news. Both sides were totally supportive. We couldn't have asked for more approval or happiness. After some heavy celebrating in Dublin, we went on to the Monte Carlo Music Awards.

We'd been on our honeymoon for nearly a week before the world discovered we were married ... and bizarrely, it was Puff Daddy who broke the news.

On our first night in Monte Carlo we went to a showbiz party. Everyone else was there in tuxedos, but Yvonne and myself were in our jeans, having a laugh and celebrating being on honeymoon. At this point I spotted Puff Daddy, the mega-famous US R&B star. I'd had a few drinks and fancied a little chat, so I went over to him.

'How's it goin', Puff Daddy!' I asked, throwing my arm around his shoulder.

'How are you doing, Ronan?' he replied.

'Myself and Yvonne have just got married,' I informed him, pop star to pop star. I must have thought he could keep a secret.

But without so much as a by-your-leave, Puff goes up to the microphone and shouts out, 'Ronan and Yvonne have just got married!' The room erupts. Everybody starts screaming and shouting.

'Oh my God, what have I done?' I thought.

After that, there was a flurry of activity as the press got wind of it. By then, we'd had our time to ourselves, so we didn't care. But I hadn't told the rest of the lads in Boyzone.

'Shit, I'd better ring them now. I want them to hear it from me,' I told Yvonne. I knew I'd never live it down if I didn't call the boys.

I've got to admit I got a kick out of making the call to Keith.

'How'ya Duster?' I said. 'I'm married!'

For once, Keith Duffy was stuck for words. 'Feck off, you are not,' he said eventually.

'I am!'

'Well, fair play to you, ye mad bastard!'

While I was away, I had time to reflect on Mam's death. I realised that it's not something you ever get over. In time, you learn to live with it, but it's always there with you. But I believe in the after-life and that has been a comfort, knowing that Mam is there watching over me and helping me to make the right moves and decisions.

My life as a married man couldn't be happier because through Yvonne I've gained another wonderful family. Her parents, Mick and Anne Connolly, are like a surrogate Mam and Dad to me, and her brother, James, is like my brother.

We are great together, all of us. It seems unlikely that we'd all get on that well, but we do. They are wonderful people and it's like I've known them forever. On top of that my father and the rest of my family and Yvonne's family have also gelled well together. We all hang out, play golf, go for beers and have barbecues. We've gone skiing with them in Aspen, Colorado – Yvonne and I are big into skiing holidays – and we had a great time. It's like we've always been one extended family.

Mick and Anne come over to our house and they spend a lot of time there, which is great for Yvonne and Jack when I'm away. I think it could be lonely, being married to a pop star, if you're not strong and blessed with a close family and friends.

Duster was buzzing with excitement. He had that twinkle in his eye I've seen so many times when he's up to something.

'What's up, Duster?' I asked.

'Ro, I need your help.'

My secret marriage in Nevis had sown the seed. Keith was trying to organise a surprise wedding – and it was going to be a surprise for Lisa too, even though they had been engaged for two years. An upcoming Boyzone trip to New York has provided him with the ideal opportunity. There was scope to take a break and fly down to Vegas for the 'quickie' ceremony.

As I had been through the whole procedure myself, I got involved in organising the official side of the event. It was up to Keith to do the rest.

We were in the Big Apple doing some studio work, just Keith, Stephen and myself and Boyzone's stylist Alex Delves, who has become a close friend over the years. He's a very laid-back guy with a wicked sense of humour. We'd arranged for Lisa and Yvonne to join us – and Yvonne was in on the big plan.

I could see that Keith was really edgy during the meal on the first night and Lisa sensed it as well. Eventually he stood up and announced that there was something Lisa should know that everyone else at the table knew already. Lisa looked really worried.

I had the rings wrapped in a piece of paper, so I passed them to Keith at that moment. He opened up the package and Lisa's eyes popped out of her head.

'We're not going home on Wednesday,' Keith announced. 'We're flying to Las Vegas and "The King" is going to marry us.' Lisa burst into tears. She didn't say, 'Yes', nor did she say, 'No'. She just bawled her eyes out. In fact I think we all felt pretty moved by then.

We flew down to Vegas and had the greatest party that you can ever imagine. I don't think I slept once during those three days. It was a real rock 'n' roll trip, sometimes you just have to live it up. We hired a limo, stocked it up with Jack Daniels and champagne, and drove around Vegas having a ball. It was boozing and gambling big time. We hit the casinos and I blew a couple of grand. I went crazy, betting serious money. 'What the hell, you only live once,' I laughed.

It was like a scene from the movies as we converged on the city's famous Little White chapel, whose motto is 'We Never Close.' Frank Sinatra, Joan Collins, Judy Garland, Bruce Willis, had all been married there.

Keith asked me to be his best man, while Yvonne was Lisa's matron of honour, so it was a very intimate occasion for us on that day of 24 June 1998. After they exchanged their vows, Stephen and I sang 'I Believe I Can Fly', acapella.

The guy who performed the ceremony was impressed. 'Hey, you guys are good. You should be in a band!' he said.

Afterwards we had dinner in Vegas's famous Stratosphere Tower restaurant, which is the equivalent of forty-four storeys high and has panoramic views of the Vegas strip and desert. We watched the sun go down on Vegas that evening and it was the perfect end to the wildest wedding I have ever been to.

The helicopter whirred through the evening sky. We had views of the valleys, mountains and woodlands and Yvonne gripped my hand tightly as if to say, 'Isn't this fantastic!'

The whirly-bird was also carrying Keith and Lisa and we were making the trip from Dublin to County Wicklow. It was the month of July and we were on our way to the grand Powerscourt House, where over four hundred people were awaiting our arrival. As we had both deprived our families and friends of a wedding, we'd decided to make up for it with a joint bash.

The balmy weather was just perfect as we touched down in the gardens of the enormous estate. As we made our way into the great hall, we could tell no one had waited for us before getting into the swing of things. With our gangs of family and friends, it never took long for the fun to get going.

To me, as well as a wedding celebration, it felt like a coming-of-age party. Within a few years, a lot had happened in my life and I had grown up fast. I had lost my mam, but I had gained Yvonne and so much happiness with her. Along the way, I had learnt a lot about myself and about what is important to me. Mam wasn't coming back, but I had a whole new future in front of me.

I had learnt a bit during the frantic last few years with Boyzone, too. From being a kid wannabe, I had grown into a confident and successful performer. I'd now got over the shock of being in a hit band and in the public eye, and at the party I enjoyed seeing friends from showbiz mix happily with my family and friends from back home.

Looking at the pictures of the party today, with the helicopter, great mansion and all, I can hardly believe I was actually there. That part of my life sometimes seems surreal. Once in a while I stop and think, Jeez, that's me on the front of *Hello!* magazine. But if I'm older and wiser, one thing hasn't changed. When events like those happen my attitude is, 'Enjoy every bit of this because it doesn't last long.'

CHAPTER 12

INTRODUCING MR WALSH

The white van rattles along the motorway en route to the Kelly TV chat show in Belfast. On board is Louis Walsh, being mercilessly taunted by five young green horns.

'Ah, lads, settle down,' he says. 'Be serious.'

No one ever knew Louis' real age, but the media would always refer to him as 'The Peter Pan of Pop'. In those days he had dark hair (we soon changed that to silver!), an excited laugh, and the crow's feet would scrunch up around his eyes when he smiled, which was often.

He thrived on the tittle-tattle of the media and entertainment worlds, adored gossip and was constantly on his mobile phone. 'Ye-aah! Ye-aah!' he'd exclaim, with his head bopping and eyes blinking at speed, as he stressed that the juicy story he'd just told was completely and utterly true. There was always a lot of fun going on when Louis was around, but he was steering a difficult line because he was also the boss and had to command respect as well.

We were like a family of unruly kids, giddy as hell, with Daddy Walsh trying to keep us under control. At that stage, we didn't have our tour manager, Mark, or chief of security, Barrie, two guys who would later become important figures in our lives.

It's around the time of the summer release of our first single, 'Working My Way Back To You', as we head for the TV studio, with Louis urging us to concentrate on stories for the interview that night. We're more interested in having a laugh.

In a desperate attempt to restore some order, Louis suddenly snaps, 'Alright, I won't manage you then. That's it! I don't need to manage you. I've enough going on.'

Mikey turns to him and asks, 'Aren't we, like, your main act, Louis?'

'Ah no, not yet, lads. You're the "B" band at the minute. You're not an "A" band yet.'

He was right, too. We were nothing at the time. Louis was still managing the Irish Eurovision winner Linda Martin and she was doing much bigger business than us.

After almost twenty years in showbusiness, as a manager and agent booking out acts, Louis had seen it all. He'd been through the boom time in the sixties and early seventies when an army of showbands toured the country, performing in every city, town and village, playing to crowds of up to two thousand people, six nights of the week. It was a phenomenon in Ireland at that time.

A country boy from the rural town of Kiltimagh in County Mayo, Louis had always had his sights set on the bright lights and a career in the music industry. At the age of fifteen, when he was still at school, he began managing a young Status Quo-style band from his area, getting them support slots to the showbands when they came to town. Louis didn't have a phone at home, so he used to do all his business from a draughty call box in the town. He wasn't in it for the money; by having his own band on the show it gave him the chance to go and see the showbands, which he loved. The fact that he ended up with ten pounds a night in his pocket – his share of the support band's fee – was an added bonus, and a huge amount of money to him at the time.

Louis saw the thriving showband scene as his ticket out of a dreary, rural backwater that bored the hell out of him. There was very little in Kiltimagh that excited him. He was a city kid at heart, but was trapped in a small town. His working life began as a barman in a country pub owned by The Royal Blues showband, one of the big names on the Irish live entertainment circuit at the time. There was a guy in the band called Doc Carroll and he persuaded their Dublin-based manager Tommy Hayden to give Louis a job in his office. There, he started off replying to fan mail and looking after the dry cleaning of stage clothes for the acts on Hayden's roster.

But, more importantly, he watched and he learned. He saw how Tommy Hayden got radio, TV and press promotion for his acts. How he got people on board and then kept them interested. Louis used to run around to the national newspapers with the publicity pictures for the acts and that way he got to know all the main Irish promoters.

Some years later, a new artist called Johnny Logan joined Hayden's stable. Louis would eventually become his manager and see him go on to win the Eurovision Song Contest twice, 1980 and 1987. Louis admits he thought they were both on their way to the big time, but international success eluded Johnny and frustrated his manager's hopes of moving up to the super league.

Then came the disco explosion of the seventies and eighties, which killed the live music scene in Ireland and left Louis in trouble. He was struggling to get dates for a new crop of Irish rock bands and it was a bleak period in his life. There were times, he tells me, when he never got paid for gigs. After experiencing the boom days, this was a bitter pill for Louis.

But it shows the character of the man that he refused to throw in the towel, even when the going got tough. Although he was still earning a reasonable living, Louis admits his savings had run out by the time the nineties arrived.

Then Take That came along. It was the start of a whole new pop phenomenon and Louis felt right at home in that scene. When they played the Point Depot in Dublin, he was in the audience and Boyzone was conceived in his mind.

He's only recently told me that, at first, he was afraid to take the plunge, terrified it was all going to fall on its arse. And when he did go for it he knew that he was being laughed at. Everybody in the Irish music business was cracking up, thinking it was a great joke. Nobody had done that kind of thing before.

When I look back I think Louis must have been mad. Brave, but mad. There was no pop scene in Ireland at the time. He went out and created it through Boyzone. It was a completely alien concept to the Irish, a band with no instruments. He had to go out and break down all the barriers. At the same time he had the nightmare job of having to deal with us and try to keep control over five totally different personalities in an industry where egos can run riot and destroy an act.

Lou handled us well. He didn't always come on the road, so I guess that helped. If he'd travelled with us all the time in the Transit around Ireland he would probably have lost his head, gone mad and killed us. Not being a dad himself, we must have been a head spinner for him because we were very childish during those early days.

Unlike the stories we later heard about Nigel Martin-Smith, the manager of Take That, Louis wasn't very strict with us. There were rules, but they were fairly loose. Fat chance of us doing everything we were told!

'Now lads, you know you can't be having girlfriends,' he'd say. 'You have too much work to be concentrating on and, anyway, the fans don't like girlfriends.'

'Ah, lads, no drink. No drink. Drink's not good,' he'd say.

Of course, some of us did have girlfriends when we started in Boyzone and Louis did a good job hiding that from the press.

'So, do you have a girlfriend?' It was a question that came up time and time again in interviews.

'Chance would be a fine thing. I'm just concentrating on my career right now. We're only young, there'll be plenty of time for that.'

The lies we told.

However, Boyzone would later go on to break all the rules by becoming dads, getting married and still retaining our popularity with the fans.

Louis looked out for us. There's a great human side to Lou. He wasn't some hard-nosed businessman using us to make a quick buck. He was the sixth member of Boyzone, in it for the fun and the laughs, all the while keeping a professional eye on the bigger picture at the same time.

In general, we were a good bunch of lads and we didn't cause him too much grief. It was great when we did have Louis in the van with us on the way to gigs, playing us tapes of The Osmonds or The Monkees, or some other song he had found that would make 'a great Boyzone song, a great Boyzone song'.

'Listen to this, lads. Listen to this!' he'd say, full of enthusiasm. The passion was always there with Louis, even after all those years in the business. He has the biggest record collection of anyone I've ever met. You could always see he was doing a job he loved.

One of Louis's strengths in those days, when Boyzone was struggling to make an impact in Ireland, was his ability to muster up publicity for the band. Promotion, image and public perception is half the battle when you're striving to make the breakthrough. And Lou got us plenty of coverage.

He's a very sociable, gregarious person, who knows anyone there is to know. Over his marathon twenty years on the Irish entertainment scene, Louis has also established a great working relationship with the local media. This was used to Boyzone's advantage time and time again in the early years. Long before we had heard of the term 'spin doctor', Louis was spinning the yarns for us and getting us acres of coverage in the newspapers.

We'd be driving along in the van and he'd get a call on his mobile, then he'd turn to us and say, 'Have you got a story for so-and-so, lads? He's on the line from the Daily something-or-other.'

Then Louis would suddenly get a brainwave, 'Well, you know, they've been involved in a crash, nobody hurt, a lucky escape, fairly minor, although a split second later and they could have been killed.'

The next day it would be headlines: 'Boyzone In Near Death Escape After Freak Car Smash!'

He always gave Boyzone one hundred and ten per cent.

Every day he was asking, 'What can I do today to get the group some publicity?' Suddenly he'd have an idea and straightaway he'd be on the line to one of his journalist friends with a Boyzone story from his imagination. 'Got a flash! Yeah! Good story, good story!' you'd hear him saying. Any photo opportunities that were going around Dublin, we were there. He'd take us to the opening of an envelope if he thought it would get our mug shots into the morning papers.

In the years that followed, when Boyzone had risen to the status of an internationally successful group, Louis' press stories became more ambitious. Linking Boyzone members to famous names was one of his regular ploys. I nearly choked on my cornflakes one morning when I opened a daily tabloid to read how Madonna fancied Shane Lynch. There, in full living colour, was a big colour picture of Shane and Madonna – not together, mind. Pop's new glamour couple. I'm sure it was news to Madonna too … Another story planted by Louis and reported as fact. But, hey, we had a single to sell and it got us into the public eye. Timing was everything.

Louis was thrilled. When I mentioned it to him that day, he said, 'Ah, sure, who's going to deny it? Madonna will never see it. Good scam! Good scam!'

We never interfered with Louis' style of promotion, although there were times when we had to warn our families that if they saw certain stories, 'Don't worry, they're not true.' One of the most sensational newspaper headlines, which Louis had a hand in, appeared in February 1997: 'BOYZ ALIVE AFTER FLIGHT OF TERROR. Plane Forced To Crash Land In Aussie Desert.'

The story in the *Star* went on: 'Pop idols Boyzone narrowly escaped death when their seven-seater plane crash landed in

Australia. "They are lucky to be alive. It was very serious by all accounts," said manager Louis Walsh yesterday. "It was a very rough landing but no one was injured. When they rang me yesterday they were still very shocked.'"

The story did have some basis in truth. We were in a small, twin-engined plane, flying over the Australian outback during the filming of the video for 'Isn't It A Wonder', the third single from the *A Different Beat* album. The aircraft had suddenly dropped four thousand feet after the turbo on one of the engines failed. It was nothing serious and we could have continued the journey, but the pilot decided to make an unscheduled landing, just in case.

We came down on the nearest small runway, which was in the middle of a wasteland. It was midnight and we had no idea where we were. The landing had been fine and when we got off the plane we were in high spirits, having a laugh about it as usual. Somebody had a video camera running and I was imitating David Bellamy, 'Well here we are in the middle of the silent plains …'

Then it struck us – Louis is going to get great mileage out of this one. So we were immediately on the mobiles to home, telling our families exactly what had happened and that we were safe and sound, just in case the reports went over the top.

Sure enough, the reports were pretty sensational. One said, 'As a result of the mid-air drama, band member Mikey Graham has developed a phobia about flying.' It was front-page news and was also carried on all the radio bulletins. There was a new single coming out and the timing of the headlines couldn't have been better.

After we appeared on a charity fashion show in Dublin,

where Shane caused a bit of a sensation by dropping his pants, Louis came up with another bright idea – Newsflash! Shane has been chosen as the next DKNY model.

That was Louis' talent, promoting his group. He did it so well, got so much exposure for us. The press wouldn't have given us a chance if we'd gone knocking on their doors looking for normal publicity. You had to provide them with an interesting 'angle' and that's where Louis was our 'starmaker'. He would probably have made a great tabloid reporter. I believe we would never had had the success we enjoy today if it wasn't for those concocted stories and all that press coverage.

Louis and myself hit it off at the very start of Boyzone; he could see the hunger and the drive I had. He knew I loved the business as much as he did and he recognised that I was genuinely passionate about the music. He could also see that I was a fashion fanatic. I loved clothes. 'You're a poser, Keating,' he'd joke.

We've always had a very honest relationship, Louis and I. He knows what I'm like and I know what he's like. He knows my good points and my bad ones, and I know his.

Despite the age gap, we like the same music. As well as pop, we both like good country stuff. We'd select country songs that we might consider Boyzone possibilities and some of the other lads in the group wouldn't be impressed.

'What are yez playin' that crap for?'

But I would always swear by Louis' choice in music. OK, I'll forgive him for 'Working My Way Back To You', but it was Louis who picked 'Words' as well. He came to me another day with the Tracy Chapman song, 'Baby Can I Hold You', and I loved it. He suggested the Anne Murray song, 'You Needed Me', which

I thought was great as well. It was also Louis who chose 'I Love The Way You Love Me', a country song by John Michael Montgomery.

The other lads in the band used to chide me in a good-natured way. 'Ah yeah, you're the boss's pet!' And they'd slag Louis, 'Of course, Ronan can do nothing wrong!'

But we both had the same goals. We both wanted to take it as far as it could go. Our shared ambition was to get out of Ireland and be on those big TV shows with the likes of George Michael and Elton John.

We have both grown together in the pop world. Even though Louis had the benefit of twenty years' experience, the whole pop industry was new to him. Boyzone has been his university of pop and now he's the professor, the man with the Midas touch. He knows the right moves and plays them so well. It's been an up and down ride for him and now he's enjoying the good times again.

When I set out on my solo career, there was never any question about who was going to be my manager. For me, it wouldn't work with anyone else. As they say, if it ain't broke, don't fix it. I am totally loyal to Lou. I'll never forget what he has done for me. I want to keep him with me all the way because he's a great guy, he's someone I can totally trust and he's one of the best managers in the business.

I think one of the main reasons why acts fall apart is that they change the whole team around them. Boyzone were very lucky to have a guy like Louis, but there were others who also made it all possible, and some of them are now with me in my solo career.

Boyzone started as a travelling five-man band, and became a major operation. That's where the tour manager comes in. Over the years I've come to know a lot of tour managers in the business, some of the best, but Mark Plunkett tops them all and when I decided to go solo, I asked Mark to be my co-manager.

I knew that Louis and he would make a good team because they know each other well through working with Boyzone for the last six years and had become good friends. Mark is a total professional and he avoided personal relationships with us lads in Boyzone because he was effectively the boss on the road and friendships can often interfere with business dealings. We used to say, 'By the end of the tour we'll have Mark telling us he loves us.' Not a chance. He always let us know, 'Lads, this is business. That's why I'm here.'

But as time went on it's inevitable that people do become close and we became great friends. I admire Mark more than anybody else I've met in the business, both as a person as well as a manager. Married with two young children, Mark is a fantastic family man. He has a wonderful wife and, as couples, we hang out together and go on holidays together.

He and I have both grown together in the pop world and along with Gar, he now runs my life. All I have to do is pick up a phone and at the drop of a hat Mark will have me on the way to anywhere in the world I want to be. If anyone wants to know where I am or what I'm doing, all they have to do is phone Mark Plunkett. I don't even know what I'm doing until I call Mark. I leave everything to him and I know I'm in safe hands.

He is the ultimate manager of the twenty-first century. He doesn't sit at home in an office, but instead he travels everywhere with me. And all the business gets done while we're on the move because he's always online; his laptop computer is constantly in use, along with his mobile phone, so the office moves with him. He is a very hands-on manager and is a decision maker in every aspect of my career, even down to selecting the artwork for my releases.

I saw through Boyzone how Mark was a very influential figure with the courage to take big decisions and make the right moves. He was doing more than just his job as a tour manager. He put all the budgets together and there were many times when he put himself on the line by taking on bigger and bigger shows.

As soon as I decided to go solo, I knew Mark would be essential as my co-manager. He knew my commitment; he could sense my hunger and he knew that I would give the job one hundred and twenty per cent. Mark admires that kind of dedication and professionalism. I also offered him a slice of the action, so we are both working for each other. We make a great team and he has earned respect from everybody for what he does. I have never heard anyone say a bad word about him, apart from the photographers he goes after when they try to take shots of me.

Then there's Barrie Knight. As well as being a great security guy, Barrie is also a real vibe man. He's the one who picks you up when you're feeling down. When you're on the road you need people like Barrie around you, because you are emotionally messed up. I don't care if he never did security, I'd still have him with me for that reason. He is a joker, but he's also a great coordinator. He keeps everything going and keeps everyone happy.

My stylist Alex Delves is another person I can confide in. He's been with me through Boyzone and I trust him completely. Like Louis, Mark and Barrie, I now regard him as one of my dearest friends. They're the people who party with me when I'm up, but, more importantly, they are also there for me when I'm down. The mark of true friends and ones to be treasured, particularly in this business.

One of our dearest friends was another Louis, a guy called Louis Parker who, sadly, lost a brave battle against cancer during 2000. I will always miss Louis and I have dedicated my album to him. He was more than an agent to me. He was a friend.

Louis was one of the top booking agents in the UK and unlike a lot of people, he believed in Boyzone from the start. In fact, he did a lot more than just book gigs for us. He put us on the road and got us our sponsorship deals. When Louis took us on we were all very new to that level of touring. We had picked outfits we wanted to wear and some of them were a disaster. I remember wearing shredded jeans and I couldn't dance because my leg kept getting caught in them and we were all falling over one another.

During another routine we had suits, but because they were all the same, Stephen's and mine got mixed up. I had Steve's jacket and it was too short and he was lost in mine. Louis Parker cried with laughter watching us.

We called Louis the 'Freebie King'. Because of the nature of his job, all the companies sent him free stuff and he wore every bit of promotional clothing that came his way. Sometimes he looked like a twelve-year-old with all the gear.

Louis Parker and myself always slagged each other about a Rolex deal. He set up a Swatch deal for Boyzone but I didn't wear them. Instead, I wore a Rolex I had bought. Every time I met him, Louis would say, 'For feck's sake, Ronan, would you ever put the Swatch on!'

Barrie Knight used to take his Swatch off and give it to me whenever I was doing press. Eventually I said to Louis, 'Look, would you just go out and get me a Rolex deal.'

He said, 'I'll get you the Rolex deal, I will.'

Louis never had the chance to get that Rolex deal off the ground. But he would have done it, I know he would.

He's up there wearing a Rolex now.

CHAPTER 13

FATHER & SON

I was in heaven. I let out a loud, contented sigh as I gazed across the County Kerry landscape. From the window of our room in the eighteenth-century hotel, I could see the cascading waterfall that gives Sheen Falls Lodge its name. In the stillness, the sound of the bubbling pool beneath drifted across the June evening through my window. Beyond the water lay dark woodlands and, on the horizon, I could make out the shimmering outline of the Caha mountains.

At that moment, it seemed the most beautiful place in the world.

I had been looking forward to this weekend for ages, and praying that the rain stayed away. We were on a rare break in one of our favourite Irish hotels. It wasn't often that we managed to get away from the madness of the pop world for a couple of days. A life of pressure. 'Good pressure,' Louis Walsh calls it. 'When things are going well, it's good pressure, Ronan,' he often reminds me.

I wandered across the thick carpet back to the bed and threw myself fully clothed on to the top cover. Propped up against a couple of pillows, I lay with my hands behind my head, thinking just how good life was at that moment. It's great to get off the rollercoaster once in a while. It's important to have the breaks to keep a balance on things. 'Everybody needs a break

'… climb a mountain … jump in a lake,' the line from Christy Moore went through my head.

'The only major decision I'm going to have to make today is what to order when I'm having dinner later on,' I thought. 'Yeah, this is the life!'

Yvonne was in the bathroom, running herself a bath after the journey. She came back in, her face flushed.

'This is great, Wiv! Isn't it!' I was pleased she looked so happy.

But she looked more than just happy, and there was a twinkle in her eye as she came over and sat on the side of the bed.

I propped myself up again and she caught my hand. 'I have something to tell you, Ro.'

'Yeah?'

As she paused, she began to smile. She seemed to be brimming with excitement. 'You're going to be a dad.'

My mouth dropped. 'I am not!'

'Yes!' she slowly nodded.

The shock was taken over by emotion, just welling up inside of me and the waterworks started to flow. I was crying with happiness and excitement and, of course, that set Yvonne off. Then, hugging each other, we started to laugh. I was overcome with joy and with love for Yvonne. It was an incredible moment in our lives. We were going to have a baby. A baby! 'I'm going to be a daddy. I'm going to be a daddy,' I kept telling myself, as if I needed convincing.

Despite my excited state, I still wasn't sure I fully believed it. They seemed just words. Daddy. Mam. We were going to have a little baby.

'Jeez, Ronan Keating you're going to be a daddy!' I couldn't wait.

But, of course, you do have to wait. Nine bloody months. It was strange knowing that there was this major event about to happen in our lives and yet nothing had really changed. The wait seemed so long – I wanted the little fella here now!

I think it was only when Yvonne got her bump that it really sank in. Now I could actually see something. A bump was a start.

By this stage the build-up to the big event was well underway. A room was decorated and kitted out and each day would bring some new brightly coloured baby contraption. I couldn't believe how much stuff comes with these little people. As the day neared, the house filled with a whole zoo of fluffy animals.

Nobody had warned me about the preparation that goes on in the months leading up to it. As well as preparing the mountains of kit, there were antenatal classes. Yvonne and I went along, but I was fat use. During one of the breathing classes I became so relaxed, I fell asleep. Yvonne had to wake me up!

'Sorry, eh, jetlag,' I stammered, trying to cover my embarrassment. But whenever I could, I went along with Yvonne, and was also able to be there when she had her first scan. The 'picture' of the baby was in my wallet for months, and shown to everyone. No one had the heart to tell me it was far too blurred to be decipherable. 'So that's the hand?'

'No I think it's a leg.'

'Oh … I thought that was the head!'

By Christmas Yvonne seemed to be growing every the day. We were told that it was a boy because of the way it was lying, at the front, sticking straight out! The little fella was due on my birthday, 3 March, and as the day approached, we made frantic last-minute checks that everything was in place. Have we forgotten something? What are we going to do? Oh, God!

But when the time did eventually arrive, he refused to come out. Obviously he reckoned that two birthdays on the same day weren't a safe bet for decent presents all round. So he hung on in there.

Yvonne got up to all kinds of antics to get him to shift. She had been advised to go for long walks and drink cod liver oil and she was doing all of those. Someone else suggested beer, biryani and, er, bonking. Still nothing.

I was hopping with excitement, and just couldn't wait to see the baby. Yvonne was just as keen. After all, she was the one who had had to carry him around for the last nine months.

By 14 March there was still no sign of the little munchkin as we went to bed. I crashed out and was sleeping very soundly when, at four o'clock in the morning, Yvonne shook me to life. Or, at least, tried to.

'Whaa! … What!' I stammered, struggling to get my eyelids into gear.

Yvonne shook me again. 'Ro! Ro! My waters are after breaking!'

'Ah, will ya stop, you're grand, go back to sleep!' I muttered and turn over.

Twenty minutes later I was being shaken again.

'Ro, are you right!' Yvonne's voice had now moved up in volume.

She had gone off and got herself ready, then she had finished packing her bag before returning to the room. And there's me still asleep!

'Ro,' she added in a voice growing more urgent by the

minute, 'I'm having a baby!'

Oh my God!

I shot out of bed and I ran around the room like a madman, grabbing the first pair of jeans and top I could find and throwing them on. Out we go, into the dark, cold night and by this stage I'm wide awake and buzzing. Once I hit the motorway for Dublin, as we headed for the maternity unit in Mount Carmel hospital at Churchtown on the southside of the city, I felt everything was under control. At that hour of the morning, there wasn't a sinner on the road.

I was so excited that the big moment had finally arrived, I began calling family members and close friends.

'It's Ro, did I wake you?'

Of course I bleedin' woke them, it was four o'clock in the morning. But I was like a child on Christmas day. 'The baby is coming! We're on our way to the hospital!'

We got there, rushed in and it was like, hurry up and wait. I didn't realise it then, but it wouldn't be until thirteen hours later that the little mallet would finally make an appearance.

The staff at the hospital were brilliant and answered our frequent questions very patiently. Soon the contractions became more regular and stronger. But everything seemed to take a long time. Yvonne tried to get some rest, and I lay down beside her on the bed, shut my eyes for two seconds and, what d'you know, I'm asleep again! The next thing I know being woken up by a nurse. The real fun is about to start.

I shake myself awake and check that Yvonne has everything she needs. She looks excited but nervous. I'm not sure what I look like – no doubt far worse! Every so often, she grimaces and arches her back slightly. I'm holding her hand and trying, unsuccessfully, to be a calming influence. Instead my worrying spins to new heights. Please let Yvonne be OK. Please let the baby be fine.

Then it is time for the pushing. Yvonne's grip on my hand gets tighter and tighter. We seem to be making progress, but it's, literally, painfully slow. Then, the midwife tells us he is stuck. Yvonne, God love her, keeps pushing and pushing, and I'm willing her on, cheering, congratulating, completely absorbed in the moment. It's very tough for Yvonne, and I'm as nervous as hell. Everything I had been taught at those breathing classes goes out the window. Eventually, after two and a half hours of pushing, out popped the little guy at last.

But the moment I had waited so long to experience suddenly turned into a nightmare. My heart stopped when I first laid eyes on Jack. The umbilical chord was wrapped around his neck; he was black and purple and he didn't appear to be breathing.

I was in a panic and felt the blood drain from my face. But I didn't want Yvonne to be alarmed, with everything she had gone through. So I just quietly asked the nurses, 'Is everything OK?'

They nodded.

Then he was whisked away in a split second; they put a breathing mask on him, and within a heartbeat I could hear a cry, a screech. I was flooded with relief and then, moments later, the excitement was bubbling over again. Jack was fine and a strapping young fella, weighing in at a healthy ten pounds and one ounce.

As the doctors did the routine checks, I held Yvonne in my arms. She was exhausted but triumphant. I was just in awe of her. Moments later, they brought Jack back to us. The whole room seemed charged with emotion as Yvonne took him in her arms. I felt so proud. This was the start of my own family.

It's the ultimate gift that anyone is ever going to receive in life. He was a little human being ... and he was all ours! We cried and cried. Life was now just perfect.

Of course, I'd forgotten that babies come with sewage works going at full blast. Yvonne was very tired for the first couple of weeks, so there was no escape for me from the daily routine of changing nappies. I had organised three weeks off from Boyzone and in that time, dirty nappies and baby wipes became the order of the day for me. It's amazing how quickly you adapt to something like that. It just suddenly happens and you realise what you have to do. Up until then I never thought I could clean up a baby's bottom. But when it's your own child it just seems natural.

It was a special time for me and Yvonne as we embarked on a new phase in our lives. The Boyzone circus seemed a lifetime ago, as we concentrated on the new life we had brought into the world. As I'm a terrible worrier, I'd suddenly wake up in the night and run into his bedroom to check on him and make sure he was breathing. We had monitors right up to his face, but I didn't trust them. Every snuffle or rattle was a deadly illness, and every sound was scrutinised. It was all new to both of us. A fantastic learning experience. But the closeness we felt as a new family made me think of the past as well. It made me think of Mam.

But I had another life to lead, and soon I had to get back to work with the band. The problem for Yvonne with having a boy is that she now has two kids to look after. Jack has taken me right back to my childhood again. I can now mess around with toys and play games because, 'Hey! I'm entertaining Jack.'

We have so much fun together playing football or computer games or chilling out and reading books or watching TV. Mummy can't say anything because Jack wants it, and Jack gets it. He's got a big Jeep that you can sit in. It's like a Range Rover, but Jack can't touch the pedals yet, so I end up driving it around the house!

Wherever possible, I take Yvonne and Jack with me on my travels. I'm so lucky to have been able to experience it all ... from the moment he was born, to his first words and his first steps.

It's much easier now that he's older but travelling with a baby at the start was very difficult. I couldn't believe how much extra stuff we had to take with us. Two more suitcases! And we were always forgetting something, which you really can't do where babies are concerned. You can no longer adopt the attitude, 'Ah sure it'll be grand.' Everything is essential, and if anything's missing you sure get to hear about it.

There are no words to describe the love I have for Jack. It's just pure, unconditional love, the same as I have for Yvonne. But I am determined that he won't be a spoilt brat. It wouldn't be fair to him. The one thing my mother always taught me was to have manners – to treat people with respect. It's the best thing I've ever been taught. And the one thing she always gave was love. That was everything that mattered and that's all I want to teach Jack. When you give love you get it back in return.

CHAPTER 14

HOME IS WHERE THE HASSLE IS

It was one of those days when it felt great to be alive. I had money in my pocket and I had a rare day off in Dublin.

The city was buzzing under a rare clear blue sky. Grafton Street was thronged as I made my way along it at speed towards the bar of The Westbury Hotel.

Duffy had been on the mobile.

'I'm on my way into town, Ro. Do you want to meet up for a couple of shots at The Westbury?'

Duster is one of the most sociable guys you could ever hope to meet. A funny, laugh-a-minute character. Just the best company imaginable.

How our lives have changed in less than three years, I had thought as I drove into town. What would I be doing now if Boyzone hadn't come along? Probably working in the States like the rest of the family have had to do at some stage.

On the radio legendary Irish DJ Larry Gogan played the Detroit Spinners on his 'Golden Hour' of oldies. 'Working My Way Back To You'. It didn't sound half bad when they did it.

'The Detroit Spinners there with "Working My Way Back To You", which, of course, has been a big hit here for our own Boyzone. All your favourites on the Golden Hour, stay tuned.'

Good old Larry, always using an opportunity to plug a local act.

I had a confident stride powering my way through the crowd on Grafton Street. The sort of confidence that comes with a little bit of success.

'We've come a long way from that first *Late Late Show*,' I smiled to myself. There were nods of recognition here and there from people on the street. I was enjoying a lot of respect in the UK and on promo tours around Europe and Asia, but I really craved it in Ireland. Then I heard something even more familiar.

'Hey! Boyzone wanker!'

'Hey! Faggot!'

The taunts were coming from behind. I glanced quickly and then turned, face forward, stepping up my speed. It was a bunch of four or five young Dublin guys.

'Yez are feckin' shite!'

'Nothin' but a bunch of assholes!'

The stream of abuse was ringing in my ears as I turned in to the Westbury, leaving them in my wake. Yeah, I thought, really great to be back!

Duffy was raging when I told him. 'That's Ireland for ya, Ro! What do we have to do here to prove ourselves?' Keith had had his own share of runs-in with drunks in city pubs, who wound him up about Boyzone. There were times when it ended in scuffles and he had to be dragged away. These days he was careful where he socialised to avoid trouble.

I couldn't believe what I was hearing from the guys on Grafton Street that day after the success we'd had. Having abuse on the streets of your home town is really unpleasant, it's too close to your family and friends. As Keith said, what would we have to do to prove ourselves?

We were also getting it in the neck from the Irish music critics. They rubbished us all along the way. It didn't matter how many awards we picked up. 'They don't write their own songs,' they'd go on, 'they don't play instruments. This isn't real music. This is manufactured crap.'

I remember one review for our first album in an Irish magazine had just two words, 'Vinyl crap.' Nothing else. It was so insulting. I'd never seen Louis so mad as when he read that. There was no justification for it.

Every time I came home in the first couple of years it was the same. There was always abuse hurled across the street at me. The other guys had similar experiences. In fact, the original Irish fans were always very supportive, buying our records and packing out venues all over the country. They showed us great loyalty and I'm sure many of them at some time were being slagged off for being into Boyzone. It was the so-called serious critics who demolished us. It was unrelenting.

It seemed like we'd never be anything in their eyes. It really upset me because we were travelling around the world telling people in foreign territories what a brilliant place Ireland is, and encouraging them to come and visit. Then we'd go home and people would give us the two fingers.

Eventually, I just got sick of the ridicule, so I started telling the foreign media what it was like for us walking down our streets; the abuse we had to put up with and the lack of respect that was being shown to us. I said, 'I'm really pissed off with people in Ireland always putting us down.'

Once I began to be open about it, things began to gradually change. I think it was also down to the fact that they realised we weren't a flash in the pan. With every passing year, Boyzone was still around, and we were growing in stature. Despite our success, the public could also see that we hadn't changed as individuals. We were still hanging on to our roots. As time went on, people began to realise that we were real people and we had a good vibe about us. Even if some people were never going to like us they could come to respect us.

Personally, I began to notice that the perception of Ronan Keating was changing. The abuse became less and less. Instead, I had young fellas shouting, 'How's it goin'! Fair play to ya!'

It became just the odd guy yelling, 'Ye bleedin' wanker!'

U2 played a major role in getting us accepted at home. U2 are the one piece of Ireland that will always be cool and magical and people will always look up to them. They are the biggest international musical superstars Ireland has ever produced, and they have made so much possible for other Irish musicians. But in spite of all their success, they have stayed normal and approachable. They like hanging out like normal people. They're not up there on a pedestal and they don't look down on young acts like Boyzone.

The first time we got to know the band was when Stephen and myself went out to Japan in March 1998 to attend the premieres for the *Mr Bean* movie. We discovered that U2 were playing there on their PopMart tour.

'Stephen, it would be great to link up with the U2 boys. I'm thinking of making contact, what d'you think?' I suggested.

'They've probably got loads on, Ro.'

'Well, it's worth a try. I'll make a call anyway and see what comes out of it.'

I tracked down their hotel in Osaka and made the phone call. Bono and the boys weren't around, so I left a message. 'Lads, it's Ronan Keating and Stephen Gately. We're in town and would love to meet up for a beer.'

It took a while, but, sure enough, we got a reply back to say, 'Hi guys, got your message, yeah let's meet up.'

That evening we went down to the bar in their hotel and Larry, Bono and The Edge came down. We had met them before, but only in passing, and hadn't spoken to them at any length.

Straightaway they made us feel totally comfortable in their company. It was just like any ordinary bunch of lads meeting up for a few beers. The drink started to flow and the conversation came easy. I remember taking a step back in my brain at one stage and thinking, 'I'm sitting here with my idols. They're treating me as an equal, having a few beers and trading stories. If I want to thank Boyzone for anything, it's for this moment.'

I have the utmost respect for all the individuals in U2 and I think Larry Mullen is one of the coolest guys you will ever meet. There is no bullshit with Larry. He has an ordinary, down-to-earth handle on things. It is so refreshing to meet people like that in this business. Fame can make people paranoid, or determined to be the centre of attention. Others can't really handle it and just flaunt the money or blow it on drugs and get very boring. But U2 are an absolute pleasure to be around. I hope that if I have twenty years of doing what I am doing that I will treat people with the same respect as U2 treat others.

We all went for it that night, hitting the sauce big time. Getting pissed with U2 at their hotel in Japan is one of those big moments for me, if only I could remember the half of it!

Bono has been supportive of Boyzone from the very start. When our first album, *Said And Done*, went to Number One in Britain, he sent Louis a fax congratulating us. Along the way we've met his wife, Ali, when she took their kids along to Boyzone concerts in Dublin. Bono also sent us a song that he thought might be suitable for Boyzone. It was called 'The Sweetest Thing'. Recording a Bono song would have had a huge impact for Boyzone. We tried it out, put down a vocal for it, but it just didn't fit in with what we were doing at the time. I wish it had because it's a beautiful track and we were all such massive fans.

But fate has a way of turning things around and when U2 recorded it themselves they asked Boyzone to be in the video. The song is basically Bono's way of apologising to Ali for forgetting her birthday, so in the video he's giving her all kinds of gifts like marching bands, male strippers ... and Boyzone!

We probably got more recognition around the world for being in that video than we might have done if we'd recorded the song ourselves. It was the ultimate seal of approval. Some of the countries where the U2 video was played were places that Boyzone hadn't made an impact in so far. But all of a sudden doors were opened for us there.

After we shot the video in Dublin, Bono sent another fax to Louis. It read, 'What do you call five lads who pull you out of a rut when you're in trouble with your wife? Manzone!' And he drew a little picture of the five of us, with big grins on our faces.

Taking on challenges outside of Boyzone, and not falling on my face doing them, also helped to overcome prejudices back in Ireland.

The Eurovision Song Contest was part of my childhood experiences. Like millions of kids I had grown up watching it. Sitting on the sofa, we'd all give our own scores for each country and be slagging off the weird ones they always have. But there were some great winners. The year I remember most clearly was when Johnny Logan won it with a song called 'Hold Me Now'. His manager at the time was a certain Louis Walsh, I later discovered.

I'd co-hosted *Top of the Pops* with Stephen and had a real laugh. It just seemed like an extension of our TV promotional work. But when I was asked to present the Eurovision Song Contest when Ireland hosted it in May 1997, I had to take a while to think about it. I would be seen by millions around Europe, and, let's face it, I was hardly an expert. But I always felt that it was a good idea to do things outside of Boyzone. It brought the group to the attention of a different audience and if you could hold on to some of them it was an added bonus.

In fact, Boyzone hi-jacking the 1997 Eurovision Song Contest was another of Louis' masterplans come good. He chased it big time. Initially, Louis went to the producer Noel Curran with the idea of getting Boyzone signed up for the interval act. After a lot of behind-the-scenes negotiations, I was selected to co-present the show with Irish TV and radio personality Carrie Crowley and Boyzone got the interval act too. It was a double stitch-up by Louis.

He saw the Eurovision as another promotional tool for Boyzone. Because it's such a huge media event, everyone in Europe would know us after it and, hopefully, everyone would remember me presenting it. The next problem was trying to find a suitable song for Boyzone to perform at the interval.

There were tracks coming in from various people, but they weren't good Boyzone material. Eventually it was decided that I should have a go at writing the song with producer Ray Hedges.

We knew what they wanted – our brief was a song with a communication theme in it. And obviously with Ray being our producer and me being a member of the band we were going to create a distinctive Boyzone track.

We knew exactly where we were going and 'Let The Message Run Free' was a mountain of a song. The performance was a big production and we spent a lot of our own money on it.

While it was an honour for me to be asked to do the show, I'd be lying if I said I enjoyed it. It's one of the most nerve-racking things I've ever had to do. For a start, I didn't like the formality of it. We were asked to work to a strict script on an autocue and every day I had to go in and rehearse the lines. There were sections in French and some of it was in Irish. They were tutoring me on how to read my lines.

'Ronan, remember it's up at the end of this sentence and down at the end of that one.'

'Ah Jeez,' I thought. 'At the end of the day, it's going to come out how I want.'

I was a nervous wreck on the night. Outside the venue there was the usual siege of Boyzone fans. Apart from having to go out and present the show, be half-decent at doing it and hopefully get some respect from it, I was also performing at the break with Boyzone and there was a lot to live up to. Riverdance had been the interval piece the previous year and expectations were high.

Both myself and Boyzone just about got away with it on the

night. And very slowly, we were changing the way people thought about the group. I felt, too, that I had moved another step forward.

That November, 1997, we released our version of the Tracy Chapman song, 'Baby Can I Hold You', and I jumped at the chance when I was asked to host the MTV Music Awards in Rotterdam that same months. Eurovision was one thing, but MTV is a far cooler and more credible event. Fortunately, I didn't have the chance to get nervous. There just wasn't the time as I flew to Rotterdam every morning to rehearse for the awards before flying back to Birmingham where we were playing five nights as part of Boyzone's Something Else tour. I woke up every morning and thought, 'Jaysus! Four o'clock and I have to get up and fly again!'

As the stars started arriving I was still calm. I was loving it being surrounded by U2, LL Cool J, Slash from Guns N' Roses, Blackstreet, Björk and the Backstreet Boys. There was plenty of slagging and plenty of attitude on show. But as the host, I was shown a certain amount of respect. Clearly, I'd gone up in people's estimation.

But when the moment arrived for me to go on stage, the nerves suddenly hit me. I was paralysed and shaking. I'll never forget the girl standing there going, 'Ten, nine ... five ... two, one ... It's you! Go!'

I stormed out of a tunnel on to the stage. I was buzzing, it was electric and the place went mad.

I thought, 'Oh my God!'

I was still shaking. 'Ronan,' I said to myself, 'Get through this first link as quick as you can and you'll be grand.'

The second link was a bit more relaxed and then it got easier and easier as the show on. By the end, I was enjoying every moment of it. It was a big show for me, with an audience of one billion people, and I was relieved to pull it off. Back home in Ireland the reaction was good. More and more people starting to treat me as a human being, rather than some laughable cartoon character.

At the end of 1997 I received an award for Irish Entertainment Personality Of The Year – and that was extra special as it was voted for by the public. There was more recognition to come, including being chosen as the Grand Marshal of the Dublin St Patrick's Day Parade in March 1998, one of the biggest honours I could ever hope to receive in my own country.

Dublin's streets were lined by half a million people, who had turned out to see the colourful Mardi Gras-style spectacle. It was a bright, sunny day and the crowds were cheering and waving as we led the procession of floats and marching bands in my open-top Mustang. The memories of the early days of Boyzone in the white Transit van flashed through my mind.

'How did we get from there to here?' I thought.

Keith Duffy, who was with me in the car, summed up the moment.

'Jaysus, Ro,' he remarked, 'things are certainly improving for us here in Dublin. They're not throwing rocks!'

CHAPTER 15

LIFE IS A BOX OF CHOCOLATES

There was no mistaking the guy with the goatee beard sitting at the table behind me during the Capital Radio awards in London in November 1995.

I had grown up listening to his music. I had been a fan from the first time I saw him perform on *Top of the Pops*, when he ruled the charts along with a fella called Andrew Ridgeley in Wham! He had remained my idol when he'd gone solo.

My heart was pounding; it was the first time I'd ever seen George Michael in the flesh and I just had to introduce myself. I had always wanted to meet him. If only I could pluck up the courage. Some time later, and after a few glasses of red wine, I was heading in his direction. My knees were going with the nerves. How would he react? Would he turn out to be a huge disappointment? They say sometimes you're better off not meeting your idols in case they let you down.

'Hi, George, Ronan Keating!'

'How are you, Ronan? Nice to meet you.' There was a friendly handshake and a warm smile. Phew!

And he was chatty, thank God. The ice was broken and George picked up the conversation. 'My mother and I were just talking about you the other day.'

I couldn't believe what I was hearing. George Michael and his mother talking about me!

He said, '"Father and Son" came on the radio and my mum said, "What is a young guy like that doing singing to his son?" And I said to her, "Nah, mum, don't be silly, he's singing to his father."'

I was ridiculously pleased to think that his mother and himself were in their house talking about me. I was like, 'Oh … My … God!'

Then he added, 'A piece of advice, Ronan, write your own music.'

Now, at that stage I had already written several songs on the Boyzone album, but I wasn't going to turn around and say that to him. 'Thank you very much, George, I appreciate what you're saying,' I replied politely.

One thing I've discovered in this business is that the people who are the best at what they do are also the nicest. Guys like George, Bono, Elton John and Barry Gibb – they are always the most respectful, self-effacing people. And that's why their careers last. It's the ones who are only half-way up the ladder that have the egos. They're the people who act like superstars. Despite his enormous success and fame, George has managed to stay in touch with reality. Gradually, as I got to know him as a person, I was no longer the fan in awe of his talent. He was a normal guy and we talked about normal things, just like anyone else. When my mother died, George was one of the people who phoned me. He knew what I was going through, as his own mother had passed away the previous year. We didn't talk about his mum because he's not the kind of person who discusses his personal life. He keeps it all very private. But he was very kind to me. When I had doubts during the writing and recording of my solo album, George was the one I turned to for help. I went around to his home and played him the tracks and I really valued the encouragement he gave me.

Yvonne and George's partner, Kenny, really hit it off as well. So, whenever we were in Los Angeles, we'd call and Kenny would come out to dinner with us. Then George started to join us too and we began hanging out, just like friends do, going out for meals or to the movies, or around to his home.

That sort of thing is a normal part of my life now. I meet people as stars, but once you get past that, everyone is just a person underneath and then it's just a question of whether or not you hit it off. But I wouldn't be normal if I didn't sometimes stop and think, 'Feck! This is a brilliant. I used to open magazines and read about these people. Now I am a part of the circle they're in and they're my friends!'

You never know what's around the next corner when you're involved in showbiz. It's like Forrest Gump saying, 'Life is a box of chocolates.' You don't know what's next, unless you read the little card inside the box. But nobody does that, they just go for it and that's the best way to do it.

Since the success of Boyzone, I've been getting all kinds of amazing invitations. The sad thing is, I have to turn down most of them because of work commitments. One party I did get to was Elton John's fiftieth birthday bash a few years ago. That was a real star spotter's night. Everywhere I turned there was a famous face, celebrities like Billy Joel, Lulu, Michael Stipe of REM, Andrew Lloyd Webber and Lily Savage.

It was in London's Hammersmith Palais and there was a big orchestra in the ballroom where people were dancing. It was a fancy dress affair, an extravagant, wild party, packed with people in mad costumes, all way over the top. I had just flown in from America and hadn't time to sort out an outfit, so Louis and I were the only two people in suits! Louis was a big fan of Elton, but he bottled out of meeting him because he was too shy. Louis Walsh shy! I couldn't believe it.

I didn't really know Elton very well at that time, but we've become good friends in the last couple of years. Yvonne and myself have been to dinner with him at his house. He's a lovely guy and very grounded, despite the image that people might have of him. I've had many conversations with Elton about the business and he's a guy who will freely dish out the advice to you before you even ask.

So many doors open for you when you're an entertainer, and you meet people from all walks of life. I've been introduced to Prince Charles on several occasions, having performed at the 'Party In The Park' concert for his Prince's Trust Charity with Boyzone, and as a solo artist. The first time we met him was a howl. It was backstage at the Hyde Park concert. We'd finished our performance and we were having a couple of drinks. Shane Lynch was in a giddy mood with the booze. He's not a big drinker and when he does take a drop you never know what to expect.

Prince Charles was eventually escorted backstage and we were all lined up to shake hands with him. He was doing the sort of tour of inspection, stopping to have a few words with all of the acts. Shane Lynch was wearing a flat cap, like you'd see on a farmer, and when Prince Charles came to us, he looked over at our Shanno and remarked, 'I like the cap.'

'Alright, Charlo! You can borrow it anytime you're goin' shootin',' says Shane, with a big, silly smile.

That was a priceless moment. Everyone, including Prince Charles, cracked up laughing. 'We have a joker here,' he said in his grand voice.

Shanno certainly made a big impression on the Prince. The following year when we performed at the same event, Charles came around and when he reached Boyzone he took one look at Shane and started laughing, 'Oh, it's you again!'

'Alright, Charlo!' says Shane.

He had stood on the side of the stage and watched our performance. I'm sure I caught him bopping and jiving from the corner of my eye. Afterwards, he told us, 'I enjoyed your music and liked what you did up there.'

It's not just royalty who has been at the receiving end of a Boyzone drunk. That mean machine of boxing, Mike Tyson, met his match when I caught up with him at the Monte Carlo Music Awards in 1998. It was at the same party where Puff Daddy announced that Yvonne and myself had just got married, after I drunkenly spilled the beans to him.

I'm weaving through the crowd when I spot a familiar looking figure drinking in a corner of the big room. 'I know that guy,' I thought.

'That's yer man, wha'sss name … Tyson … Mike Tyson.'

So I staggered over with a vodka attitude. 'How'ya Mike, how's it goin'?' says I.

He gave me a look, as if to say, 'What's a gnat like you doing in my web!'

I point my finger and tell him, 'Michael Collins will kill you!'

He stared at me with a face like a bulldog chewing a wasp. 'I think you mean Steve Collins,' he scowled.

Another killer punch from Tyson.

I had just made a total ass of myself, confusing Michael Collins, an Irish patriot, with Steve Collins, the Irish boxer, as Tyson had so rightly, and smugly, pointed out. I staggered off with my tail between my legs, feeling like a right eejit.

It all came back to me the next morning and I was cringing with embarrassment. But all was not lost. As I wandered through the hotel, wondering if the construction works in my head would ever end, I spotted Mike Tyson again. He was out cold and lying on a bench.

I went over, slapped him on the face, and ran off up the stairs giggling to myself. At least I'll always be able to say, 'I hit "Iron" Mike Tyson and lived to tell the tale.' Even if it was the gentlest of slaps.

Getting the opportunity to sing our hit song, 'No Matter What', with Pavarotti in Modena, Italy, should have been an occasion to be treated with total reverence. But the prestigious event followed straight on the heels of our major stadium concert at Dublin's RDS on 31 May 1999. The result was that five seriously hungover guys turned up for our flight out of Dublin Airport the following morning.

Things got off to a bad start when I saw the private plane that was awaiting our arrival. It was like a tin of beans with wings! 'I'm not getting on that!' I said. 'No way am I getting on that! I value my life.'

Keith, who is still pissed from the post-concert party the night before, says, 'I don't mind. I'll get on it.' He would have got up on a broom stick at that stage. So he goes off on the plane alone, I get two scheduled flights and the other three lads go home when they discover that they're really not needed in Modena until the following day.

Eventually I arrive in Italy, very hungover, and I turn up to do my sound check with Pavarotti. He, of course, doesn't do a sound check, so I perform with his stand-in.

I have to do Stephen's bit of 'No Matter What' as well as my own, as he's not arriving until the following day. Duffy, meanwhile, is on the side of the stage, with a bottle of wine in his hand, shouting, 'How'ya Ro! Are ya alright!' while I'm trying to sing the damn song. All I'm thinking about at that moment is, just let me get to the pub, I don't want to be here. It turns out to be a bit of a rock 'n' roll weekend.

Next day, before the concert, everyone Keith meets tells him that Luciano wants to say hello and is looking forward to meeting Boyzone. When the big man finally arrives and is introduced to us as Luciano Pavarotti, Keith turns to me and says, 'So that's who that Luciano bloke is! Everybody has been talking to me all day about Luciano and Pavarotti and I thought they were two different people.' Well done, Duster...

We were always game for a laugh, always taking the piss out of someone, mostly ourselves, and I think that's been the secret of our friendship and that's why we never broke up. One time we dressed up as the Spice Girls on *Live And Kicking*, the BBC Saturday morning TV show. The Spice Girls themselves were on the show and they didn't know anything about it until they saw us on a monitor while they were live on air in the studio. I was 'Baby Spice' with a long blonde wig, Shane was 'Posh', Keith was 'Scary', Stephen was 'Sporty' and Mikey was 'Ginger'. We were singing 'Wannabe' with our backs to the camera and as the shots flashed to us and then to them, you could see the look of bewilderment on their faces. They hadn't a clue what was going on. It took them a couple of seconds to realise that it was actually Boyzone imitating them! Then they cracked up.

Boyzone always got on well with the Spice Girls. I remember meeting the Spice Girls after they came on the scene all of a sudden. Boyzone were going well at the time; we were one of the more popular pop acts coming out of Ireland and the UK. We were out in Germany appearing on an MTV show and the Spice Girls were also guests on it. The girls turned up in clothes they'd been travelling in for weeks. They were filthy dirty and absolutely hyper. They were so enthusiastic, flying around, loving every minute of it and obviously all great mates. Emma and Geri are the two girls I know best. When Boyzone played a big outdoor concert in Dublin in May 1999, Emma came over for it and she stayed with me and Yvonne. All her Irish family live in Ferns, County Wexford.

What a pity they didn't all manage to stick together. But then the pop world, is a crazy, crazy life. I've seen people fall by the wayside because they can't deal with it. And I see people in the business who have lost the plot because they believed the hype and allowed themselves to lose touch with real life and real people. One of the saddest individuals has got to be Michael Jackson. I got a surprise invitation to come to his room, along with twelve others, for a private audience with him at the Monte Carlo Music Awards 2000.

Yvonne and myself were sitting at Prince Albert's table with an incredible group of people that included Jean Claude Van Demme, Elle McPherson, Billy Zane and Ursula Andress. Michael Jackson, who was on the show, should have been there, but, of course, he wouldn't join guests for a public dinner. Instead, he summoned us, the people at the head table, to a private audience with him.

That, to me, is quite hideous. I thought, 'Go to a room just to say hello to him? Feck that! What would I do that for? What would I talk to him about?'

I think Michael Jackson's music is great, but the way he carries on is just freaky. So I said, 'No, I'm not going to that.'

Later on, Yvonne and myself, along with Mark Plunkett and Alex Delves, were making our way through the hotel. We were on our way to a back door exit, leaving to go on to another party, when we walked in to a load of very intimidating-looking security guys.

'Sorry, you can't come through here,' said one.

I saw red and kicked up a stink. 'I'm going through here. What do you mean I can't go through here? You just watch me.'

As luck would have it, an Irish guy – they're everywhere – was one of the security team. 'He's alright! He's alright!' he told his colleagues. So the Irish guy was escorting us through and I still didn't know what all the fuss was about.

It was only when we got near the end of a corridor that I discovered the reason. Michael Jackson was standing behind no less than twelve bodyguards, who were formed in a semi-circle with their backs to him. It would have been comical if it wasn't so sad.

As we were going past, I said, 'Alright Mick! How's it goin'?'

He just nodded his head.

That, to me, is how it all goes wrong for some people in this business ... when they start believing this whole superstar myth. I'm not the talent Michael Jackson is and I never will be, but even if I had his success I wouldn't behave like he does. Not in a million years.

Nobody ever gave me a book on how to be a pop star; I never

did find *The Beginner's Guide to Survival in Pop*. But from the moment Boyzone started being a serious pop contender and I began meeting the stars who had travelled the road before me, I was hungry for information and knowledge. I met Matt Goss of Bros, a group I had been a big fan of when I was growing up. With hits like, 'When Will I Be Famous', they were the Take That and the Boyzone of their time. Matt taught me the ins and outs of not getting screwed in the business. He now knows the pitfalls. He had all his money taken off him. He lost the lot. It was very scary to think that is what can happen to you in this business if you don't watch what goes on around you, watch your money and watch people. I try to be as careful as I can.

My brother Gary and myself were also huge fans of the band, Del Amitri, and I've become good mates with their lead singer and songwriter Justin since we met on our travels. We did some songwriting together and I'm constantly learning from people like him.

Justin is a mad hatter and we've had some great nights out, one of which was particularly eventful. They were playing at a venue in Hammersmith and Boyzone had been on *Top of the Pops* the same evening. I arrived in time to catch the last three songs of Del Amitri's set and then I spent the rest of the night in the bar with the Justin and the lads in his band.

The drinks were flowing, and when Justin and I finally left the place at about one o'clock, we were both steaming and in very high spirits. Out in the street, we spotted a tree, and Justin decided that it would be a great idea to try to climb it. I'm hanging on to his leg, trying to pull him off a branch when the police car arrives.

It pulls up alongide the tree and one of the policemen gets

out. Hands on hips, he calls out to us, 'Are you alright there, lads? Come on now. The game is over.' Then he takes a closer look at me. 'I know your face, it's Ronan Keating.'

'How are ya?' I said, trying to stop the ground from moving about under my feet.

'Can I have your autograph,' he says. 'My daughter …'

I make the man an offer. 'I'll give you an autograph if you give us both a lift home.'

He pauses for a moment and exchanges a glance with his mate. 'Fair enough,' he says eventually.

So we hop in the car, and I say, 'Chuck on the siren, there!'

Fair play to him, he switches on the siren and we belt through London to the hotel. It was like something out of *The Dukes of Hazzard*. Except that Justin and myself are in the back, hammered drunk, giggling and rolling around the place, with me trying to put pen to paper and keep my half of the bargain.

Michael Jackson doesn't know what he's missing.

CHAPTER 16

THE NEXT GENERATION

25 March 1999: A banner headline in the *Irish Star* declares: RONAN'S WEST COMES TO LIFE. The report goes on to say, 'Boyzone star Ronan Keating showed off his new "baby" to an international press corps last night. But newborn son Jack was nowhere in sight. Instead, Ronan unveiled his other baby – Westlife, the boy band he hopes will find fame and fortune.'

It was just a week after Jack was born and, as the *Star* had pointed out, my second baby was finally out there.

I had come full circle. I was stepping outside a boy band to help create another boy band. I was being given the opportunity to use the experience I had gained through five years in pop to guide five more young Irish guys along the tricky path to success. I was hugely excited about the project. Not only would I get the chance to share things I learnt the hard way, but also the prospect of creative input into the group gave me a real buzz.

But I didn't foresee just how successful Westlife would become … virtually overnight.

Louis phoned me one day. 'Ronan, I've just found another group of guys and I think they're really good. They definitely have something. I'm thinking about taking them on.'

Lou was giggling a lot, a sure sign that he was really excited. I knew Louis was keen to work on new acts, having tasted success with Boyzone. Lou has an incredible drive. Like me, he eats, drinks and sleeps the business. It's his whole life.

After Boyzone had made it to the top, he wanted to experience the kicks of breaking a new act again, 'Starting something and getting it going. I love all that, Ro,' he told me. 'Finding the act, getting it right, getting the record company deal, the first TV exposure and getting to *Top of the Pops*, that's a fantastic buzz. You can't beat it. You know that, Ronan.'

He told me how he had been having an average day, trying to fit in nine meetings and a thousand phone calls on his mobile, when he had a call from a stranger.

'Is that Louis Walsh?'

'Yes.'

'Louis Walsh from Kiltimagh, County Mayo?'

Louis hadn't been to his home town for years. But his interest had been aroused. 'Yes, that's right. Who is this?'

'My name is Mae Filan,' the woman went on. 'I'm the mother of Shane Filan. He's in a brilliant group called IOU. They're based in Sligo …'

Louis was immediately interested. He had already spotted IOU on a short TV news clip when they appeared at a local charity event performing one of their own songs, 'Together Girl Forever'. His mind started whirring.

The Backstreet Boys had a concert lined up for Dublin's RDS arena on St Patrick's Day, 17 March 1998, which was a few weeks later. As soon as he had come off the phone from Mae Filan, Louis contacted the Irish promoter, his friend Peter Aiken, and asked him to try out this new act he was thinking of managing. Peter agreed to give IOU a support role to the American boy band. Louis was delighted and got in touch with the boys straightaway.

I can imagine the excitement among the lads when Louis told them, 'Guys, you're playing support to The Backstreet Boys.' They had been doing small shows around their area, performing in little halls and clubs, but now they would be facing an audience of 8,000 screaming girls and sharing a bill with international superstars. Mind-blowing stuff.

Fair play to them, IOU rose to the occasion. Louis said they went out, performed a tight little routine and the girls loved them! I wasn't in the picture at that stage, but Louis was won over. Unfortunately, since there were six members in the group at the time, and Louis has always believed the best number is five, he had to make the tough decision to drop one. Then all he had to do was get them a recording contract.

Louis was keeping me up to speed on everything that was happening with his new project. During one of our regular chats he suddenly suggested, 'Why don't you come in on it with me, Ronan?'

I laughed. 'I'm serious, Ronan, come in on it with me, why don't you?'

My mind started to race. This wasn't something I had ever considered. Management? It was a whole new area to me. Would I know what to do?

I didn't commit to it straight off. 'I don't know if I could be a manager, Lou,' I said. 'But, I'll tell you what, I'll go along and meet the guys and I'll tell you what I think.'

'Listen, Ronan, they have very little experience, so any advice you could give them would be great. They're a good bunch of lads, all they need is a bit of confidence.'

The meeting was arranged to take place at the U2-owned Clarence Hotel. 'How'ya lads!' I said, bounding into the bar of the hotel a week later.

The Clarence is a quiet, classy hotel by the river. The oak panelling on the walls and subdued lighting gives the bar an exclusive atmosphere. Polite, sharp-suited staff glide by and it could easily seem intimidating. Meeting the guys in there made me suddenly feel ten years older than them, even though our average age difference is probably about two years. There they sat in the corner of the bar. The five of them looked kind of shell-shocked and fidgety, and were glancing awkwardly at me now and then before looking back round the expensive interior of the hotel. I was immediately conscious of the fact that they were uncomfortable around me. For them, I was Ronan Keating, the big star from Boyzone, the guy they saw on *Top of the Pops*, on the MTV Awards and in *Smash Hits*.

I couldn't help putting myself in their shoes, remembering my hopelessly star-struck meetings with Take That, East 17, and later, George Michael. As Louis introduced me I saw that Shane was clutching a newspaper with an article about their support gig for The Backstreet Boys. I was reminded of excitedly showing Louis our first newspaper story.

It seemed like a million years ago at that moment.

But it doesn't take long to see the person, rather than the personality, and we were soon chatting. At that time, there were two other guys from Sligo in the line up, which didn't yet include Nicky Byrne and Bryan McFadden. They were all quiet and polite, looking scrubbed-up but street-smart. You could tell they were sparky as hell underneath.

'Look guys,' I said after a while. 'There's a big prize out there for you if this works. But it's not going to be easy. This is not about fame or glamour. It's all about hard work. And you have got to really want it more than anything in the world or else forget about it.'

The lads sat quietly, listening intently and occasionally nodding. 'If you go down the road I followed, be prepared to make a lot of sacrifices. I have. This will take over your whole life, every day – and I mean *every* day – will be a working day with the group. You'll be away from home, you'll hardly ever see your family or friends and it's going to be a very tough regime. A lot of late nights and very early mornings and being tired all the time.'

I'm sure it's not what the lads wanted to hear. But I felt it was important for them to know what they were getting into. As we talked, I really warmed to the boys.

When they had gone, Louis gave me a questioning look.

'I'd love to get involved with this, Louis,' I said straightaway. 'I'll do it. I'll use my name to help them along, to help them get a deal, and I'll tell you what I feel is right or wrong.'

'OK, Ronan,' Louis replied, and I walked away the co-manager of the group that became Westlife. It was as simple as that.

Louis moved quickly, and the next week, top A&R man Simon Cowell of RCA, who has signed up good acts like Robson & Jerome and Five, came to see them. But it was bad news for IOU – he only wanted Kian Egan and Mark Feehily and he was offering them places in other groups. He didn't even rate Shane Filan whose mam had contacted Louis in the first place!

Louis decided it was time to go back to the drawing board, to sort up the line-up, feel and look of his new band. So once again he held Boyzone-style auditions at the Red Box in Dublin. When I arrived at venue to help with the selection process, it was like someone had pressed the rewind button. Three hundred young hopefuls had turned up, looking nervous but buzzing. Everyone was eyeing up the competition and comparing clothes and looks. I totally identified with their nervous energy as they stepped up to sing solo in front of Louis. Suddenly I was that naive young pop wannabe fighting for my place in Boyzone again. My heart was jumping as I relived that moment.

By the end of the day, the decisions had been made. Just as there had been at the Ormond Centre, there was jubilation and bitter disappointment. When I heard the final line-up singing together I thought, 'These guys have amazing voices. They are something special.' Kian Egan and Mark Feehily had survived from IOU. Louis had also stuck by Shane Filan, in spite of Simon Cowell's reaction to him. They were joined by two Dublin lads, Nicky Byrne and Bryan McFadden.

I couldn't help comparing them to Boyzone when we were just starting out. I cringe now when I think how much we had to learn. These guys seemed so polished in comparison. Certainly these lads had the same hunger. I could see how much they craved success and I knew they'd work hard at achieving it. There would be one hundred per cent commitment and that was just as important as their ability. But they had amazing talent as well.

I·started to work on them straightaway. Along with Louis, I picked their songs and I concentrated on their look. All the time, we're looking for that break, that exposure. They did an Irish radio roadshow, the 2FM Beat On The Street, and then started getting some gigs in the city. Then Louis heard that Simon Cowell would be in the audience of their next show. He still wanted a deal from RCA, even though there were other record companies interested. Remembering Simon Cowells' objections to Shane Filan, Louis quickly arranged for Shane's hair to be dyed blond to make him look like a different singer! Westlife were in great shape at the gig. They looked right together, they had polished up their act and they had amazing harmonies. Simon was impressed and he even liked the new blond guy this time round!

Those are the sort of antics that make Louis Walsh one of the most colourful and successful managers in the music business today. When Louis told me what he had planned to do with Shane, it took me back to the day that producer Ian Levine had written me off. Louis stood by me then and now he was doing the same for Shane. It was only after Westlife had had four Number One hits in the UK that Louis told Simon the stunt he had pulled. Simon saw the funny side of it. I think …

24 March 1999, was the day Louis and I unveiled our new boy band to the media. Yvonne and myself went down to the Red Box to watch them rehearsing during that afternoon. They were in the middle of singing the Garth Brooks song, 'If Tomorrow Never Comes', and when we arrived, it threw them completely.

I listened and offered some advice on how the emphasis in the songs could be enhanced, but they were brilliant already. Once again, listening to those voices made the hair stand up on the back of my neck. Yvonne whispered in my ear, 'They have voices of angels.' She was right, they were incredible.

When Westlife set out to build their fan base abroad, it was a natural progression for them to join the Boyzone tour that autumn. I travelled with Westlife in their coach, listening to the banter between the five of them, thinking, 'God I'd love to be starting all over again.' Everything was going to be the first time for them. Those were the best experiences for me.

But I also knew that there were going to be tough times ahead. That's where I can support them. If you're going through something traumatic, it helps when there's somebody there at the end of a phone line who understands. I know only too well that there are times when being in a pop band feels like going through a war zone. You are cut off from family and friends, thousands of miles from home, with seemingly no end to the daily grind. It does mean giving over your entire life to the business for as long as it is happening. That's the sacrifice you have to make going into a pop career … and you have to be prepared to roll with that.

We were the first pop group out of Ireland to go this route, so there were no big brothers for Boyzone to look up to for advice, guidance and support. There were times when I was going crazy in my hotel room because I didn't realise that what I was experiencing – tiredness, loneliness, isolation and insecurity – is all quite normal in this lifestyle.

So, travelling on the coach, I had long conversations with Kian, Shane, Mark, Nicky and Bryan. My aim was to inform so that when they started experiencing those lows they would remember, 'Hang on, it's not my fault, it's not just me, this happens to everyone. Ronan told me that this is what happened to him. It'll get better.'

In many ways, there's an uncanny similarity between the personalities of the lads in Westlife and us guys in Boyzone. Shane Filan and Nicky Byrne are both very similar to me. Shane is probably a little quieter than I am, but he's totally focused on the business side of the pop industry. He knows where he wants to reach and what it takes to get there, just as I do. Nicky is a real talker and sees the best side of everything. He tells me I'm his role model, which is a real honour.

Bryan McFadden is the Keith of Westlife. He's full of fun and devilment; always game for a laugh and always winding up the other lads and playing tricks on them. But when there's work to be done he quickly switches into that mode. Kian is the Shane Lynch of the group. He's totally chilled out and cool and it's hard to faze him. Like Shane, he's also into his cars and has an order in for a Porsche Boxter. Finally, the voice may be deeper and bigger, but Mark Feehily is the Stephen of the group – a quiet and thoughtful chap. Doesn't say a lot, but when he does it's always worth listening to.

I told the Westlife lads about all our experiences as I sped around Europe in their sleeper coach with them. We got to talking about the first time we played Wembley Arena. 'Lads,' I told the Westlifers. 'Just wait till you get there. It's an amazing sensation. Just the whole buzz of being able to say, "We're playing Wembley." It's one of those cool moments.'

Having Westlife on tour with Boyzone gave me the opportunity to concentrate on honing their act. Several nights while they were performing on stage, I put a hat on and pulled up a hood around my face before slipping out to the side of the stage to watch them.

I reviewed every aspect of their stage show in my mind and then I went straight back to their dressing room afterwards to pass on my comments, have a chat with them … and they listened. In fact, they were very, very slick from day one, I have to say. They gelled well as an act. But there were small things they weren't aware of.

'Be more friendly with the audience, a few more smiles won't go astray,' I told them. 'Watch your hand moves, watch what you are doing, watch where you are going and don't turn your back on the audience.' Little tips like that.

I'd be in chatting away and all of a sudden Barrie Knight would come rapping on the door of the dressing room, 'Ro, are you right, man! Five minutes to stage! Five minutes to stage!'

That made me realise how far I had come. Here I was, minutes before I was due on stage with Boyzone, giving a school class to my own boy band! There was a time when I would have been a nervous wreck waiting to go on. I'm still nervous before a show, but I take it in my stride more and more these days.

It feels odd being big brother to the Westlife lads and having all this experience to pass on. I'm still only twenty-three years of age! It really struck me one night when I took them around to George Michael's house to meet him while I was recording in Los Angeles. I had known George for a couple of years and at this stage we're mates, rather than me treating him as an idol. But I could see how the Westlife lads were totally in awe of him and thrilled to be hanging out in his house playing pool.

From the moment I first heard Westlife singing, I knew they were going to make a huge connection with people. It was those voices. All they needed was the right material. In some respects, I was envious of the start that Westlife got. Their record company put huge resources behind them. They got killer songs from the top songwriters and producers in the world today from day one and no expense was spared on choreography and styling (they initially got Kenny-Ho who had worked with the Spice Girls). They even had 'classes' about how to deal with the media and the paparazzi.

'Don't be surprised if you go out some morning to find a camera lens sticking out of the bushes and pointed at your home,' I warned.

Boyzone had to struggle for a long time before we got close to that kind of support. A newly formed Westlife had to choose between eight record deals. I'd been working in the shoe shop. But, in a way, I wouldn't change what we went through. It was a fantastic learning process and a solid grounding that will hopefully keep us down to earth.

But I don't think the Westlife lads will go too far wrong, either. They have a fantastic attitude. They may have had everything handed to them on a plate, but they are the hardest working band in pop today.

From the off, Westlife took the pop world by storm. I sat back and watched them notch up the Number One hits with 'Swear It Again', 'If I Let You Go' and 'Flying Without Wings'. I know that in years to come, they will look back at 1999 and wonder, 'Did that really happen?' It has been an incredibly hard year for the boys, as I had warned them from the outset. They only got a total of twelve days off during those twelve months. But, man, did it pay dividends for them!

Even I never dared hope, when I first set them on the pop road along with Louis, that they would end up scooping the Number One of all Number Ones in the UK at Christmas 1999. 'One-derful', said the Irish *Star*. They had knocked Cliff Richard from his perch to scoop the last Number One of the Millennium. Amazingly, it was also four Number Ones with their first four singles.

Louis told me he never imagined back in 1993, when he was

thinking of putting together 'Ireland's answer to Take That', how far that dream would take him. He had enjoyed watching Boyzone grow and grow, now he was getting instant thrills from Westlife.

Such is their success at home, they have now broken the record Boyzone set for the biggest number of gigs in succession at Dublin's Point Depot. We registered nine – and they've gone one better! Little gits! They've even taken over our column in Ireland's biggest selling newspaper, the *Sunday World*.

I feel really proud of being part of their success, and I will be there with them, every step of the way, doing what I can to give advice and support. Although I have a business interest in the group, that's not what it's about for me. I care about what they are doing as artists and I care about them as people. If they came to me in the morning and said, 'Ro, we don't want you to be involved in this any more,' I'd say, 'Fine!' and I'd walk away.

I've been really lucky to have had advice from the likes of George Michael and Elton John. Working in this business is like nothing else, and only those who have been there can really understand and guide younger and more inexperienced performers. George Michael, in particular, has given me real soul support, as I know he has to Geri Halliwell, too. He gives back to other artists what he has learned. That's one of the things I have taken from him. Like George, I want others to avoid the mistakes I made.

I'm also conscious that I was given an opportunity in Ireland by Louis Walsh and I want to return that favour as many times as possible. That's why I have helped Westlife. I hope it won't stop there. One of my ambitions for the future is to manage other acts.

My beloved Harley. St. Anne's Park, Dublin 1997

Emergency show supplies

The golden boys

That's Australia behind me!

Mute Stephen

Behind the scenes, 1997

Where am I now?

Transport in style

Looking cool in USA

Looking less cool…

Shopping I

That Swatch watch...

Asian tour 1997

Performing our way round the East, 1997

Video Story

'All That I Need'

'No Matter What'

'So Good'

Me and Yvonne in the Seychelles (in between filming Miss World 1998, the MTV awards and appearances in Germany, London, Dublin, Milan and Rome)

Together with Emma

Me and Mark Plunkett on the move in Japan, 1998

The one and only Mr Louis Walsh

Shopping 2

With Maurice Gibb and Yvonne, backstage at Bee Gees show, Dublin 1998

Me and one of my best mates Glin Donnelly, on the way to Australia, 1999

© Hipclash Ltd

Performing on the Kelly show with Brian Kennedy, Belfast 1999

Relaxing at home in County Kildare, 1999

'The problem for Yvonne, with having a boy, is that she now has two kids to look after.'

The three of us, 1999

The night I made Julia Roberts cry. The *Notting Hill* premiere, 1999

'Life is a Rollercoaster', LA 2000

June 2000, Sanderson Hotel, London, during the build up to the single's release

'The party's only just beginning'

I will always be proud of the fact that Boyzone created a pop industry in Ireland. Pop was never treated seriously in my country until we went out and broke all the rules by becoming successful on the international scene. A lot of people had to eat their words. It took a while, but Boyzone finally gained respect at home. By doing so, we opened the doors for others to follow. Because of us, acts like B*Witched, Samantha Mumba and Westlife got the breaks. Who would have thought six years ago that Dublin would become one of the pop capitals of Europe?

How many other kids are out there, waiting to burst onto the scene? Perhaps I'll ask Mr Walsh...

CHAPTER 17

ITCHY FEET

I felt a tingling sensation running down my spine and the hairs stood up on the back of my neck. It had been the most eagerly-awaited British film for a decade. The images of Julia Roberts and Hugh Grant had lit up the big screen in the London cinema, transfixing everyone, and as the credits started to roll I heard the opening bars of 'When You Say Nothing At All'.

Yvonne, sitting on my right, grabbed my hand and gave it a little squeeze. Rowan Atkinson, on my left, elbowed me in the side. 'It doesn't get any better than this!' I thought. 'Man, this is just perfect!'

I sat there with a grin from ear to ear until the final credit had gone and my voice trailed away. 'Keating, you lucky bastard!' I thought, leaving the cinema. I do consider myself a lucky guy. Things have fallen my way and I've grabbed hold of them. You have to know when to take the luck and when to let it go. It's about taking your chances.

The song, 'When You Say Nothing At All' and the link up with the movie, *Notting Hill*, was the perfect launch for my solo career. But it wasn't something that I had carefully planned ages beforehand. The thought of doing a solo album had been going through my head around that time. I had felt that the timing was right. But I hadn't made any decisions and I had nothing set up.

Then I got a call from Louis to say that a movie writer and director called Richard Curtis wanted me to do a song for a new film, starring Julia Roberts and Hugh Grant. It was going to be put together by the same people who had done *Four Weddings and a Funeral*. I was told there were a lot of big names in there. It looked like it was going to be a big movie. I had no hesitation, and told Lou that I was definitely interested. A meeting was arranged with Richard Curtis. I knew and loved *Blackadder*, I knew that Richard Curtis had written *Four Weddings* and that the Hugh Grant character was supposedly based on him, but I didn't know what to expect as I headed for his west London home. In fact he instantly put me at my ease. He was unassuming, funny and relaxed but it was clear straightaway that he knew exactly what he was doing. He had chosen a song, and he had selected me to sing it. It was good business all round.

And he had chosen the right track. 'Would you sing this song for me?' he asked. As soon as he mentioned the title, I was hooked. I knew the song and I knew it was perfect for me, for my voice. 'When You Say Nothing At All' is a big country ballad, written by a guy called Paul Overstreet, who is based in Nashville. It had been a huge hit around the world for the country singer Allison Krause, but it wasn't very well known in the mainstream music scene. I jumped at the opportunity.

Some people did think that I was actually hanging out with Julia and Hugh during the making of the movie. It sounded like someone has done a Louis Walsh with the tabloids. But you don't have to go anywhere near the shooting of the scenes just to do a song. I actually met them both for the first time at the film premiere. I was looking out for Julia, and spotted her in the crowd at the party. There was no mistaking the tall, slim woman with the shoulder length hair and a smile that lights up a room. I had that Roy Orbison song going through my head: 'Pretty Woman, walking down the street ...'

Later, as I was chatting with some people, Julia came over and whispered in my ear, 'It was my favourite song. I cried when I heard it. It was wonderful.'

'Can this get any better?' I thought.

I mentioned to Julia that we had a mutual friend called Mick Devine, Ireland's favourite star chauffeur. Mick has been working with Boyzone ever since we moved on from the white Transit van. But he's more than a driver. He's your dad, your brother, your friend, all rolled into one. He is a very warm, jolly fella, full of charm and with a big, ever-ready smile. And he's the perfect tour guide for any visitor, as he seems to know the story behind every stone in Dublin. It was Mick who had driven my mam back from the hospital for that last Christmas together.

'Oh Mick's a wonderful man,' she agreed, and it was a moment that we really bonded. Mick's always been a useful man to know!

A few years ago when Julia came over to Dublin, he was her driver and the two really hit it off. Julia enjoyed his company so much that she ended up becoming a family friend. Meeting her at the premiere, I could see why she found Mick so appealing. She's a very warm, down-to-earth person herself.

Hugh Grant turned out to be a nice, earthy fella as well, not at all like the bumbling character he plays in films. 'Ronan,' he said, 'would you mind coming over to say hello to my cousins who are here? They tell me they'd love to meet you and they'd like your autograph.'

Hugh Grant is asking *me* to meet *his* family. If only Mam were here!

I had got to know Rowan Atkinson when Boyzone did 'Picture Of You', a song I wrote for his *Mr Bean* movie. The people behind the film sent me the script and I read it on a plane while on tour with Boyzone. Later, I called up the producers, the respected Absolute Brothers, and we discussed how I should approach it. So, I ended up writing the song around the movie. It turned out to be a big hit for Boyzone as well in July 1997, and I picked up an Ivor Novello award as the songwriter. I was amazed and a bit overawed. Previous winners included George Michael, Elton John, Sting and Rod Stewart. I couldn't ask for better than that, but, to be honest, I don't feel I deserve the award yet. I'd like to think that I might get one off my own solo album.

Rowan agreed to be in the video and it's probably the one that Boyzone enjoyed the most making. We laughed for the whole two hours that Rowan was there. I've always been a big fan of his work, particularly *Blackadder*. I love that agitated humour. He is a very clever man, but is quite shy. He stays in the background and doesn't talk to too many people.

Having a song on a movie was a great boost for Boyzone at that time because we got exposed to markets we might otherwise not have got into. When *Notting Hill* came along two years later, I knew it would do for me what *Mr Bean* had done for Boyzone. But I was still very nervous the week that the single was released. It was so vital to me that my first solo effort got to Number One. I was thinking to myself, 'What if this doesn't work, I'm going to end up with egg all over my face.'

There was a lot to live up to. Boyzone had had fifteen hit

records and four Number One albums up to that point. My own self-imposed pressure was to duplicate that type of success, achieved over years, with my very first single. This time I was out there doing all the promotion on my own. The one thing I was very conscious of in interviews was making a remark that might sound like Boyzone was breaking up. I knew that people would be trying to read between the lines when, in fact, there was no story.

Up to then, I had probably appeared on *Top of the Pops* about thirty times. Yet I was surprised at how nerve racking I found it for that first solo single. The whole time around the track's release in July 1999, my natural worrying really took off. It was the pressure of trying to get everything right and making sure there were no slip-ups. I was working with a different band to the one we had in Boyzone, because I wanted to get a new sound. So I was very, very edgy.

I couldn't let this go wrong for me.

There were sleepless nights as the pressure mounted and the moment of truth drew closer. I'll never forget the relief when the word came through that 'When You Say Nothing At All' had gone all the way.

The first moves towards the solo step had really been made back in mid-1999 when I noticed that we were all struggling as individuals in Boyzone. There was nothing really new or inventive happening in the group. So there was no real stimulation or feeling of pushing through the barriers any more. We all needed change to maintain the interest and keep things fresh. We had the Greatest Hits album, *By Request*, but that was all stuff we had done before, so there was nothing new for ourselves or for the fans on the live shows. I felt that the healthiest thing to do would be to take a break and reinvent ourselves as individuals, so that we could throw more experiences into the Boyzone pot afterwards.

The solo success I tasted with 'When You Say Nothing At All' and the freedom of working as an individual had given me the hunger for more of the same. I had had a Number One hit on my own, so the waters had been tested. It wasn't a case of wanting to leave Boyzone and break up the group. That thought hadn't entered my head. But I now had a growing desire to get out there and prove myself as a solo performer. As always, I needed new challenges and I wanted the freedom to go seek them out.

I think I was right that we needed a break. We had done it all, there was nothing left except more of the same. America hadn't been broken, but we had left it too late. We did go out and try it, but they wanted us to be kids again, doing all the silly stuff we'd done starting off and it wasn't in us. I didn't want to put on those silly shirts once more and jump off chairs, or stage pillow fights in hotel bedrooms. We'll leave that to Westlife.

We all had different solo projects hovering in the background, yet no one was prepared to make the first move. The body language between the five of us was an indication of the tension that was building up. Gone was the old team spirit. The jokes and the laughs were becoming a rarity and we were beginning to rattle along like an old banger.

Eventually, I broke the ice one day with Steve. 'How are you feeling, Steve?'

He looked at me. I couldn't tell what he was thinking.

'I mean, how are you feeling about the band? I think the

time has come to do something else. I want to do something.'

Steve seemed to take it in his stride. Then again, I knew Steve was also keen to work on his own solo projects. He had talked about doing an album and so had Mikey. I knew Keith was interested in doing TV work and Shane had his cars. Yet no one had seemed prepared to make a move or even seriously discuss it.

'Yeah, I'd like to do an album, too,' Steve said.

We left it at that.

I knew that everyone wanted to talk about it, so a few weeks later when we were in Amsterdam for a TV show, I decided to finally confront the issue. We were all hanging out in a room together and having a very loose conversation, a lot of chit-chat, when I suddenly announced, 'Listen lads, I want to say something here.'

A silence suddenly fell over the room and they all turned and stared at me.

'I'd like to move on and do something, lads. I want to do my own album.'

I could sense the shock, as if I had dropped a grenade. I glanced anxiously at each of the boys.

Shane asked, 'What exactly are you saying here?'

'I'm saying I'd like to make a solo album if I get a cool offer, that's all. Nothing more. I'm not saying I'm leaving the band or anything like that.'

There was a pause.

'Fair enough.'

The ice was finally broken. Steve then said how he wanted to do a solo album as well. Mikey said he had plans. There was an air of mounting excitement. Everyone was suddenly agreeing that it was the right thing to do at that stage ... and it was what we *all* wanted to do.

Keith interrupted, 'Can we, as friends, promise each other that we are not leaving this band?'

'Lads, just watch me,' I said. 'Watch and see what I want to do. I'll promote this band as long as I'm promoting myself and I'll always be in this band as long as we're friends.'

We had such a brilliant night together afterwards. The tension had been defused and everybody was relieved that there was no question of any individual leaving Boyzone. It was like being back in the white Transit van again. It was one of those nights that you'd love to capture and put in a bottle, so that whenever you're feeling down you could open it up and jump in. PolyGram in Holland had thrown a party for us because we were their biggest selling act. As part of the entertainment, they had a group of five comedians who went on stage and were mimicking Boyzone songs. They were absolutely brilliant and it was a great laugh.

The five of us hung out together in our little corner, ordering drinks and laughing and joking. Then we went back to our hotel and continued our own private little party. We were still going at nine o'clock the next morning. It was magic. Everything went right. Everything we did we laughed at. There were no smart remarks, it was just fun between the five of us. That's why I know we will always survive together as a band, because we can have nights like that.

Clearing the air that night in Amsterdam was a weight lifted from everyone's shoulders in the band and we went on to really enjoy the winter tour as friends together on the road. Nowhere was the fun atmosphere more in evidence than the night we hit

Glasgow and completely took over one of the band's favourite hotels in the world, The Devonshire, a Victorian town house in the West End of the city. We had come to love The Devonshire during our six years with Boyzone because it was like a home away from home, so different to most impersonal hotels.

It has only fourteen rooms, so we would lock the door behind us and have the run of the place to ourselves. The manageress there, Jeanette, mothered us and made allowances for the fact that she was going to have a bunch of kids on her hands and lots of drinking and late nights. All the staff in the hotel had got to know us really well as individuals and became our friends. They knew what we liked and what we didn't like and we could completely relax. Gradually the fans had got to know that it was our favourite haunt in Glasgow and they were always outside. But there was never any wild scene and, anyway, the fact that there were no other guests in the hotel during our stay meant that we weren't annoying any visitors.

It is a beautiful and spooky old building, with many back staircases and crooked passageways. Sometimes it conjured up for me the same thrill Gar and I felt as kids exploring the Old Shieling Hotel in Raheny. As the years went on we all came to have our own favourite rooms. Mine was right at the top. My mam would have loved it. It's decorated in cream and beige, with a fantastic four-poster bed and a blazing fire.

Jeanette always sat with us and had a drink and a laugh. She knew all the little things we liked. I'd always find a couple of whiskies in my room. Some of the other guys might find bars of their favourite chocolate. After the concerts we'd head back to The Devonshire and stay up all night drinking. There was one time when the staff found Mikey and myself still playing monopoly at six o'clock in the morning and the two of us hammered drunk.

But whilst we would rent the whole hotel, Boyzone were never totally on our own. Legend had it The Devonshire was haunted. During our Christmas '99 tour we were having an early night there for a change. It was freezing cold and wet outside, so we wanted nothing better than a warm-up by the fire. I think we were all worn out from all the late ones that had gone before. As the wind howled around outside, we had been talking about the ghost in the hotel. We'd heard a lot of stories from Jeanette over the years. Apparently a previous owner had been horribly murdered in the room that Keith always slept in. Unable to find a resting place, this poor soul had been reduced to terrorising the occupants of that room.

Soon we went our separate ways to bed. Yvonne and myself were on our way up the stairs, when I turned and said to her, 'Wiv, let's hide in Keith's room and frighten the life out of him when he goes to bed.'

All the keys are always left in the doors when we're there. So I open the door and the two of us are sneaking around in the dark looking for somewhere to hide when suddenly there's a roar of, 'Whoooooo! Whoooooo!'

'Oh Jaysus!' I roared, my heart in my mouth.

'Is that you, Ro?'

'Shane! You frightened the crap out of me!'

'I was waiting to give Keith a scare.'

'So are we!'

All of a sudden the door opens and Stephen comes into the room. He has the same idea. We all find places to hide, behind the sofa, behind the TV, behind the curtains.

We didn't have to wait long. The door opened and we jumped out going 'Whoooo!'

'Stephen! Stephen! What's happening?' the voice in the darkness said.

It was Eloy, Stephen's fella. So we explain it to Eloy and he, too, finds a place to hide.

After waiting for what seems like an eternity, there was still no sign of Keith. He'd been drinking downstairs with my brother Gary when we left the pair of them. I suddenly thought, hang on, Keith is probably windy after all the ghost stories and he's afraid to sleep in his own room.

I tiptoed around to Gar's room and, sure enough, there's Keith sleeping like a baby on the couch.

CHAPTER 18

THE FAME GAME

This was hell.

I had that horrible, sticky feeling that comes from twelve monotonous hours cooped up in the cabin of a plane. 'Man, I'd give anything to stand under a hot shower right now,' I thought.

But I wasn't going anywhere and neither were the rest of the Boyzone crew. We were being held prisoners in Taipei airport, Taiwan. Having flown in from Manila in the Philippines on our 1997 tour of South East Asia, the Middle East and India, we had run into trouble at customs. There was a problem with some of the visas.

'I need this now like a hole in the head,' I said to myself.

Mark Plunkett, as usual, was on the case, calmly but forcefully sorting things out, so I knew everything would be alright. Eventually.

'How long is this going to take, Mark?'

Mark is always straight with us. 'Don't know, Ro.'

Airports are the most miserable places in the world when you're tired and cranky. What's more, the hot air in Taipei was a killer. Give me the coolness of an Irish summer any time. The minutes turned into an hour. Two hours later we're still in limbo and I'm doing my nut with boredom. It's evening in Taipei, but the crack of dawn in Ireland. I need contact with the outside world, so I call home and I'm surprised when Gar immediately answers.

'It's Ro, Gar, you're up early.'

'Yeah, have you heard the news about Princess Di?'

'What news?'

'She's been in a bad car crash, I've been watching the reports on TV.'

'Jesus!'

Nobody knew that she had died at that stage. Gar quickly filled me on the sketchy details. It was a car crash in a Paris tunnel. Dodi had been killed and Diana was in hospital. It didn't look good.

I was stunned. Diana, of all people, you'd never expect it. I rushed back over to where we were sitting to tell the others. 'Diana's been in a car crash,' I shouted.

'Wha-aat?'

All of us in Boyzone loved Diana. She was more of a pop person than a royal. We had been looking forward to meeting her for the first time the following weekend, when we were due to perform at a concert in aid of her charity at Wembley Arena.

There was a stunned silence. It took a few moments for it to sink in with everyone. The whole thing seemed unreal, like one of Louis' silly stories for the tabloids. It was impossible – we'd all grown up with Diana everywhere, smiling, being photographed. She was an icon, a talisman, there was no way she could have been in a crash. By the time Mark announced that everything was sorted, I had forgotten all about the problems with the visas. When we finally got to the hotel, I turned on the television and the news came across: Princess Diana Dies In Crash.

It felt like a bad dream, too tragic to believe. I wandered around the room in a daze. The tiredness and the longing for a shower that I had felt at the airport were now the last things on my mind. Instead, I sat at the end of my bed with tears in my eyes. On the TV, it was wall-to-wall coverage of the crash. When I saw the pictures of the mangled car, and imagined Diana's body crushed inside, I just felt sick.

I called Keith. 'Man, are you watching this on the TV! Can you believe it?'

Keith was going, 'Jesus, man, it's unbelievable.'

'Come round to the room,' I said.

We sat at the end of my bed, totally fixated. An hour passed and we didn't notice, we were so into the minute details of the accident. The initial reports of the paparazzi's involvement were sickening. And frightening. We didn't know then that her driver had been drinking as the investigation into the crash would later reveal.

People believe that stars like Diana are unique, above ordinary worries and tragedies. But their very celebrity can make them vulnerable. The TV reports that night painted a picture of Diana and her boyfriend Dodi Al Fayed being hunted like wild animals. It was like the hounds after the fox. It was hideous.

Of course, the paparazzi didn't kill Diana and Dodi, the drunk driver did. But the reason their driver had been speeding was to lose the photographers who were in pursuit. The image of that car racing through the tunnel that night was terrifying, like something from a film. But all she was trying to do was have an ordinary meal out with her man.

Is stardom really worth being hunted down? Does being a

celebrity mean that you are owned by people you don't know, tracked down for photos they think they have a right to take?

I'd hate for fame to spoil everything that I have. I wouldn't like to have to put up with the stuff that David and Victoria Beckham deal with on a daily basis, never out of the goldfish bowl. It's a difficult line to walk, but I have always played the game with the press and the general media. I have let them into my life, time and time again. I have opened my door and said, 'Here I am, this is my world, this is who I am, a normal bloke with a normal family.' I've done the *OK!* spread. I've let *Hello!* through my doors. The reason behind that is to take the heat off. One photo shoot, here it is, here's what you want to see!

Someone in my position cannot ignore the press entirely. It's a two-way street. When I've got a single to sell or an album or concert to promote, then I need the media to give me as much exposure as I can get. I'll be out there on the publicity trail, having my photograph taken, opening up my life for all to see. Unfortunately, it's not something that can be switched off when you go back into your own private world. There is always someone hiding in the bushes, hoping to make a quick buck from a picture.

It's not a nice feeling to discover that your privacy has been invaded, that Peeping Toms have been spying on every move you make. I couldn't believe it when I opened a British newspaper to find a photograph of Yvonne and myself getting married on Nevis. It was a picture of the actual ceremony taking place. I hadn't noticed anyone around at the time and I'm normally fairly quick to spot a lurking cameraman. The same thing happened when we had a church wedding ceremony back home in Straffan, County Kildare. Two years after our wedding on the beach, we wanted to renew our vows in a more traditional setting. What was a very private ceremony and reception for my family and a few close friends ended up in one of the morning newspapers. It was like something private had been taken from us and made into public property. I was furious that someone had been hiding in the shadows watching us.

I'm always very aware of what is going on when I'm on the road and behind the wheel of a vehicle. When Jack was born and I was at home in Ireland, the paparazzi guys were on the trail big time, desperate to get a picture of the little fella. I was wise to them. There were two, in particular, that I had copped. Being a car fanatic, I memorised their cars and their registration numbers ... and I don't forget a face. I picked them out no problem when I was out and about in the Range Rover. I even had a bit of fun with them, winding them up. I took them on tours around blocks and down lanes and I lost them by parking in a driveway out of view. They never got anything that day, which made me happy, and I actually enjoyed the excitement of that chase.

I would rather drive myself than have someone drive me because I like being in control. I can handle myself well behind the wheel, as those two guys discovered. The mobile also helps. I've called friends, 'It's Ro, are you home? I'm in the area and there's a couple of guys tailing me. Do you want to go for a drive?' My pals know the routine – they join me on the road, then cut off the guys who are following me, holding them back so that I can lose them. I love that kind of stuff, winding them up and giving them back a bit of their own messing. In spite of what happened in that tunnel in Paris, I refuse to change my behaviour or stop having these bits of fun with photographers. There's no point in being paranoid. At the end of that road you become like Michael Jackson.

Boyzone have had a very good relationship with the tabloids. From the moment we arrived on the scene, we were different to Take That. There was a wall built around them. They couldn't look out and nobody could look in. With us, it was very open. Everyone could see us for what we were, five young guys from the Northside of Dublin. And we were so young! One of the biggest mistakes I made in the early days was telling a reporter that I was a virgin. That questioned followed me around until I married Yvonne and had Jack sitting on my knee. Every interview from Sheffield to Sydney was the same. 'So, are you still a virgin, Ronan?'

You feel like saying, 'Ah, would you ever go feck off!' But, of course, you don't.

It was my own fault for making that statement in the first place. But I was a naive sixteen-year-old at the time, and I let the media and the press straight into a part of my life that should have remained private. I soon learnt that you could be too open with the press.

Guided by Louis, we kept quiet about the fact that some of us had girlfriends, even though the papers were always keen to break that type of story. Eventually, it was Keith and his girlfriend, Lisa, who made the headlines when they went on a holiday together to the Canaries. Lisa opened a British tabloid one Sunday to see a photograph of herself sunbathing topless on the beach. She was devastated. Keith said she cried for a week afterwards. Lisa was not in a band and had never willingly revealed herself to the media. It was just so unfair to show intimate pictures like that.

There was one area that we fought particularly hard to keep away from the media – Stephen's private life. We all knew from the start that Stephen was gay. Early on he came and told us the way it was and how he felt. It was his decision to keep it quiet and we respected that. It was a personal thing and it was none of our business, or anyone else's for that matter.

We were all growing up in the public eye, changing from boys to men, finding out who we were. For Stephen it was especially difficult. He didn't need telling how big a story it was that he was gay. He was an idol to thousands of girls, and a hero to lots of young boys. For five years, he had to live a lie, conscious always that it had to be only a matter of time before one of the snoopers found out the truth. In a way, the longer it went on, the bigger the story became. At times the pressure for him was horrendous.

When a newspaper eventually approached Stephen it was a difficult time for him and for us. We were all dodging journalists because it wasn't up to us to be talking about it. It was a tough decision for him to admit the truth, but, I have to say, fair play to Stephen, he coped with it very well.

In the end, the fact that he was forced to go public was probably the best thing that ever happened to him. At last he was free to be himself, and no longer had to cope with running a fictional life for the benefit of the press. Overnight, we noticed a change in him. He was relaxed and at ease with himself at last.

Stephen had always relied on us to be there for him and we tried to be supportive. But, God love him, we will never really understand what he went through and how hard it was for him.

For any young person, male or female, finding out you are gay and coming out to your friends and family must be hard enough. But to go through all that, whilst in a boy band and under the microscope of press attention, must have really taken some doing. All those close to Stephen were incredibly impressed.

'How is Brian?' an acquaintance asked.

'Brian?'

'Yeah, how's Brian?' he said again and walked away laughing.

Strange fella, I thought. Must be losing his marbles.

A couple of weeks later a guy on the street was shouting over to me, 'How's Brian?'

'What the hell is going on?' I muttered to myself.

The penny eventually dropped when Louis broke the news to me as we crawled through Dublin's bumper-to-bumper tea-time traffic. 'Listen Ro, I didn't know how to tell you this, but there's a rumour doing the rounds that Yvonne caught you in bed with Brian Kennedy.'

'Shut up!' I laughed.

'I'm serious, Ronan. It's spread like wildfire and people actually believe it,' he said.

There were various versions of the story, but the gist of it was that Yvonne arrived home to find me in bed with my good friend Brian Kennedy, the Irish singer. She was then said to have freaked out, picked up a golf club and smashed up my car. Everyone apparently knew someone who knew a cop who investigated the case.

It had become one of those urban myths, a story from someone's twisted imagination that had developed legs.

Everyone was talking about it, apparently. Taxi drivers, shop assistants, bar staff, accountants, you name it, they were discussing it during tea breaks and over a pint at the pub. I could see that Lou was uncomfortable about having to drop that bombshell on me. I laughed. 'Lou, for God's sake, who gives a crap about stuff people make up? No intelligent person would believe a mad story like that!'

'I'm telling you, Ronan, they do.'

'I couldn't give a toss.'

'That's OK, Ronan. I just thought you should know.'

I laughed, 'At least it's not one of your stories this time, Lou.'

When I told Yvonne later that night she thought it was the funniest thing she'd ever heard. Brian was a good friend of both of us. I was on a foreign tour when it was supposed to have happened, which made the story even more ridiculous.

We thought nothing more of it. Then the Irish *Sunday World* contacted me about it, so I said, OK, I'll make a statement to put an end to the completely untrue gossip once and for all. In the interview I said, 'I shouldn't have to come out and say this, but this story has been going around for weeks and it looks like it's not going to go away until somebody puts the record straight.

'I've never had an affair with Brian. We have been pals for a long time, but there has never, ever been anything between us other than friendship. To suggest otherwise is just unbelievably nasty and vicious.

'Yvonne and myself have never been happier. Things are going so fantastic. Our baby Jack is healthy and strong, thank God, and we are having a wonderful life.'

Could I make it any clearer than that? But the story, of

course, didn't go away. Brian and I discussed it and, while he said he didn't care and was laughing it off, to be honest, I really felt for him. He's one of my best friends and, as it happens, while I am straight, Brian had revealed that he is gay. Because of this, Brian was getting the worst of the slagging from people while he was out and about on the streets. He told me that guys were rolling down their car windows and shouting it at him as he went about his business in town. But at least he was still laughing about it. Sometimes that's the only way to respond to this sort of story.

We continued to be asked about it in interviews, particularly after we later did a duet together called 'These Days'. Doing that track wasn't my way of giving the two fingers to the rumour mongers. I did it because Brian is a great artist and I was proud to get the opportunity to make a record with him. Brian has got an amazing singing voice and he pushed me vocally in the studio, so I learned a lot.

I also wanted to support Brian because he has been a dear friend to Yvonne and myself. When Mam died, he sang her favourite song, 'Carrickfergus', in the church at the funeral mass. It was a really beautiful and poignant moment. He also came down to see us when Jack was born. That is what he is like, he's just a very kind and thoughtful individual. That's why it made me so angry when people – and it was the public rather than the newspapers and media this time – spread that seedy story about us.

But what can you do? It's just one of the downsides of fame and it doesn't really bother me as long as it doesn't affect those who are dear to me. Fortunately, Yvonne laughs at all of that celebrity rumour-mongering. She has a clear head on her so, thank God, my family will never be affected by stupid things they see in the press.

'Barrie, I'm a really lucky bastard!'

'Why do you say that, Ro?' Barrie Knight asks.

'Well, just look at me!'

'What's wrong with you, Ro?'

'There's nothing wrong with me, Bar, I'm just thinking, here I am, driving around London on a sunny summer's morning in my Porsche. My Porsche! This was my dream and it's come true.'

'Yeah, Ro, but surely now that you've got used to having a Porsche it's just another part of your life.'

'No. you're wrong, Bar. I never want to get used to it. You've got to always remember where you came from. I'm going to make damn sure that I enjoy all of this and don't take it for granted.'

This is the other side of fame. The homes, the cars and the Harley. Eating in the top restaurants and flying first class. I want all of this. I love it and I'm not going to pretend that I don't. I'm no liar. People have supported me to help me earn this and it'd be disrespectful to turn round and say it's worthless.

I was on my way in the Porsche to Surrey to see the work in progress on the second family home we've just bought there. It's going to be our base when I'm working out of the UK. I'm determined that it will be a real home, a family home, just like the one in Ireland.

The situation when I was growing up was very different, but I'm here now and I'm enjoying it. I'm a spender. I believe in enjoying the money and living the life. Once Yvonne and Jack and any other children we have along the way are looked after, I'm going to enjoy the rest. I can't take it to the grave, so I'm going to make the most of it right up to the end.

But don't be fooled by my public lifestyle. In some respects it is an illusion. The private jets, the chauffeur-driven cars and the glitzy star-studded parties are what I get when I'm doing my Ronan Keating Pop Star stuff. I'm not directly funding those luxuries myself. There's another strange spin-off to fame – you get lots of stuff for free. I'm basically a product, Ronan Keating Pop Star, and people sign me up to promote their products, like motors, so I get the use of them for nothing. My mam always used to say, 'Money follows money.' It's so true.

How you're perceived by the public is very important in showbusiness. Appearances are everything. I can't be seen going down the street in bare feet on a push bike. People have to see people in the limelight living the dream, otherwise it looks like you're not successful. And, as the saying goes, nothing succeeds like success.

Chasing after the finer pleasures in life probably comes from my mother. Mam had a flair about her; she was a very stylish woman in the way she dressed and presented herself. She liked the good things. She had her standards and the certain ways she liked to live her life. It was a different scale to what I now enjoy, but it was the same principal. It's all relative.

I came from a working-class background, but we strived for a middle-class standard of living because of Mam's hard work and sense of style. She always had us looking our best and we were a very well respected and presented family. You could put us in any circle and we wouldn't look out of place. Interestingly it was only when Boyzone were away from home that we were real muck slappers. We would get very Irish, and develop even more of a Dublin accent than we had at home. When I got back Mam would say 'Where did you get that from, your dits and dats?'

As the youngest in the family, there's no denying I was spoilt and I always had what I wanted. My mam gave me a taste of the good things in life and I wanted to hang on to them. I always wanted it all. I wanted to do something with my life. I didn't want to be just another number.

Mam liked her homes, just as I do. It took Yvonne and myself a year to find the one in Ireland. But it was worth the wait. Everything we want in life is in that house for us now. It's got character and space and comfort. There's a beautiful big garden with a barbecue area and the house has a great kitchen and lots of rooms to relax in. It's got a bar and swimming pool, everything I ever dreamed of.

The garage has my classic cars, another of my passions. It wasn't until I started making real money that I could afford them. My first pride and joy was the green '66 Mustang the Boyzone lads gave me as a twenty-first birthday present. Then I bought myself a '61 Chevy Corvette, which is beautiful, my baby. What a car! I've flirted with others along the way, but those are the ones I've been faithful too.

One day I'd like to think that I'll have my own helicopter to fly around in. I've been learning to fly a chopper whenever I get the chance, which isn't very often. The lessons were a Christmas gift from Yvonne. Every now and then I get up in the chopper, take the stick and off I go. I love engines, planes, helicopters, cars and bikes. A big child, that's what I am, and I hope I'll always stay like that.

Despite being blessed, I hope I don't act the star. The strange thing about showbusiness is, when you start out you think straight away that you're a star, but when you become successful that feeling isn't there any more. I may lead the celebrity lifestyle, but I haven't changed as a person. My family and friends have always kept my feet on the ground. I surround myself with real people, rather than the 'yes' people in the business, so there is that sense of normality there in my life all the time. One by one all my siblings came back from America. Ciaran is now managing a hotel in Westport, County Mayo; Linda has a restaurant in Naas, County Kildare; Ger is a stockbroker in Dublin and Gar runs my life.

It's just like our childhood days, Gar and Ro, back together as a team. Brothers in arms. Gar is my personal assistant at home and the fact that he is my brother is such a comfort to me. The biggest problem in my life is finding people I can trust. Because I'm constantly on the move and away from home most of the time, Gar is the man who takes care of business.

I have an office in the house and he works out of there, a regular nine-to-five job. He deals with all the faxes that come through, pays the bills, taxes and insures the cars, all the day to day things I don't have time for.

When he was a teenager, Gar was a real loose cannon. He broke all the rules; went out drinking, stayed out late and didn't give a toss about the consequences. I'm delighted he did all of that because it broke the ice for me. Anything I ever did after Gar was insignificant by comparison. But these days Gar is a picture of maturity and responsibility. He's a terrible worrier, just like me. But mostly, when he's not being wound up by the work load, he's quite chilled out.

The one thing Gar had wanted in life was for Mam to see him graduate from Iona College with his marketing degree. She knew that he had got it, but she died before his graduation day. That was so hard on him, but the rest of us all went to New York for the occasion and we made the most of it.

I know that Mam would have wanted to give Gary the sun, moon and stars for his graduation, so, instead, I surprised him myself with a BMW. When we were kids, and Gar was twice the size of me, he used to joke, 'Ro, when you're big and famous will you buy me a BMW?'

Dave Warhaftig, a friend of Gar's in New York, organised it all. He's another car fanatic, so I knew I could call him and he'd do the business. And he did. It was a three series BMW with all the works, stereo, car phone, sun roof … it was a cool machine, a black one. The weekend before we went out to New York, I had gone to Gucci and bought a lot of clothes for myself. So I wrapped a couple of the shirts and told Gar that was his present from me for graduating.

He opened the parcel and was thrilled. 'Oh, I don't believe it. Gucci shirts to go with my Rolex watch. I can't believe it.' I had given him a Rolex for being my best man at the wedding on Nevis.

Then I handed him a smaller parcel and said, 'Open that one!'

So he opened it and it was the keys to a car, but the BMW badges had been removed. We took him outside and said, 'Walk down the street and hit the alarm button.'

The lights flashed on the BMW and he was stunned. Then his eyes watered up. It was a great moment. When you can spend money in that way, it makes all the hard work seem worthwhile.

He didn't get the Gucci shirts, of course. I said, 'You can feck off if you think you're getting them as well. They're mine!'

We are all very alike in our family, all softies and very emotional. Ciaran is the softest. Linda is like an egg, hard shell and runny inside. Gar is the bulldog in the family, while Ger is the brain, he thinks everything through. He's conservative, but he can be a real party man at times. I'm also very emotional and not afraid to show it.

None of us has left Ireland since Mam died. We needed each other around. It's very important to us that we are here. With the exception of Ciaran, we all live within fifteen minutes of each other.

None of them has ever had to take me aside and tell me that I'm getting too big for my shoes. They'd promptly let me know the moment I overstepped the mark.

Whenever we get together, all the old stories from childhood days are retold and we have the laugh. It's good to reminisce and I can get very nostalgic. I have even driven past my old home in Bayside several times and that's quite an emotional experience for me because it brings back all the memories of the happy times we had there as kids, with all of us together and Mam and Dad.

It's funny how much smaller everything there now looks. It seemed such a big, vibrant home. There are a lot of memories for me in that house, a lot of good times and a lot of fun. I'd actually love to own that house now to keep a bit of the past safe.

I am wary of becoming close too quickly to people I meet

now, because all some of them want to do is ride the waves and jump on board, fly the jets and take the money off you. It happens, and many people have warned me about it. This industry has its downside as well as everything else. There are a lot of nasty people out there who can cut you down. I am lucky that I have so many old friends from before all of this kicked off. I intend to hold on to them.

Glin Donnelly is my best buddy and has become like a brother to me. Everyone thinks we're childhood pals, but, in fact, we first met in 1997 when I hosted the Eurovision Song Contest in Dublin and he was one of the chauffeurs. He's a young guy like myself and we really hit it off. It's fantastic having a really good friend like Glin as I know he'll always be there with me during the bad times as well as the good. His wife, Elaine, and Yvonne get on brilliantly too, so as soon as I get home we call them up and make arrangements to meet and catch up with each others' lives. My cousin, Trev, and his girlfriend, Sally Anne, are also part of our close-knit circle. Trev, of course, was my best buddy during school days and we have remained close ever since.

There are a few friends that I've made in music who are dear to me as well. I don't let a lot of people in. I'm not that type of person. But together with my family, I hold these people very close to my heart.

If I didn't have Yvonne and Jack I'd be lost. Yvonne keeps me going and gives me the hunger to continue. Wivvy understands my business so well and understands that it takes me out of family life and away from home at times. I have found the perfect partner to handle this strange life. I don't know what I'd do without her. God's knows where I'd be … I'd be a mess.

We all need an anchor. I come home and Jack and me kick a ball around, or jump in a car and go for a drive.

I'm a big barbecue head. When the sun is shining I'll buy the steaks and the chicken and skewer them up. Then I'll put the barbecue on and open a bottle of wine. Jack is out playing in the garden, Yvonne and myself are joking around as we get the food on, our friends are chatting and relaxing. It's a real family.

I feel like I'm getting back what's been taken away from me.

CHAPTER 19

DOING THE BUSINESS

Everything in Los Angeles is business, business, business. And more serious business seems to be done at meal times that at any other stage of the day.

'We'll have breakfast at ten and we'll talk about it.'

'We'll have lunch at two and we'll talk about it.'

'We'll see you at dinner at nine and we'll talk about it.'

After that hungover flight to LA straight from the Boyzone tour, and the early snags with the studio dates and Pat Leonard's illness, I had settled into life in LA with Yvonne and Jack. The work was going well in the studio with Pat and I was also having various business meetings, trying to set up management and promotion back-up for my future solo career in the States.

Most people say that New York is fast, but I found myself being swept along by the speed of life in LA. If you lack motivation in your life, a good dose of LA will sort you out, I guarantee you. Everyone is shooting around trying to make an impact and climb another rung up that ladder. It's the city of hard sell. Everywhere you go, you get interrogated. The bar tender asks, 'So what do you do, man?'

'I'm a singer!'

'Hey, man, I'm a songwriter! Maybe I have something you might be interested in.'

Every second person seems to be an actor or actress. I lost count of the number of times I got served by a Courtney Cox or Matt Dillon lookalike. Everyone is looking for a script, everyone wants a gig in the industry. This is definitely the city of stars. It's just that most them just haven't been discovered yet.

Pat's style of working really suited me. From the outset he told me, 'Ronan, if it suits you, I work regular hours. We'll start off around eleven or twelve in the day and finish up around six o'clock. How do you feel about that?'

'Pat, that's spot on,' I said. 'That's me at peak time.'

Pat liked to get the job done during the day, leaving the nights free. That was fine by me. I'm not someone who works late into the night. I've hooked with producers before who've said, 'Come in around ten or eleven at night and we'll work till three or four in the morning.' Of course, I've done it, but it kills me. I regard my nights as a time for chilling out.

When I'm in America I get up around six, particularly in the first week or so while I'm getting used to the different time zone. By eleven in the morning I'm primed to go, so Pat's schedule was a dream.

Yvonne and Jack also settled into the lifestyle. We moved into a large, well-equipped apartment at the back of the hotel and it soon became home. The whole secret to our survival was to try to make things as comfortable and as homely as possible. The first few weeks in particular were an exciting time for Yvonne because the whole place was new to her. We were in a really pretty area and there was a lovely park nearby where she took Jack for walks during the day. We were also close to Rodeo Drive, Beverly Hills, so Yvonne enjoyed endless hours window shopping.

The weekends were great when I had time off and we got to do a lot of stuff as a family. We'd take the car out of the city, driving for miles through the sprawling suburbs. It was like a little holiday every weekend as we went to places like Disney and Seaworld. It was just a shame that Jack wasn't a little older so that he could enjoy them more. Instead, it was me who was getting the kick out of the amusements!

Having the evenings off, too, meant that I could spend some time with Jack every day before he went to sleep. Our nanny looked after him through the night, which left Yvonne free to come out with me, as I had business dinners most nights. As I said, eating time is a meeting time. I was seeing people from the William Morris Agency, one of the top publicity and promotions agencies in the world for creative acts. I was meeting record company heads. And I spoke to a lot of managers, because I was looking for someone to take care of business for me in America. It was a very productive time for me out there. A great town to get work done. Make four or five phone calls and you have everything happening.

One of the good things about LA was the food: it was fantastic out there. Coming off the back of the Boyzone tour, I felt I had put on a lot of weight and I needed to get back into shape. It was something I wanted to do, even though nobody was telling me I needed to. But in LA it was easy, you can get the healthiest food any time of the day. I'm a big sushi fan, so I had plenty of that, and I swam and jogged every day.

But going to Los Angeles also dragged me down to earth again because it made me realise that I am nothing in America. Nobody knew me, nobody really cared. It was up to me to prove myself to them before I left. And I did. It was a very interesting time for me. I had to learn to market myself; to forget about being modest, go out there and sell the talent I believe I have.

I was obviously convincing. By the time I was leaving, I had people in record companies and promotion agencies calling me. I was confident I had laid the foundation for the launch of my career there. Now all I had to do was produce the goods for the album.

Halfway through the recording I began to fall apart. My confidence had been very strong going in, but within a few weeks I started to question everything. What was I doing here? Had I deserved my success so far? The songs were coming together, but were they the right ones to kick off my solo career? I knew that the decisions I was taking would affect the rest of my life. Some of the time I was still buzzing, soaking up the starry LA scene, but at other moments I felt I had more in common with the city's other side, all those people desperate for success and not at all sure it was going their way. My mood would swing up and down depending on whether my confidence was sky-high or rock bottom. It was a very stressful time.

Some nights I'd lie awake in bed fretting like mad over the album. Then I'd drop off to sleep, only to wake up in the middle of the night in cold sweats, having anxiety attacks and really, really panicking.

'Wiv! What am I going to do? What am I going to do?'

'It'll be fine, Ro,' she kept reassuring me. But I knew she was worried about me.

I couldn't stop thinking how much was expected of me. I'd had four Number One albums with Boyzone, and was involved with the success of Westlife. I'm supposed to be the man who can do everything. What if this doesn't work, I thought, if I fall flat on my face? It'll be all over for me and what else can I do with my life? I have nothing to fall back on. This is my life!

Maybe it was that worrying thing of my mam's again.

It was tough on Yvonne as well. Thank God, I had her with me. Just having herself and Jack around definitely helped to distract me from all those negative thoughts. Gradually, as I worked my way through the songs I started to get more confident about what I was doing, and comfortable with the tracks I had recorded. I started to calm down.

Pat and myself established a great relationship. The fact that he had been Madonna's producer soon faded into the background for me. Madonna was mentioned in conversations a few times, but Pat's a total professional and he would never betray a confidence or talk in detail about his clients. Now Pat was my producer and we hung out, slagged each other and had a laugh.

I'm in it for music, first and foremost. With me, it's not about the gimmicks or the fame. It's the music. I really love the creative side of the business. I can put on a CD and find a track and get lost in it. It takes me away. If I'm feeling down it picks me up, and when I'm feeling up it straightens me out. Music does that to me any time of the day. If you've got music in your life you'll never be without a friend. I love making music.

I'm passionate about what I'm doing and I think I pass that on to other people. Pat could see that in me. Despite his reputation and track record, I went into Pat as an equal. But I'm by no means cocky. I listen and I take advice. I let Pat go for it, but I also came in with my own ideas. It became a partnership. He'd play something and I'd come in with a melody and he'd say, 'That's cool. Let's work on that, I like that.' So he'd work on that melody and we'd keep going.

I don't play instruments and I wish I did. But thank God the producers and songwriters I collaborate with accept that, otherwise I'd be lost when it comes to songwriting. I have ideas in my head and that's where the songs come from. The people I work with can understand how I work.

Q Magazine sent a guy over to do a feature on me while I was working with Pat in Los Angeles. One night we all went out to dinner and when I left Pat turned to the *Q* guy and said, 'I've worked with a lot of different artists, but every now and then you meet a Madonna and you meet a Ronan Keating. That's why you do it.'

When I was told about that later I was really pleased. It's those sort of compliments that make it all worthwhile. I work really hard and for me that's the pay-off, for Pat Leonard to say that.

Along every journey there are milestones. The Bee Gees' song, 'Words', was one of Boyzone's.

We had been waiting a long, long time for a Number One hit single in the UK and we finally got there with our version of that number. Many of The Bee Gees' hits were before my time, but their music was always around. When I went to discos as a young fella, the DJs were playing 'Saturday Night Fever' and 'Stayin' Alive'. But it was their song 'So Little Time' that was a big hit when I was starting to really get into music. So they were very much a part of my life.

After 'Words' was released we appeared on the *Richard and*

Judy TV show in the UK. We performed the song and were then interviewed. During the conversation, Judy said, 'Actually, I think we have a little surprise for you. Are you there, Maurice?'

'Yes, Judy.'

It was Maurice Gibb of The Bee Gees. 'How is it going, guys?'

'Great.' We were gobsmacked. Nobody had warned us.

Maurice said, 'I just called to tell you that we've had a lot of people cover our songs, but we feel this is the best cover of any of our songs that's ever been done.'

I'm sure the Richard and Judy viewers could see our heads swelling with pride. To hear Maurice Gibb pay us that compliment on national TV in the UK was a great thrill.

A year later we were invited as guests on the TV show, *An Audience with the Bee Gees.* Only two acts would be performing, apart from The Bee Gees themselves, and we were one of them. Celine Dion was the second, but she was doing a satellite link from the States. So we were the only act on the show, which was a huge honour.

But it didn't end there. When The Bee Gees tour arrived in Ireland in August 1999, for a performance in front of 40,000 fans at Dublin's RDS outdoor arena, they invited me to come along as their special guest and join them on stage to sing 'Words'.

This would be the biggest audience I'd ever performed before in Ireland. Getting up there on stage with these legends in front of my home crowd would be a serious job for me.

During the day of the concert I went in to the RDS to rehearse the song with The Bee Gees. 'How are you, Ronan?' they greeted me. 'Great that you can do this. Let's go out tonight and have a good time on that stage!' We began to rehearse and for a moment, I took a step back in my mind and looked at these three legends around me. 'God!' I thought, 'How did I get to here?'

But Barry, Maurice and Robin were completely unpretentious and made me feel very at ease. Yvonne was with me and they brought us over and introduced us to their families. Everyone got on really well.

I went home, had a shower and got dressed and then headed back to the city for the concert.

'Jesus, Wivvy, can you believe I'm actually doing this?' I said, as I drove through the gates of the RDS and into the backstage area. It wasn't a question. I was just trying to convince myself that it was actually happening.

I met Barry, Maurice and Robin in the dressing room and we chatted briefly about how everything was looking good for the show.

'See you later,' they said.

I watched the three legends trail off towards the stage. 'Looking forward to it,' I replied. The prospect of singing in front of the 40,000-strong crowd had me shaking all over. If there had been a roof on the venue, the roar of the crowd would have lifted it when the lads made their entrance. When I went up to the side of the stage and looked out over the audience, there wasn't a space to be seen around the stands or on the field. It was one massive party of swaying bodies. And everyone was singing along to the songs.

I took a deep breath as the set list came around to 'Words'.

'Right,' I thought. 'Here goes. Just remember the words, Ronan.' That's what normally goes through my head at concerts. 'Remember the bleedin' words.' I forget the words of songs a lot. It's happened to me a million times.

Boyzone had also done a slightly different version of 'Words' to the one that The Bee Gees do. Thank God they were singing that extra little bit. But I had to remember to stop singing at that point. So all that was going through my head as I prepared for my big moment.

There was a shot of me on screen first, singing the song … and then I walked out. The boys let me stand in the middle as I sang the song with them. It was just magical. I was in Dublin, my home town, singing with The Bee Gees. Everyone in that audience knew 'Words' as a Boyzone song and they were all singing along with us. There are moments you want to go on forever and that was one of them.

Afterwards, Yvonne and myself had drinks with the lads and their families and Barry and myself really hit it off. He brought me in to his company like a son and looked after me straightaway.

'Why don't we do something together,' he suggested that night, before we parted.

'Jesus I'd love to do something with you, Barry.'

'Well, then, come on over to the house and we'll write.'

I went home that night and thought no more of it. People say things like that in this business. They might mean it at the time, but it rarely happens.

Not Barry. He rang me a week later and asked, 'Hey Ronan! Are we going to do this?'

It all fell into place. I went over to his home in Miami the following month and we started working on a song called 'Lovers & Friends'. We didn't get to finish it as I had to leave to pick up with Boyzone. But the working relationship, as well as the personal one, had been established.

Then in February I had a break from working with Pat Leonard, so I arranged to go on to Miami and finish the song for my album.

Compared to Los Angeles, Miami is a lot more fun. It's more of a party town. There is always something going on. The people there are really cool and they have their own individual style, whereas in LA everyone is wearing what they see in the shops.

Miami has a big gay community, which, as usual, adds to the fun and the party vibe in the city. I also loved all the little coffee shops and bars around the city and the whole Cuban/Latin influence. After the full-on business drive I'd been doing in LA, it was time for me to relax. I needed to chill out and Miami was the perfect place for that.

We rented a beautiful mansion with six bedrooms and lots of reception rooms and sitting rooms. To get to it you had to troop up a big, palm tree-fringed drive and the house really jumped out at you with its flash pink colour scheme. Very Miami. Inside it was decorated in art deco style, with big marble floors and glass tables. Its location was perfect. It sat on the water and it had its own jetty, leading to a yacht down below.

I turned that trip into a little holiday and Yvonne and I were joined there by the Irish painter Terry Bradley. Terry is an artist I really admire; I have a lot of his paintings around my own home and he has become a dear friend. There was also a pool table in the house which Terry and me held up every night till five or six in the morning.

Terry and his partner, Ashley, got married while we were in Miami and Yvonne and myself acted as their witnesses, so there was a great fun vibe going on during that period. The work got done as well. It was just the one track I did with Barry. We felt we didn't want to sit down and write four bundles of crap. Instead, we wanted to concentrate on producing one great song. We wrote the lyrics in Barry's house and the Bee Gees have a studio in Miami where we recorded it. Maurice got involved. Then Robin came down. We all worked out the vocals together and it was a brilliant experience for me, although a bit surreal.

But, just like during our time together in Dublin, they made me feel so welcome. We had a lot of fun. I got into a groove with them, we slagged each other, we hung out, we laughed and we talked about the business.

We had a mad party in Barry's place the night before we left. As always, the last night is always the best fun, you're high on excitement and tiredness. Anyway we were all in high spirits, especially Yvonne, who decided late into the evening that she wanted to go for a swim in Barry's swimming pool, but that she couldn't quite be arsed getting changed. So she climbed up on to the twenty-foot diving board and jumped off … fully clothed. We all thought that was as funny as hell.

Steve Lipson, the producer on all the Boyzone albums, confronted me in the studio one day. I was singing a track when he rounded on me. 'For God's sake, Ronan! Forget about this bloody American twang!' he said.

I looked at him, with an embarrassed grin. Steve, who's best known for his work with Annie Lennox, and I had become good friends.

'Right, we have got to get rid of this bloody twang, you bastard,' he stressed again.

I laughed.

'No more of this awwww, like an engine on a car, awwww."

'Right,' I said. 'Fair enough.'

It's what I wanted to do anyway, but it was Steve who urged me on and made me do it. 'Just stand still,' he said. 'And don't try too hard. Just sing the song and stand still.'

And I did. It was a track called 'Once Upon A Lifetime'. So I sang, 'Once upon a lifetime I looked in someone's eyes/And felt the fire burning in my heart/For the very first time …'

'Keep going!' Steve said.

So this is me now. I think that 'awwww', that growl, whatever the hell it was, was me busking a note that I couldn't hit or couldn't get into. It was my way of getting around it and it was a cop out. But Steve Lipson came along and finally got rid of it. Steve was one of the people I co-wrote with in Nashville when I went there to create material and source songs for the album. We did a song called 'If You Love Me' and I was backed by a full Nashville band. On that track, in particular, you can hear the change of tones in my voice. I love the song, it has a Bruce Springsteen feel to it. The groove in it is really solid and it sees me in a different light.

It was quite strange how 'If You Love Me' came about. We were working on some chords for another song and Steve was messing about on the guitar and he hit this cool chord and then another, two chords back to back. I loved them, they sounded so good together. I said, 'Play that again!' and from there we wrote 'If You Love Me'. It's one of my favourites on the album, it could have been the first single, and it's easily one of the best to perform live.

Some songs definitely belong to women. 'When The World

Was Mine' is going to be a favourite with some because it's a man saying I had it all, but I was so confident and so cocky that I took advantage and lost it all. And there is nothing better than to hear a man say he has failed, because we never admit it. The track is Nashville born and bred, written by country guys Gary Baker, Steve Diamond, Steve Lipson and myself. I was really keen to do some writing in Nashville, not to make it into a country album, but because the music is fantastic down there, and so many country songs have crossed over to pop.

I love country songs. 'When You Say Nothing At All' is a country song, and it has done me nothing but good. It stayed around all year on the radio after its release. Everybody has loved it. People have come up to me and thanked me for that record, saying how much it means 'to me and my boyfriend' or 'me and my husband'. It's a hatches, matches and dispatches song, something that gets played at important moments, from births and weddings to funerals.

'In This Life' is the most incredible ballad. One of those ones that you can't forget, that just lingers in your head. It's another country song, written by Mike Reid and Allen Shamblin. I also teamed up with Gary Baker and Jason Bloom, two brilliant country writers who have done stuff for Garth Brooks, for two other songs on the album. I'm a big fan of Garth. I believe that 'If Tomorrow Never Comes' and 'The Dance' are some of the best love songs ever written.

Each song on the album means something to me, reflects a different bit of my taste and life. 'Brighter Days' is one of the Nashville team's that I fell for immediately. No messing. The lyrics are about how people use the term 'love' too freely. They think they are in love, when in fact they're not. They don't understand that until they actually find real love and 'that's the day, the brighter day, when I found you'.

I worked on songwriting in a few places in Nashville, including the BMI building (BMI is the convention of songwriters). They have 'writing rooms' there. It was a very weird experience. You walk into a room and team up with the writer there. There's a keyboard and a guitar and off you go with a tape recorder. It's like a conveyor belt; you leave and there is someone in there after you. Although I learnt a lot in Nashville, it wasn't quite what I expected. The town had no vibe to it, which is odd considering it's legendary. It seemed like one big corporation, not a living, breathing city.

Greg Alexander of The New Radicals called my house in London.

'Ro, I have these songs, I know you are making an album and I think they're just right for you,' he said. Greg had given up the whole New Radicals thing because he didn't want to be in the limelight, but he remains a very talented songwriter. When I listened to 'Rollercoaster' and 'Heal Me', I got that gut feeling, that instinctive buzz when you know something's right.

I got that feeling again with Bryan Adams' 'The Way You Make Me Feel', it's so mellow with a really seductive groove. I've always got on well with Bryan so it's great to have him on backing vocal. And it's equally good to have a song by LA writer, guru Diane Warren, the lady responsible for everything from Celine Dion's 'My Heart Will Go On' to Aerosmith's 'I Don't Want To Miss A Thing'. She wrote 'If I Don't Tell You Now' for the big American smash hit movie, *Boys & Girls*, and I was asked to sing it.

'Only For You' takes my vocals to another level. For that one I teamed up in Sweden with Anders Bagge, who wrote and produced Stephen's first single, and my Westlife connection on the album is a track called 'Addicted'. It's about a love-junkie and was written by Wayne Hector, who has penned a lot of stuff for my boys.

In the final shake-up, only two of the six tracks I wrote with Pat Leonard in LA actually made it on to the album. 'Believe' and 'Keep On Walking'. Albums take shape slowly and they grow on the way, so sometimes things have to be held back for another time, like the Bee Gees track, 'Lovers & Friends'. In the end it was just too different to the other tracks on the album. But it will appear somewhere along the line because it's a wonderful song. Watch this space...

I wanted my first solo album to have that a bit of an edge, to use real instruments in all the songs. Even the ballads are stronger for it. Where Bryan Adams was in his denim jacket with 'Kids Wanna Rock' and 'Summer Of '69', that's where I wanted to be with this album. I wanted all the kids to get into it, to love it and for it to be a part of them because I am one of them. I want to hear this. I would buy this album.

Recording this album was one of the most exciting experiences of my career. I literally stood in the studio with my cans on, the guys in the band there, and it was, 'One, two, three, go ...'

With Boyzone it was very different. I'd turn up and put the vocals on something that a producer had worked out. But this now was the way Elvis Presley did it. Working with real musicians was a total buzz for me. It made this a more organic album than any other. It started life in LA and I shaped it alongside great songwriters and fantastically talented musicians. Like Boyzone's, they are songs with great pop melodies that people can sing along to. They are big anthems and songs with beautiful strings, just this time I was involved in every last note. The songs are me, even though I didn't write them all. I'm not this precious artist who feels he has to write the whole album. I just wanted to have the best pop album that I could have. That was more important to me than anything else.

Of course, when the album was finally finished all the insecurities came rushing back again.

Have I chosen the right songs?

Is my voice up to it?

Do I look right?

There is always something to worry about. But I kept thinking about the words a good friend once said to me, 'Ronan, the footballer who trains the hardest will reap the rewards.'

I've given it my best shot.

CHAPTER 20

THE BIGGEST HURDLE

The morning sun casts shadows across the garden from the trees and shrubbery. On the lawn, rabbits hop and I can see some of Jack's toys have been left out overnight. Beyond the garden, through the early-morning mist I can see the vivid mid-summer green of the fields and trees.

It's an idyllic, peaceful scene which contrasts with the inside of our conservatory, which is littered with Jack's debris. I'm enjoying the oasis of calm here after a seven-day storm of publicity and travelling, which picked me up last weekend and has spat me out a week later. I'm exhausted and, although I'm trying to hide it by looking out of windows, very tense.

'And it's still not over,' I think, as I head down the hallway for a sauna and a morning swim. It would pass the time while I nervously wait for the phone call to confirm the UK chart placing of 'Rollercoaster'.

It's not that the single hasn't sold. Far from it, it's the best-selling single of the year. It's just that there's been an industry cock-up and my chances of a Number One hit still hang in the balance.

'Best laid plans and all that,' I think to myself, still furious at the mistake that had put me in this position.

Until then, everything had been going so well. I had come through the stress of the early months of 2000 in America when

I fretted day in and day out over the decisions I was making on the songs that would define me as a solo performer.

It had been such a relief when Greg Alexander came to me with 'Rollercoaster', a track that was up-tempo and in your face, a totally different vibe to the ballads that are the trademark of Boyzone. It was a song that perfectly captured how I see myself now – full of excitement and out there, having the time of my life like any young guy. I had been in deadly danger of being perceived as a boring old pop star at the age of twenty-three!

It was my own fault. When I was thirteen I acted like an older guy because I wanted to go drinking with my mates. Then I went into the music business at sixteen and started presenting myself as a more mature bloke so that people would respect me. I spent seven years trying to convince people that I wasn't a baby.

Now that I am twenty-three and I have a wife and a child I don't have to pretend any more. I feel that I have come a long way for someone my age. Not only am I a husband and father, I've also got six years of Boyzone behind me. But I am relaxed to be in this position. If anything I feel younger now than I have for years. Whereas once upon a time I grew my hair long to look more mature, now I have cropped it short.

I wanted to portray this 'look' in the artwork for my single and album and I discussed it with Terry Richardson, one of the world's top photographers. Thinking back on that photo shoot with Terry gives me hot flushes and brings the blood rushing to my cheeks. Sometimes I open my mouth and the daftest things come out …

Terry had found the perfect backdrop for the shoot in an old, run-down, rambling hotel in a seedy area of Los Angeles. I could imagine some of the characters from Bono's *Million Dollar Hotel* hanging out in this ramshackle neighbourhood. There was a real air of decadence about the dusty old interior and you could dream up all kinds of strange goings-on there that might have happened in a bygone age ... that's the kind of vibe it gave off.

It had amazing looking pieces of furniture all over the place and there was one particularly funky room which had red wallpaper and Terry had suggested this as the background for the cover of the album.

I looked at the room and agreed, 'Yeah, cool Terry, this looks the business.'

Terry has an arty look about him, but he is very open to his subject and takes on board any ideas you have to offer. One of the striking features of the room was a wonderful old chair in the corner. I said to Terry, 'Maybe we should do a shot by that mangetout over there.'

He hesitated, then looked at the 'mangetout', didn't bat an eyelid, and then said, without batting an eyelid, 'Yes, yes, that's an idea,' and went over to sort through some of his camera equipment. Mark Plunkett had been standing nearby and I noticed that he had suddenly developed a fit of the giggles.

'What are you laughing at, Mark?'

He could hardly answer he was cracking up so much. Eventually, between sharp breaths, he pointed to the 'mangetout' and said, 'I think you mean chaise-longue, Ronan!'

Oh shite!

Plunkett is doubled over with the laughter at this stage.

'I knew it was one of them double-barrel French words,' I muttered, turning bright red with embarrassment.

Once I was happy with the songs on the album and had the first single all wrapped up, I couldn't wait to get back out there again.

I had been waiting for this moment for a long time, the freedom to do my own thing.

Sure, I missed not having the guys around me, but I loved the personal control I had over the music I was making. It had been a scary ride right up to the end with the album, a race against time to meet the fast approaching deadline. But I got there. Now all I had to do was convince people how much I believed in each and every one of those songs.

I knew the release of the single was going to be another nerve-racking time for me. This was the start of my new career, so I was back at square one. People probably thought, 'Ah, sure, he'll have no bother getting a hit. He's already successful with Boyzone.' But you can't take that for granted. I really believed I had to convince people all over again. I couldn't rely on my success in the past with Boyzone to make it happen. So I went out and I worked harder than I have ever done before. Because I didn't have the guys with me, I felt I had to do the work of five people.

If it failed, all eyes were going to be on me. There was going to be no one around me to take a shared responsibility for failure. It was just my head on the block this time. Expectations were high – the biggest selling album in the last year of the twentieth century was Boyzone's *Live By Request*, our greatest hits. Our four albums all went to Number One. The Beatles were the only other band that's ever happened to.

Could I have all that success again ... on my own?

There is no telling how your material is going to be received, so you have to get out there and work your socks off. As the single release approached, I went out and I did all the stuff that I'd done in the early days of Boyzone. Some of it I hadn't done in six years – regional radio stations, small TV shows and less high-profile magazines. But I did them all because I had to go out there and make my own mark as a solo artist.

There wasn't a spare minute in my day during the build-up to the release of 'Rollercoaster'. But I was no stranger to that kind of pressure. I had been living with it for six years. One of the interviews I did during the 'Rollercoaster' promotion was with Irish radio DJ and TV presenter Dave Fanning, who asked me, 'There are twenty-four hours in a day, why are there forty-eight in yours?'

I knew what he meant. It's a crazy, crazy life and it takes a certain kind of person to be able to do it. And not everyone can. I've seen people fall by the wayside because they cannot deal with the pace. I was once asked for the five words that best described me. 'Happy, tired, busy, cautious and approachable,' I said. Most days that was the appropriate order, but sometimes we were busy first, tired second and happy third. Looking back, I sometimes wonder how I ever got through some of those days and weeks in Boyzone.

The Miss World event in the Seychelles during November 1998 nearly killed me. It was in the middle of our publicity campaign for the 'I Love The Way You Love Me' single, which was just coming out. Our third album *Where We Belong* was in the shops so we were also promoting that everywhere from Europe to Asia. It was one of the busiest times ever in the band.

We were finishing off the single in the studio when Mark

Plunkett arrived in with the new Boyzone itinerary for the month of November.

'There are a few things happening next month,' he quipped.

'You're not feckin' kiddin',' I said glancing at the schedule. 'Is there any time for a pee in there!'

Mark disappeared laughing.

In fact, I hadn't been kidding. I picked the schedule up again and scrutinised the various events that were going to fill every moment of my time during that period.

Nov 10: Working in France.

Nov 12: MTV Awards, stay in Milan.

Nov 13: Fly to London.

Nov 14: Live And Kicking, London.

Nov 15: Planet Hollywood, Dublin.

Nov 16: Ozone and Electric Circus, London.

Nov 17: Big Breakfast Live, Gt. Ormond Street Hospital, Pepsi Chart Show.

Nov 18: Radio promotion all day in London.

Nov 19: Fly/drive Omagh (Ireland). Record *Top of the Pops*, London.

Nov 20: Radio 1 Breakfast Show, Radio 2 interview, Children In Need TV.

Nov 22: Golden Europa Awards, Saarbrucken, Germany.

Nov 23: Fly to Seychelles via Rome.

Nov 24: Arrive Seychelles 7.35am. Rehearse pm.

Nov 25: Rehearse pm.

Nov 26: Miss World Live Show.

Nov 27: Fly home via Frankfurt.

Nov 30: Fly to Los Angeles via London.

On top of all this, *OK! Magazine* contacted me to set up a photo shoot with Yvonne and myself while we were in the Seychelles. Wiv was five-months' pregnant with Jack at the time and they presented us with the idea of doing 'My Real Miss World And Our Baby'. Happy to do anything that would help promote Boyzone, we agreed, so it was more pressure to cope with during the trip.

I hadn't fluffed too many lines on the Dublin Eurovision show, so me presenting Miss World had come from that. I hadn't learnt my lesson, though, and I was also performing 'I Love The Way You Love Me' with Boyzone in the middle of the show as well. It meant additional pressure, although I was glad to do it because it meant maximum exposure for both the group and the single.

'Just get me through this,' I thought on the flight over. It was going to be a mental time. There was a huge amount of work crammed into three days. The flight was long and tiring. As Yvonne was pregnant, she had to keep getting up to walk around and keep the circulation going. When we arrived it got worse. Yvonne and myself wait, and wait, and wait for our suitcases to come through on the conveyor belt. No suitcases! So we have no clothes … and we're doing a photo shoot for *OK!*

It is hot in the airport, and Yvonne is suffering. The last thing we needed was for our luggage to be lost. Wivvy gives me a look. This is all my fault.

Because the rest of the guys in Boyzone only had to worry about the rehearsal for the interval song, they were free to relax and take it easy when we arrived. I, on the other hand, had to go straight into rehearsals for the presentation.

'Eh, Ro, pal, don't worry about us, we'll be alright on our own. We're all heading off to do some scuba diving!'

'Rub it in, Duster!'

'Oh, Ro!' It was dependable Mark.

'Yes?'

'I'm going to try out this scuba diving myself.'

'Whaat?' Even Plunkett was taking time off working for the band and leaving me. I couldn't believe it.

I went off and met all the people involved in the production of the show and I was handed a script to learn off. 'Now, this is work!' I thought. I needed a lot more time to prepare for the event than was possible the way it had been organised. I was being thrown in at the deep end, sink or swim. Furthermore, at the same time as working on the show and learning the script, which kept changing all the time, I was rehearsing with Boyzone and doing the shoot for *OK!* with Yvonne.

In the end, I just about pulled off my role in that show, but it was all a bit too thrown together for my liking. The 'Miss World' contestants were all gorgeous, but trying to interact with them on stage was incredibly hard work. Sometimes my questions seemed to hit a brick wall and leave the girls' glazed expressions entirely unchanged. I was glad when it was all over.

There are obviously times in those sort of pressure chambers when I feel like exploding, particularly when I'm being pushed too far or asked to do something I'm not comfortable with. I'm only human after all. I have my moments when I go mad, but I do it behind closed doors.

I'm lucky that I have a brilliant team around me, so I never have to be confrontational with people. But if I did have a problem I would try to deal with it quietly and in a civilised fashion. Sometimes in TV studios I get asked to do things that I don't want to, but I'm never the one who turns around and says, 'I'm not doing that!' I'd quietly mention it to Mark and he deals with it. And that's the way it should be dealt with. When you're the artist, it can be a very delicate situation. If I simply said, 'No!', it could cause trouble or offence.

I like getting on with people and it makes the whole business so much easier. If you treat people with respect, you get it back in return. After I went out on an Asian trip to promote my first solo single, 'When You Say Nothing At All', Mark got e-mails and faxes saying 'It was a pleasure to work with him.' I get a real kick out of hearing things like that. However rich or famous you are, you can't buy stuff like that. There are many times I bite my lip when my patience gets tried, but it's worth holding back.

People ask me how I survive in the business and I tell them, 'I love what I do. I love the flights, the jets, the hotels, travelling around the world and getting up in front of 20,000 people.' I accept that when I walk out the door people will stop me and ask for autographs, or to pose for photographs or hand me their child to hold for a souvenir picture. I know all that comes with the territory and I accept it. It's part of the deal.

The main push of the promotion for 'Rollercoaster' begins several weeks before its release and I'm swept along, from studio to shoot to event, as the momentum builds. I'm starting to really enjoy myself, and people are noticing a change in me now I am a solo performer. With Boyzone, I would usually slip into a room unnoticed, but now that it's just me, I bound in, smiling broadly, greeting everyone, as all eyes turn towards me.

I feel younger and healthier than I have for a couple of years, and my confidence is on full throttle. The word in the industry is that 'Rollercoaster' is set to become a monster of a song.

But the acid test for me was going to be Capital Radio's 'Party In The Park', the Prince's Trust gig in front of 100,000 people in Hyde Park. It would be the defining moment for me as a solo performer. I had done the 'Party In The Park' in the past as a member of Boyzone (when Shane and Prince Charles hit it off!), but this was different. This was going to have to prove something to *me*. Like my mother, God rest her, I'm an awful worrier. I had a live tour lined up, venues booked and tickets sold, even before the release of the single or the album. If I flopped in Hyde Park, it would be a nightmare. But could I do a major set on my own?

I was gutted when I woke up on the day of the big open-air concert and saw the rain pouring out of the heavens. 'Oh man!' I thought. 'This was not good.' But when I arrived, I could see it hadn't dampened the spirit of the crowd, who were like a great multi-coloured brolly brigade. Backstage before the performance I was suffering from nerves, the likes of which I've never experienced before. Elton, Bryan Adams, The Backstreet Boys, my own boys Westlife, and Bon Jovi were all there, and the atmosphere was brilliant, despite the weather. Everyone was hyper. David Beckham was there messing around with Victoria.

I was itching to get out on to that stage. I was going to be working with my own band and I wanted to know my fate, good or bad. The suspense was killing me.

As I waited for my cue to go on stage, I suddenly felt very strange being without the rest of Boyzone. Normally at this time, we'd be bantering, making jokes to keep us calm and focussed. Duster would be slouching about at the back, Shane would be downing a bottle of water and Mikey would be running through the dance steps in his mind. We'd have each other to gain support and confidence from, we were a team.

Now it was just me. This was crunch time.

I burst on to that stage like a lion out of a cage and straight into 'Rollercoaster'. The audience came straight back at me, and as soon as I heard their first roar, I was on a roll. The *Notting Hill* track, 'When You Say Nothing At All', was the sandwich of my three-song set and the popularity of that song stood up brilliantly, the crowd singing the chorus back to me. By now I was well into my stride, and was even beginning to enjoy being the only one out there at the front. I felt like I had come of age. This was freedom.

Then I hit them with a new number, 'If You Love Me', which I had written in Nashville, and, yes!, they loved it. They were singing along, and it was at that moment that I realised, 'I can do this. I can definitely do this.'

Prince Charles came around later on to meet the artists and we had a bit of banter about Shane Lynch. 'How is that lunatic? How is the old boy?' he asked.

Buoyed up by the triumph of the 'Party In The Park' gig, I was feeling good on Monday morning, the day 'Rollercoaster' finally hit the shops in the UK. I got a further boost later in the day when I learned that I had double the sales of the current

Number One, which happened to be my mates, The Corrs and their song, 'Breathless'.

It was the best possible start, but this business is a bit like Wall Street. Fortunes are made and lost overnight. Mark broke the news to me on Tuesday as I was getting set to pre-record 'Rollercoaster' on the *Pepsi Chart Show*. I could sense that he was a little edgy when we met. 'Everything OK, Mark?' I asked. I just knew there was something up.

'Errr, yee-ah!' he said. 'Actually, there is a problem. I've just heard about it from the record company.'

There was a knot in my stomach. 'What problem?'

'The CD1 format has been disqualified from the chart.'

'Get out!'

'I'm deadly serious, Ro. They've disqualified it because it's got three tracks and the CD-Rom interview, which they view as four tracks, meaning it's not eligible.'

How could they make such an obvious mistake? Didn't they know the rules? 'I don't believe it! Jesus Christ!' I said to Mark.

I thought the game was over at that moment. The CD1 format was the most popular one. I was totally gutted. 'What's going to happen, Mark?' I asked. 'Is there not something we can do?' I was totally deflated. All that work...

'They're going to move the earth for damage limitation, but it's definitely going to affect the chart position.'

'Oh Mark, how could this happen?'

After everything I'd been through to get to this point, I was going to be the loser on a technicality. I couldn't believe it. But it was done and it was beyond my control, I just had to keep going, work through my schedule and hope for the best.

On the Wednesday I flew from London to Manchester to

perform on the *Midweek Lottery Show*. Then on Thursday, when I was due to appear on MTV Select, there was another little problem.

'What's wrong this time Mark?'

'I don't want to alarm you, Ronan, but there are going to be some special guards and armed police down at MTV today.'

'What's after happening now?' I asked.

'A death threat.'

'What do you mean a death threat? A death threat against whom?'

'You.'

'What the …?'

The threat had been issued through the Boyzone web site and it said that 'someone will go to MTV with a gun and shoot Ronan while he's on MTV Select'.

It's probably some spotty little kid with nothing better to do, I thought. But, of course, you have to be cautious about something like that. However, I decided to go ahead with the show, which I co-hosted with presenter Kelly Brook.

As I arrived at the studio, I could see armed-response police officers carrying Heckler and Koch machine carbines on duty outside. I felt like a mafia supergrass as I scurried into the building, glancing around, half-expecting to see the police diving behind their cars and starting firing. It was a pretty heavy scene.

The show is normally hosted from an 'outdoor' glass studio where fans can look directly in at guests. As a result of the threat, it was moved to a safer location indoors, although computer trickery made it look like the fans were behind me.

Obviously the day went off without incident, but the threat

still hung in the air and I waited until I got home until I could tell Yvonne in person. I wanted to make sure she wasn't scared in any way. Threats are the flip side, the dark side to success, but then it goes with the territory.

But the threat was not going to slow me down. On the Friday I was up at the crack of dawn and performed 'Rollercoaster' live on GMTV, before flying to Belfast to perform on the *Patrick Kielty Almost Live* show. As soon as that was done, I was heading for Edinburgh in a private jet. As I landed I learned that 'Rollercoaster' had gone to Number One in Ireland. It was fantastic news. But I couldn't enjoy it because I still wasn't out of the woods in the UK. I was ahead of The Corrs by about 19,000 CDs, but that's nothing in this business. It was going to go to the wire. The next day's publicity events would be crucial.

From the moment I got up on Saturday, my feet hit the ground running. In Edinburgh I did a major signing session at the Big W store. After an hour, I sped to the airport and jetted to Rotherham for another signing session in the Big W store there. I was exhausted by the end, but it was on to Bristol, again by jet, for a third signing session. At each of the three stops the airport was about forty minutes by road from the event, so it was a constant race against time.

By the time I arrived home to my house at Celbridge I was a basket case, completely knackered. But I had done everything I could to repair the damage of so many sales not counting towards the chart.

I woke up on Sunday morning aching and with butterflies in the pit of my stomach. The day seemed to creep by as I waited for the news of the chart that evening. Yvonne and Jack did their best to calm me down, but I continued to pace about, unable to settle to anything. 'It wouldn't be your fault if it doesn't make it. You've done all you can,' Yvonne kept saying. She was right of course, but it didn't help.

At last the time the call came. I felt sick as I answered my mobile.

I'd done it. I'd gone straight to the top. Sweet Jesus ... we'd done it. 'Rollercoaster' had gone into the UK charts at Number One.

I was so relieved I just burst out crying. All that tension escaping. And then I hugged the breath out of Yvonne. The song had sold 200,000 units that week, making it the then biggest selling single of the year, but due to the mistake with CD1, only about half of those counted for the chart.

But by then, I didn't give a toss. It was time to celebrate.

In no time I round up the family and we head out to take over a country restaurant for the night. I'm just over the moon about 'Rollercoaster'. I love this job, I think to myself as we all make out way to our seats around a large table. I want to be doing this in ten years' time. But I will never take my good fortune for granted. In the music business, you can fall as fast as you can rise.

Everyone is pleased for me. I suspect they knew more than they let on about how stressed I was about the solo project. Gar keeps shaking me by the hand and banging me on the back. Loud chatter reverberates around the room, broken by great uproars of laughter.

I sit quietly for a few moments, letting it all sink in.

Everything has changed so quickly over the last six years. So much has happened. Music has helped me to live life to the full. I think back to the atmosphere at The Party in The Park, and to earlier times, with Boyzone, when we seemed about to bring the roof down. I love hearing an audience sing your song back to you, watching them surging towards the stage. Nobody can imagine what pleasure it gives me. It's magical.

I remember being with Boyzone in the Far East, watching the fans streaming in to a gig. Holding their tickets in their hands, they were so excited. They wanted to get T-shirts as souvenirs and the concert programme to remind themselves of the night they went to see Boyzone. That to me is what pop music is all about. The enjoyment we gave people is more important than anything else. We brought fun into people's lives.

The gang around the table is getting noisier. I see Yvonne looking at me, smiling gently. I know she's really proud of what I've achieved. My dad has been telling everyone that he never doubted for a moment that 'Rollercoaster' would be Number One. Jack is there, although it's past his bedtime. Holding on to his uncle Ger, he is tired but happy. What will the future hold for him?

Louis passes me some food. He is telling a tall story involving a tabloid journalist and a deaf cat. I am reminded of the first time I met him, and I get a flutter in my stomach, an echo of the nerves of that first audition. It seems like a lifetime ago.

I am so lucky to have my family around me, I think as Ciaran congratulates me again on the Number One. Success is always for your family, and to be with them is the only way to celebrate it. By now we are filling the restaurant with our happiness.

Mam is there, too. I can feel her presence.

I look around the table. Gar is refilling Yvonne's glass, and Linda is telling a story about her restaurant. My nephews and nieces dash around the table, squealing and giggling. Louis is calling out for the waiter, 'Where's the music? More sound, turn up the volume!'

The party's only just beginning.

CHAPTER 21

A NEW BEGINNING

Achieving the number one solo single might have been like scaling a great hill, but there was still a mountain to be conquered. The first week's success of 'Life Is A Rollercoaster' had been a massive relief, but in the cold light of day, I realised there was still a long way to go. Just a few days after the jubilation I had a knot in my stomach again. What if the album stiffed? A hit single was no guarantee that people would flock to the record store to buy the album. And if they didn't buy the album then I would be history. As they say in the industry, you're only as good as your last record. 'Jeez, I'm not out of the woods yet,' I thought.

Wiv caught my pained expression one morning a few days later. 'What's the matter, Ro?' she asked

'Just feeling a bit tired,' I lied.

As I stumbled around the bedroom picking up the trail of clothes I had discarded on the floor when we arrived home in the early hours of the morning, Wiv could sense that there was something more going on. She knows me so well.

'Ro, there's something up.'

I started to brush her concern away, but then stopped and sighed and just admitted it. 'Ah, I'm just worried about the album.'

Wiv looked at me and smiled. 'Stop worrying. You're number one in the charts today. Enjoy it.'

I knew what she was saying. And, as usual she was right. I should be living for the moment. I should be lapping up the success of 'Rollercoaster'. It was where I'd always wanted to be. But I couldn't help dwelling on how a single was so temporary. Next week it would be somebody else up there. Whereas with an album, you have a longer life. You have a career. A single is only the shop front. You step inside and the real foundation for any artist is the album.

'Ro, enjoy the moment,' Wiv insisted.

She knew, of course, that I would work myself into the ground to make sure that the album was a hit. And she was also aware of the fact that I had a fantastic team of people behind me.

Eventually I thought, 'Wiv is right. The album is another day's work. I am going to enjoy "Rollercoaster".'

'Life Is A Rollercoaster' was one of those gems of a pop song. Thank God Greg Alexander came to me with it and that I had the sense to see it for what it was: my ticket to solo success.

That single was such a huge hit and it brought me to places I'd never experienced before. Believe me, after nearly seven years going around the world with Boyzone, there weren't many places I hadn't touched on.

I'd never been to Russia or Poland before, but 'Rollercoaster' took me to those territories. I was meeting different people, experiencing new cultures. Suddenly I began to feel the kind of excitement I used to have in the early days when I got used to life on the road with Boyzone. Except, I was doing it all by myself.

One afternoon, on a rare break between promotional commitments, I was enjoying spending a bit of time at our new home in England. A car snaking up the drive caught my eye. It was Barrie Knight.

'Something for you, Ro,' he said, handing me a jiffy envelope.

'What is it?'

'Well, you've waited seven years for it,' he said, flashing the big white smile that's become his trademark.

'The album!' I shouted with delight, ripping the packaging to shreds.

God it looked good. I couldn't stop staring at the art work with my face and my name on the cover. I scanned through the list of songs that I'd been involved in. 'Look at all of those titles. They're my songs,' I marvelled. I may not have written them all, of course, but they were my adopted babies.

Barrie was right. I had waited seven years for this moment. This is what had always been my fantasy. Recording an album. I had done it with Boyzone, but it wasn't quite the same. Then I was one-fifth of a group that had made the music and I could never be sure how much of the success was down to me. Now I had my own baby. It was called Ronan.

Inevitably, the pressure came back on my shoulders in the build up to the album's release. The butterflies in my stomach were having a party. All that self-doubt I'd had in the early part of the year while making the album returned with a vengeance.

There was some relief down the line when Mark Plunkett arrived down from his hotel room one morning and announced that he had good news.

'I can always handle good news,' I said.

'The pre-sales are good, Ro.'

'Good Mark? Jeezus, tell me will ya.'

'They're up there around the half-a-million mark.'

'Half-a-bloody-million!' I roared, dancing around the foyer of the hotel.

A couple of elderly Yanks gave me an odd look as they passed through.

'Mark, that's fantastic!'

But ever the pessimist, I was brought crashing back to earth with the realisation that advance sales were only to the stores. There was still no guarantee that the music fans would rush in and buy it.

We discussed it in the Range Rover on the way to an interview on one of the radio breakfast shows.

'Jesus, Mark, those are the kind of advance orders that bands like U2 get in the UK.'

'The industry is behind us, Ro. That's half the battle,' Mark pointed out.

He was right. Unless the major stores were showing some confidence in your album you'd have a real fight on your hands. If they don't splash your album in their window or put them out on the big displays, then the fans will walk on by to the next album. Luckily, all the stores were backing me like a favourite in the race. And I lived in hope of being first past that winning post.

Even though I now had the industry behind me, it wasn't the time to relax. You only reap what you sow, so I went on a really punishing schedule to publicise the album. My record company had done a fantastic job securing the major TV and radio shows for me. I did *The National Lottery, This Morning, CD:UK, Live and Kicking, The Pepsi Chart, Top of the Pops* and anyone else who would have me.

While I was doing all of that, Europe was going wild for the 'Rollercoaster' single and there were demands for me to be there as well. So I was trying to fit in countries like Germany and Holland as well as doing all the UK stuff. I didn't dare look at the itinerary at the time because it would have scared me. I just put my head down and kept going.

'Where are we tomorrow, Mark?'

'Rotterdam.'

'What's happening the day after?'

'Press and radio interviews in Birmingham.'

'Right.'

And on and on I went, like a dog chasing it's tail.

In the midst of all that mayhem there was some really encouraging news for the album.

'The tour has sold out, Ronan!' Mark told me one afternoon after trawling through his e-mails.

'Feck off! I said, laughing.

'Seriously, Ro.'

'You are fecking joking!'

I couldn't believe it.

For reasons best known to my managers Louis and Mark, they had decided to put the tickets on sale for my solo tour two week *before* the album went into the shops. I thought it was a crazy idea myself. Why would people buy tickets for a concert when they hadn't heard the songs?

Obviously we had to book the venues months in advance of a tour, but when the tickets went on sale I didn't have a show. I didn't even know what kind of support was out there for me because the album was still in store rooms. Ever the pessimist, I thought we were taking a huge risk. What if no one bought tickets for the shows?

They had all sold in *two days*!

It's just as well that I stick to the music and let other people get on with managing my affairs!

If all of those fans had bought tickets for the twenty-six shows, then surely they would buy the album. It was a great position to be in as the release date approached.

The week the album went into the shops was brilliant. I careered around the place doing in store signings. That's when I got a real sense of how good it felt to be out there standing on my own two feet and selling my music. Going into the stores and seeing the album racked up gave me such a buzz. No drug could compare with it. Hearing the music playing over the PA system in shopping malls and record outlets sent tingles down my spine. During one signing session I actually stopped doing what I was doing to listen to some of the songs.

'Jaysus, I haven't listened to this song. This is a great song,' I said, forgetting where I was.

The fans in my vicinity laughed at my reaction.

Suddenly I went puce.

'Well, it is a good song,' I winked.

Unlike the heart-stopping situation I found myself in with the single, when the industry cocked up and eliminated half the sales, the signs were good all week that I would have a number one.

I had poor Mark pestered every day.

'What's the up-date? How many sold yesterday? What's happening today?'

But I still held my breath until the final confirmation came in on the Sunday afternoon, a week after *Ronan*, the album, went into the shops.

The relief was unbelievable.

'Yeesss! Yeesss! Yes!' I screamed as I punched the air.

Jack, who was in my arms at the time, started crying.

'Ooops! Sorry pal. Didn't mean to scare you,' I said, close to tears myself. I had worked so hard to get to this moment. Now I found myself on the brink of a major solo career. The foundation was finally in. It was rock solid. Now I could build a life in music from it.

The realisation that all of those people had put their faith in me; believed in me and voted for my by buying the album was humbling. 'Jesus, do I deserve this?' I thought.

I remember being gob-smacked when Mark told me that 45,000 had been sold on the first day. But I wanted so much to get to number one. A number two position would have been a failure in my eyes. I suppose I was competing against myself. All of the Boyzone albums had gone straight to number one. I wanted to be able to achieve that on my own. And I did.

Later I would learn that my album had out-sold all of the individual Boyzone albums, with the exception of *By Request*, the greatest hits. If ever I needed affirmation of my appeal as a solo performer outside the group, then that was it.

The success of *Ronan*, the album, told me that I had taken the right path, chosen the right music and surrounded myself by the best people in the business. You don't become a success in this business on your own. Everyone from management to the record company staff and the people who work in the stores are a part of it. I wouldn't know where to begin thanking them all.

Asia went crazy as well when I toured there on my own. I had enjoyed the ride of Boyzone-mania in that amazing part of the world, but I didn't know what was in store for me when I returned to promote my solo album.

As soon as we touched down in Hong Kong I knew that these would be happy days. There were thousands of fans waiting for me, waving banners and screaming my name. I had hoped that there would be a respectable turnout of supporters when I entered the airport. But, according to airport security, there were 3,000 girls swarming all over the building, trying to catch a glimpse of me.

It took my breath away. Instead of five people sharing the attention, all eyes were on me. All hands were on me, too, as I fought my way towards the exit and into the safety of a waiting car.

I thought I was going to die laughing as I spotted Mark being swept along in the heaving crowd, his glasses crooked on his face and him clinging on to his mobile office for dear life. Barrie Knight is the best crowd control man in the business, but Hong Kong even beat him. There was no way he was holding back that stampede.

'Run Barrie!' I shouted, and we left skid marks out the door. I lost my baseball cap along the way as one of the girls bagged a souvenir.

'That was great craic, lads,' I said when we were all safely on our journey to the hotel.

'Great craic, Ro?' Barrie remarked, raising an eyebrow.

I was on a high. Every territory was working for me now. It was all falling into place.

Back in the calm silence of my hotel room I reflected on the scary months leading up to that moment. LA at the start of the year seemed like the dark, distant past. It had been a nightmare at the start, but now I was enjoying the fruits of that hard labour.

I looked around the room.

'Holy shit!' I thought. It was double the size of our old home in Bayside. All the hotels in Asia are mega. They lay on massive suites for you and you even have your own butler in attendance. It's way over the top, but it didn't stop me enjoying the luxury of it.

The only downside to the Asian trip that August was being torn away from Yvonne and Jack. I'm nothing without my family and just love having them around. Obviously it wouldn't have been fair to drag Jack all over the place on that trip. And of course there was another reason for their absence from my tour party. Yvonne was pregnant with our second child.

That trip wasn't one for the faint-hearted as I spent every waking hour – and a few when I was asleep – travelling, signing autographs and doing interviews. There were days when it was so insane I was literally brought to my knees and on the verge of crying. I was exhausted and missing Wivvy and Jack like mad.

As soon as the time difference was okay I would get on the phone.

'Everything alright, Wiv?'

'No problems, Ro.'

'How is Jack?'

'I know he misses you, Ro. But he's fine.'

'Love you both.'

Everytime I heard Wiv's voice it hurt so much.

'Why am I doing this?' I asked myself again and again.

Of course, I knew the answer. It was all for the benefit of our future. There was a career to tie down here. And once established I would never have to work so hard in the future. I could come back on my own terms; do a signing session, a big MTV show and the main magazines and newspapers. That would be then, but for now I had to plough every field.

Mark, Barrie and my stylist Alex Delves picked me up several times when I was in the depths of despair from tiredness. I don't think I could have survived without them.

There was a reprieve in the middle of it when I had to fly home after ten days to take care of some business. Those few days were just the tonic I needed. Walking through my own hall door was like entering the gates of heaven.

I put my bags down and walked into the kitchen. There was Jack. He looked at me, frozen on the spot for seconds. I got a sinking feeling, thinking he didn't recognise his dad. Then the arms went up and he ran towards me. God it felt so good and I whisked him up in the air and drew him down into my chest.

I clung on to Wiv as I watched Jack waddle through the kitchen and into his toy den in the conservatory. Once again I reminded myself how lucky I am to have found this perfect partner in my life and become a dad to a lovely little boy. These were the people who gave my life real meaning.

All too soon I was back in Asia and the Far East for another ten days. This time around my band came out to join me in Japan where I did two massive showcase shows. That broke up the trip for me, so the time away from home didn't seem as long on this final leg of the promotion.

Everywhere I went there was a fanatical reception, with thousands of fans turning up. Our jet-set trip took us to Hong Kong, Singapore, Manila, Kuala Lumpur, Taiwan and Tokyo. I'd go to sign albums in the massive shopping malls and discover that there were up to 10,000 people in the queue.

'Ten thousand!' I gasped, the first time Mark told me.

'You've only got three hours to do it,' he pointed out.

I sat at a table and they all filed by. Very polite people. I was honoured to be in that position. But there was no way I was going to be able to make every one of them happy.

I'd take a break and sing some songs. Then I'd go back to the signing. By the end, my hand was hanging off me.

One evening I arrived back at my hotel to find a fax waiting for me. It was from Elton John. I read the words, but my brain couldn't seem to absorb them. I read it over and over again.

Elton John was asking *me* to sing with him at Madison Square Garden in New York.

'Holy shit!'

I had remembered the conversation months earlier when we met up. 'You'll have to do Madison Square Garden with me.' he'd said then.

'Love to, Elton,' I'd replied, thinking no more of it. So many people say those kinds of things in this business. You're never really sure if they're serious - and mostly they're not. So I take it all with a pinch of salt.

True to his offer, Elton was now giving me the official invite.

'Madison-fecking-Square-Garden' I said over and over.

Then a lump started in my throat and moved all the way down into my stomach, tying it in knots. I had suddenly taken notice of the dates; they clashed with the opening night of my solo tour in Liverpool on Saturday 21st October.

I was gutted.

'I'll see if there's something we can do,' Mark said later, realising my devastation.

'But it's the opening night of the tour, Mark. The tickets are sold out and I couldn't disappoint those people.'

'Let's just see if there's anything we can do. Leave it with me.

Mark is brilliant in those situations. He's a real lateral thinker. Time and time again he has found his way through seemingly impossible situations.

I didn't hold out much hope this time, though.

Polydor, my record company, were jumping around the place with excitement when they heard that I had landed Elton's gig. They saw it as the perfect launching vehicle for me in the States, where I'm an unknown artist. Boyzone had never taken on

America in earnest, so it was the one territory we didn't crack. I needed to get my name out there, and what better way than to link up with Elton's fan base.

There were other considerations. Lots of other artists were dueting with Elton. The show was going to be televised all over the world and it would be released as an album. It was a promotion team's dream for an artist like myself.

'Ronan, we'll have to do it, it's too good an opportunity to miss,' Louis told me on the phone from home.

'We're all working hard to make it work.'

It piled on more pressure for me. I was living on the phone, linking up with everyone on conference calls, trying to sort it out and the twelve hours time difference between the zones didn't help the situation.

It was being handled right from the top, with John Kennedy and Lucien Grainge from Polydor taking a very hands on approach. I was so worried by the situation that I was even ringing friends at home to talk it through with them. But in the end a solution was found. It was decided to move the Liverpool shows to Manchester at the end of the tour and provide coach transport for the fans.

It wasn't an ideal situation, of course, but the people in Liverpool were extremely gracious in their response. They stuck by me and took the Manchester ticket.

New York, New York, so good they named it twice. And that's exactly how I feel about the city that never sleeps. It's the coolest place in the world to me. I love everything about it; the atmosphere on the streets, the colourful people milling around, hot dogs on the corner and an endless supply of cabs. I want to live there one of these days.

The Elton concert was a three-day trip for me and I was determined to make it a rock 'n' roll experience. Yvonne and Gar travelled with me and Mark was accompanied by his wife Clare. I could have crossed the Atlantic without a plane I was on such a high going out! It was late at night when we arrived and the sight of the Manhattan skyline all lit-up set my heart racing. It's a scene straight out of the movies.

Gar couldn't wipe the smile off his face. We had designated him as our tour guide and driver because, having worked there, he knew the Big Apple like the back of his hand. And he was returning in style. Hey! We were taking over Madison Square Garden. It was a long way from Bayside, but we were ready for it!

Elton's people had made all the arrangements for his guests and we were being put up at the famous Waldorf Hotel. 'I'm staying at the Waldorf,' I said in a very posh accent.

'It's far from the bleedin' Waldorf you were reared Ronan Keating,' Gar slagged in his best Dublin accent.

Our suite at the Waldorf was like a soccer stadium. The bed was so big an army could have shared it and still have space left over. We quickly sorted out our clothes and had a shower. It was getting on for midnight.

'Party time,' I declared.

There's a little pub in Manhattan called McCormack's. You'll find it on 26th and third. It's a haunt of mine anytime I get the opportunity to go to New York. I had arranged with the gang that we would head on down there as soon as we got sorted. Our body clocks were all over the place and we were wide awake anyway. Plus, I didn't want to miss a minute of the New York experience.

There are 17,000 restaurants in the Big Apple, but none of them does a Shepherd's Pie like McCormack's. It may have been after midnight, but it was still on the menu. It wasn't long before I was tucking in to one, washing it down with a Jack and coke. You can take the boy out of Bayside, but...

When we got up the next morning the first plan of action was a mad dash around the shops. You can't go to New York without shopping; at least I can't. I always end up buying an extra suitcase to bring home all the new clothes. I have a feeling I'll always be a fashion victim.

We hit all the big department stores like Sachs on Fifth Avenue and Bloomingdales, of course, putting a serious hole in the credit cards. But we also took a trip down Canal Street which is jam-packed with little shops flogging fake designer gear. There you'll get everything from fake Rolex watches to Gucci bags, which make great fun presents. Ten dollars for a Rolex... you can't go wrong. You could spend hours sifting through the massive trays of watches, but unfortunately I was working against time.

My rehearsal at Madison Square Garden was in the afternoon and Gar drove me up to the venue.

'I can't believe me little brother is playing Madison Square Garden,' he said.

'Pinch me, Gar,' I replied, trying to get my own head around it.

Arriving at the venue reminded me of the first time I played Wembley Arena with Boyzone. You knew you were doing something right when you got there, and this was a similar experience. Mention the names of either venue and they have a special magic. It was like another landmark in my career.

The magnitude of the moment hit me when I went inside and heard Elton and American singing star Anastacia's voices reverberating around the venue. 'This really is happening,' I thought to myself.

The stage staff escorted me to my dressing room. When I went through the door and saw plush carpeting, beautiful decor and the sheer size of the interior I thought they had made some mistake.

'Are you sure this isn't Elton's?' I asked the staff.

'No, this is your dressing room, Mr Keating.'

Glancing around at the massive couches, huge wardrobe, mirrored wall and all kinds of fruits and drinks, I wondered what sort of luxury they had provided for the real star of the show.

'You are next up, Mr Keating.'

'Oh Jezus!'

I strutted off to the arena with an outward show of confidence, concealing a very shaky character underneath. In my favour was the fact that Elton and I knew each other as friends, so I didn't have to go through that awkward stage of making a connection with him. But, at the same time, I had never sung 'Your Song' with Elton before, so I was apprehensive.

There was a hive of activity around the stage. Guys in black jeans and matching T-shirts were crawling around the place like an ants' nest. TV cameras were homing in on the stage from all angles. It was like the set of a Hollywood movie. It was all very unnerving.

'How are you doing, Ronan. You got here,' Elton said, giving me a hug.

'Wow! this venue is something else, man,' I enthused, trying to project an air of ultra-confidence.

'Wait till it's packed with people, then you'll see just how good it feels,' Elton told me.

Here was a pop legend who was no stranger to Madison Square Garden.

'OK, will we give it a go?' he asked.

'Yeah, I'm up for it.'

The band suddenly kicked in and the sound just blew me away. I was totally energised in an instant. All of a sudden I found myself telling Elton how we should perform the song.

'Elton, how about me singing this bit and you sing that part?'

'Yeah, Ronan, whatever.'

Then it struck me. Keating, what are you doing? You're telling Elton John how to sing his song. But Elton is a really cool guy like that. He lets you get involved and it really helped my confidence.

We performed the song and I didn't really hit the mark. Elton, on the other hand, was brilliant. But then, he had been singing the song for 30 years. It came out in 1970, seven years before I was born!

'Let's give it another go, Ro! Elton said.

This time around I felt a lot more comfortable and the duet really started to happen. I knew by Elton's reaction afterwards that he was happy. It was a great feeling getting that kind of approval from someone of Elton's stature. But even though I was excited, I knew that no matter how many times I rehearsed the song, nothing was going to prepare me for my appearance on stage that night. Even the thought of it was a killer.

There were another couple of hours to kill before the show that night, just enough time to cram in some more shopping. It would take my mind off the big event that lay ahead of me. Afterwards, I chilled out for an hour in my hotel bedroom, had a shower and stuck on the threads.

We were like a wedding party in the foyer of the Waldorf before leaving for the show.

'You scrub up well, Mark,' Gar slagged.

My brother was getting such a kick out of this night. New York was like his home town, his patch and he was the man showing it off. It felt good to be surrounded by close family and friends on this special evening in my life.

'Your car is here, Mr Keating,' the concierge announced.

We all trooped out into a massive limousine (they're ten a penny in the Big Apple). Inside it had every mod con, TV, video... the works.

'I could get used to this, Ro,' Gar announced, tumbling back into his plush seat.

Inside, Madison Square Garden was buzzing. I could hear that Elton had already started the show. As I was led through the corridors I noticed a sort of hall of fame, there were pictures of some of the artists who had played the venue. The Beatles, John Lennon, The Rolling Stones, George Michael, Elton John. I was about to take my place among some of the biggest superstars in the world. How did I make it all the way from Bayside to here?

Backstage, Billy Joel was chatting to Bryan Adams. Anastacia was having a chin-wag with Kiki Dee, the lady who teamed up with Elton for their big hit, 'Don't Go Breaking My Heart'. I was really chuffed with myself to be a part of this golden circle.

Bryan Adams spotted me and strolled over. I had recorded one of his song, 'The Way You Make Me Feel', on my album. It was actually my favourite track of the whole collection.

'How are you doin' Ronan, good to see you,' he said.

'How's it goin' Bryan?'

'What song are you doin', Ro?'

'"Your Song".'

'My song?'

'No... oh, go on, ye messer!'

Bryan laughed. We went through he entire song list, talking about the different duets and why the various singers were chosen. We reckoned that Mary J Blige would really complement Elton on their song, 'I Guess That's Why They Call It The Blues'. Anastacia had the perfect in your face voice for 'Saturday Night's Alright (For Fighting)'. Bryan was doing 'Sad Songs (Say So Much)'.

'I'm really looking forward to it, Ronan,' he said.

'So am I,' I replied, trying to sound confident and enthusiastic.

Racing through my mind was the awful realisation that the audience out there didn't know me. I was a complete stranger to them. Boyzone had never made an impact in the States, so they didn't know Ronan Keating. They hadn't bought tickets to see me. They were here to see Elton. How would they react when I walked out on stage?

My knees were beginning to go. I went to my dressing room to get my head around the whole thing. On the way I bumped into my good friends Geri Halliwell and Kenny Goss. Geri and Kenny were visiting New York, so they decided to pop around to the concert, as you do. They dropped in to my room and within seconds Geri had me falling around the place laughing. She is such a mad-hatter.

'Enjoy the moment,' she said on her way out.

My big moment finally arrived, all too soon for me.

'OK, Mr Keating, you're up next,' I was told.

I inhaled deeply, pumped up my chest and headed for the stage. It took all the energy I could muster up to get my feet walking in that direction. And I was sweating really badly. Backstage, the crew put my ear monitors on and then I was ushered to the wings.

Elton had stopped singing and I was frozen on the spot as I heard him say how he would like to invite somebody on stage.

'The most promising pop star from the new generation.'

It was a very surreal experience. It almost felt like I wasn't really there. This was something I was watching on TV.

'Ronan Keating!' Elton announced.

'Oh Christ!'

I tried to walk, but my legs wouldn't carry me up the few steps to the stage. I was weak at the knees. My mouth was dry. 'Why did I say yes to this,' I asked myself.

Then I was on the stage, the crowd was applauding, Elton started playing the piano and suddenly I was in a groove with him. Bam! It suddenly hit me and I went for the song big time. It just rolled off me and my confidence was soaring by the second. I felt elated. Glancing over the audience I could see little candle lights flickering over their heads like a massive birthday cake. The audience was loving it.

There were a few moments when I felt like I was *The Man*. Forget Elton, this was my gig. Of course, before I knew it the song had finished and it was time for me to leave the stage. Just when I was really getting into it. I could have stayed there singing all night. Fortunately there was a second show the next night to look forward to.

I knew by the beaming faces of Yvonne, Mark and Gary back in the dressing room that it had gone well. I hadn't even appeared nervous at the start, which was good.

'Let's go party!' Gar declared.

He didn't have to say it twice.

The second night up with Elton was more enjoyable for me because I was in control and totally confident going out on stage. I had a real grip on it. Again, it was over all too quickly.

After the show, Elton was very complimentary.

'I really enjoyed it, thank you very much, Ronan,' he said.

'Jeez, Elton, I'm the one who should be thanking *you*. It doesn't get much better than this. It's all downhill from here.'

He laughed.

Elton is such a great guy. He has been very supportive of me and I have learned a lot from him. He's one of the masters. Elton also introduced me to an audience in America that had never seen me before. The timing for me was great. I was gearing up to launch myself on the American market.

'Party time!' Gar announced afterwards.

'You must be joking. I'm off to me bed at the Waldorf,' I declared.

There was a flight to be caught the next morning. Although I felt very proud of myself to think that I had pulled off my gig at Madison Square Garden, yet again it was tempered by the thought that another major challenge awaited. My first solo concert in two days time in Nottingham.

The rehearsals for my show had been painless. I already had my band from way back, so I didn't have the extra pressure of getting to know new people and how they worked. I would have hated going cold into a tour, meeting a band I'd never been on stage with in the past. We had all gelled way before then and they were a great bunch of musicians.

I was still with Boyzone when I had my first outing with them. They backed me on 'When You Say Nothing At All' when I performed the Notting Hill track at the 1999 Party In The Park in London's Hyde Park. I was singing with Boyzone at that Prince's Trust concert and then did my solo song with the band.

Between us, Louis, Mark and myself hand picked the group. Louis wanted some people in the band that he knew. Mark had a couple of good guys that he head-hunted. And there were a couple of musicians I'd met along the way.

We ended up with a group fronted by Calum McColl. He is my

musical director and a brilliant musician who plays guitar in the band.

The bass player, Paul Turner, had been one of Boyzone's band, so I already had a good relationship with him. James McNally, who plays keyboards, bodhrán, tin whistle and accordion had worked with The Pogues and The Afro Celt Sound System.

Kieran Kiely, on accordion, tin whistle and keyboards, also worked with The Pogues, amongst others. I have another great guitarist called Steve Jones and the whole machine is driven by a superb drummer, Liam Bradley. My backing singers are Janet Ramus and Jo Bryant, who worked with George Michael.

I wasn't daunted at the prospect of working with all of those professional musicians when we were putting my show together. In Boyzone, I was always the one who hung out with the band to make sure the music was right. That was very important to me. I'd spend half the time at dance rehearsals, but for the most part you'd find me down in the studio singing with the band.

During those Boyzone days it was important for me to exercise my vocal chords every day. When I went on tour I was singing all the time, every night. You are demanding an hour-and-a-half of your voice and unless you have been working it during the previous weeks it will tell you 'feck off, I can't do this' and it'll clam up.

Nottingham's Royal City Hall was my first port of call on the tour. On the afternoon of Wednesday, October 25, Mark and Barrie took me down there in the Range Rover for the sound check. It felt a bit like my first day at school, entering the echoing hall and catching the musky scent in the air. Going out into the empty auditorium, a series of pictures raced through my mind, little snap-shots of how I envisaged the audience reacting to the songs later that night.

I was on tenterhooks in the countdown to my curtain call that night, but no more nervous than I had been before the Boyzone concerts. It's quite normal to have some pre-show nerves. I always think they give you an extra edge when you kick into the show.

It was only when I took my first few steps out on stage as the band struck up the music to 'Heal Me' that the nightmare began to unfold. I couldn't get a grip on the show at all. I was nervous and every ounce of confidence had drained from my body. My legs were going from under me and there was a knot in my stomach. I could hear myself singing, but the song wasn't coming out as it should have done.

The tempo was lifted with the second track, 'If You Love Me', but my spirit was gone. And so was my voice. I could hit the higher notes, but anywhere else just bottomed out. My heart was pounding against my chest. 'Jesus Christ, it's all over for me,' I thought, feeling slightly faint. The blood drained from my face and I couldn't even force a smile.

In that instant I was in a living hell. All kinds of pressure was pummelling at my brain. I was looking out at all of those people in the audience who had bought tickets for this show and were expecting me to give them the night of their lives. I was thinking about all of the other concerts that had been sold; then there was the band and all the crew who were depending on me for their wages. It was a massive weight on my shoulders. I had no idea it was going to hit me with the impact of an express train.

This was the crossroads in my career and real failure was staring me in the face. 'If I can't do this it's over,' I thought. It's like a carpenter's hand being broken. I could go around the world talking about the songs I'd recorded in the past, but I couldn't sing them anymore.

I knew I was in the biggest disaster zone of my life from the looks on the faces of the band. Glancing towards the wings I caught sight of Gar and Barrie. I could even see the panic in their faces. I was freaked out.

'Mam, get me through this,' I prayed.

I ran to the side of the stage and Barrie handed me a hot honey and lemon drink. I skulled that.

'Mark, I'm skipping 'Believe In Me' and going straight into the Boyzone set,' I croaked.

I looked at Mark and could hardly recognise him. I had never seen that kind of anger in his face before, there was fire in his eyes.

'Who the hell do you think you are? There are people out there who have paid money to see your show. Now get out there and sing,' he bellowed.

I was gob-smacked. Mark had never spoken to me like that before...*ever*. In fact, I'd never heard him use that tone or language with anyone else.

'But, Mark...'

'Get your arse back on stage, start smiling and sing the bloody songs,' he roared.

Now I was angry. 'Feck off, Mark!'

'No, you feck off. You are throwing away your whole career... after all that work.'

That confrontation was just what I'd needed. It got the adrenaline pumping again and fired me up. I stormed back on stage.

'Let's party!' I roared.

The crowd went wild and before I knew it there was a big, silly grin sweeping across my face. My voice had miraculously returned, the songs were flowing like clockwork and I was on a one to one with every person in that audience. It was really rocking.

Afterwards I was physically exhausted. I went straight back to the hotel, had a cup of lemon tea and retired to my bed. It wasn't a night for the bottle of Jack or major celebrations. I had salvaged potential disaster, but the second night would be the acid test.

The next morning over breakfast we did the post mortem on the show. Apart from me getting my act together, there wasn't much tweaking to be done to improve it.

Mark and myself laughed over our little side-show.

'Don't you ever talk to me like that again!' I mocked.

Mark giggled.

'Jesus, Mark, what went wrong? I've done hundreds of shows with Boyzone and never experienced that. Not even on the first Boyzone show.'

'It was just nerves, Ro,' he said.

Mark could see immediately what was wrong with me. He knew that the only way to snap me out of it was to lash into me. It could have gone either way; I could have completely disintegrated from what he said to me. But Mark knows me so well. He read it right and it worked. Thank God!

I was apprehensive going on stage for the second show. The impact of the previous night's trauma was still affecting me. But as soon as I started singing the opening track I knew I was going to be OK.

After the shaky opening, I soon realised that I had a hit tour on my hands. It had been a trek into the unknown for me. I had no idea starting out what the audience expected of me or how they might react. I didn't know if they were going to be a Boyzone audience, expecting all the hits from that era of my life, or a whole new fan base.

The fact that the tour had sold out before the album was released indicated to me that it might be a huge Boyzone thing going on. I wanted to bring the Boyzone fans with me, but I was also hoping to attract a new core of people to the music I had made . on the Ronan album.

I couldn't have been more thrilled when show after show confirmed that I had crossed over. The Boyzone fans were there, but I could see lots of older couples, all of them singing the new songs back at me. I had achieved what I'd set out to do.

I wanted the concert to stand or fall as a Ronan show, so we put just one Boyzone set into it. Making the link between the past and the present gave me the chance to wear my cowboy hats.

As a kid, I always loved the old Cowboys and Indians movies. There was always something about those cowboy hats that really took my fancy. They had a macho vibe and I always thought they were cool. They were never something I was going to wear in real life. But the beauty of showbiz is that it allows you to get away with most things.

The first time Boyzone went to America, I picked up a cowboy hat. But it was like buying an elephant; what do you do with it? I wore it on stage for a laugh one night and it got a reaction. 'This is it. This is perfect. I can use it in the show,' I thought. So, from then on, the cowboy hat became a Boyzone showpiece.

When it came to planning out my solo show, the cowboy hat was the perfect prop to make the connection with Boyzone. In the middle of the performance, a mirrored box arrived out on stage. I looked surprised, went to investigate and when I lifted the lid it lit up inside. From the box I slowly produced the hat... and the audience went wild. Suddenly we were all back in Boyzone time. It was a three-song set featuring 'Picture Of You', 'Father And Son' and 'Baby Can I Hold You'. I had chosen well, the crowd loved it.

The tour gave me the opportunity to dust the cobwebs off those hats. I have rows of them in my wardrobe. One of these days I'll pluck up the courage to strut down Dublin's Grafton Street wearing one.

Bringing the show home to Ireland was the ultimate thrill for me. 'If I can make it there, I'll make it anywhere,' I thought. That's the thing I love about being Irish, we're not impressed by hype. Prove yourself and then we'll love you. Of all the concerts, the Dublin one took the longest to sell out. So I expected to have a tough time winning over the crowd.

I couldn't have been more wrong. From the moment I hit the stage the show took off like a rocket. The crowd let it be known in no uncertain terms that they were mad for it. Every time I tried to talk between songs their wild screams drowned me out. And I couldn't contain my excitement, telling the crowd, 'This is some gig!' It was a dream homecoming for me as a solo artist.

'Don't believe everything you read, I love Ireland more than any other place in the world,' I told the home crowd, referring to reports that I had turned against the country that had made me. 'I walked down Grafton Street today and never felt more at home,' I added. I was in the middle of a great big love in, enjoying every second and on my tippy-toes dancing with delight. It was the best show of the entire tour.

Mark arrived down at breakfast in the hotel one morning with a delivery for me. It was the Madison Square Garden album.

'Wow! Mark. I can't believe this,' I said, checking the credits.

Track number ten was: *Your Song (Elton John with Ronan Keating)*. To see my name on an Elton John album was incredible to me.

'Mark, I don't know how I got to this point in my career. This is just fantasy stuff,' I said, unable to take my eyes off the album.

It was another major milestone in my career. Whatever happened from there on, that night in Madison Square Garden could never be taken away from me.

Just when I thought it couldn't get much better, Louis phoned me one morning with the news that MTV had invited me to perform at their 2000 awards in Stockholm. And I had been nominated for a Best Solo Artist award as well. I was up against the likes of Eminem and Ricky Martin. It was where I wanted to be. This was always a part of the dream. I just didn't dare think that it would happen... and so soon at that. Louis' phone call completely threw me for the day. I couldn't think of anything else.

I had presented the MTV Awards a couple of times, but those honours paled into insignificance by comparison to the call to be one of the live performers on the night. This is one of the most glittering showbiz events of the year and it was going to be a fantastic shop window for me around Europe. As if it wasn't exciting enough for me, I was to learn later that my idols U2 were also going to perform that night. 'Doing the same show as U2, Jeez!, this is unbelievable,' I thought. Then the word came through that Madonna was going to be there. It was just getting better and better.

The night before the show was a sleepless one for me. I was too excited. That day I was running on sheer adrenaline. It was the most incredible feeling. I could have taken on the world.

There were no nerves going into the venue that afternoon. Just pure joy. Other artists were shouting my name, 'How are you doin' Ronan?'. Bands like the Backstreet Boys were congratulating me on the 'Rollercoaster' single. 'We love what you're doing,' they said. To be acknowledged like that by your peers was a good feeling.

Bono, The Edge, Larry and Adam arrived in a little later and, without ever seeing them, you could sense their presence. Other people in the music industry are in total awe of them. No one can touch what they have done in music. It's such a privilege to know them.

'How's it goin' Ronan?' Bono asked, when I popped into their dressing room next door to my own.

'Oh, Jeez, I'm buzzing,' I said, clearly showing my delight at being a part of this league.

'How is the missus?' Larry piped up. 'When is she due?'

That's the thing I love about U2, they are real people. They may be the biggest rock band in the world, but they have their priorities right. It's people and normal life that matters to them above all the bullshit of the business. That's one of the reasons why they have been around for so long and command so much respect. Every artist in the industry should learn from them. And it's the way I want to handle my life.

As I waited for my turn in the spotlight later that night, there were no nerves. I was buzzing with nervous energy, but I felt that I was in total control and I was determined to enjoy the moment. I walked out on to the stage feeling like a million dollars. There wasn't one negative thought going through my mind. I stepped back for a moment and sized up my show. The stage looked great, my band was in position and I was in the best form ever. I felt I looked cool and had the right gear on me. It's all part of the performance.

I shot out singing 'Life Is A Rollercoaster', strutted down to a little circuit that went round and round. It was a great pop moment. There were fireworks going off and a blizzard of confetti falling around me like a New York celebration. The music was firing off at ear-piercing decibels. For a few minutes I was the King of Pop.

Afterwards, I was so wound up I thought I'd never come back down to earth. I didn't pick up an award that night, but I hardly noticed. Afterwards, I sat in a corner with Bono and we got drunk together. 'I've definitely died and gone to heaven,' I thought.

Coming just before the end of my tour, MTV was the perfect wrapping to my solo launch. I finished with two shows in Manchester and the understanding Liverpool fans finally had their night as well. Hopefully, for them, it was a case of saving the best till last. I'm told the reviews in general for the show were fantastic. I never read them myself, unless someone says, 'Here's a good one.' If it's bad it can crush you, playing on your when you're mind on stage.

I was on a real roll when I released the follow-up to 'Rollercoaster'. There was no doubt in my mind that I had a sure-fire hit on my hands with 'The Way You Make Me Feel'. I considered the Bryan Adams song to be one of the best tracks on the *Ronan* album. When the mid-week position indicated that I wasn't in the top five, the bottom fell out of my world again.

'What's happening, Mark?' I asked, desperately seeking some kind of reassurance. But Mark seemed just as perplexed.

When the official chart was released on the Sunday, my worst fears were confirmed. Sales hadn't picked up and it came in at number six.

'How did I get it so wrong?'

It knocked the stuffing right out of me. After getting everything so right, suddenly I was back in a danger zone. I was baffled as to why the public didn't like the song. It was only when the following week's album chart was released that the jig-saw was complete again. *Ronan* the album had jumped twelve places. By attracting an older audience I had become an album-selling artist. That's what I'd been trying to achieve and it happened for me.

I felt I had the world in the palm of my hand when 2000 drew to a close. Elton John was hosting Channel Four's *TFI Friday* on December 22 and invited me to open it with 'Rollercoaster'. It was a great end to the year and, as I flew home to Dublin that night I was looking forward to my best Christmas ever with the family.

When I woke up the next morning, my body felt like it had been crushed by a steam-roller. Every muscle ached and my head was spinning. Once again, life was showing me who was boss. I had the 'flu.

Over the last twelve months I lost one 'baby' but gained another. Having been at the birth of Westlife and nurturing them along the way in the early stages, I was having less contact with them as their popularity soared. I was there for them as a friend, someone they could lean on whenever they needed me. I had set up their first album with Louis, but after that there wasn't a whole lot more I could do. The lads worked really hard and achieved phenomenal success. The ship was sailing itself and it had five great captains. With the demands of my own career occupying all my time, we decided in the true style of gentlemen to part company. The Westlife lads are a great bunch of guys and I'm proud and honoured to have played a part in their amazing success story.

With our second child due on February 8, I had arranged to take time off during the first couple of months of 2001. Babies, of course, rarely stick to a schedule. A week passed and nothing happened. In the second week there was still no movement, so we reckoned that it was safe for me to work for one day. I had been invited to appear on a TV show in Germany called *Wetter Das* which has twenty million viewers and a private plane was organised for the day trip.

Throughout the morning and afternoon I kept in regular contact with Wiv by phone. When I rang her around eight o'clock in the evening I sensed that something was wrong.

'Is everything OK, Wiv?' I asked.

'Everything is fine, Ro, don't worry,' she assured me.

'Are you sure?' I asked, not totally convinced.

'Everything is grand, don't worry,' she insisted.

My TV slot was running late at the German show. I rang Wiv on her mobile at nine o'clock and I knew by her voice that she wasn't her normal self.

'Wiv, there's something wrong,' I insisted.

'I'm grand, Ro,' she said unconvincingly.

'Wiv, tell me...'

'The contractions have started.'

'Where are you?'

'In the hospital.'

'In the hospital! Holy Jeezus! Wiv, I'm on the way.'

I raced down the corridor of the TV studio to Mark Plunkett.

'Mark! Mark!... get the plane, get the car ready, we're out of here,' I said barely taking a breath.

Mark quickly explained the situation to the TV director. He came back to me and said, 'They're arranging a police car to take you to the airport and they say you'll have the song over by the time it arrives.'

'I'll only do it if they put me on this minute, Mark,' I said.

There was no time to change into my gear. I raced on in my jeans and T-shirt and straight into the number, an album track called

'Addicted'. As soon as I killed the last note I was out the door in a flash. We raced at high speed in the police car with the siren blaring. When I got on the plane I wanted to be home in that instant, but there was an hour-and-a-half of a journey ahead of me. I was sweating and agitated. Mark gave me a large Jack Daniels to steady my nerves, but it had no effect. I so desperately wanted to be there for that special moment.

Gar was waiting for me at the airport when we arrived. It was midnight on Saturday and, just my luck, traffic was heavy on the motorway.

'What is going on here!' I roared.

Gar shot up along the hard shoulder at high speed. We were hoping a Garda car would see us and lead the way. Twenty minutes later we arrived at Mount Carmel Hospital and I burst through the doors.

'Is Wiv OK? Has the baby arrived?'

The nurse reassured me that everything was under control. And, yes, I had made it on time. In fact it was two hours later that our little daughter finally entered our world. I cried my eyes out when I saw her, she was so perfect and so beautiful.

Our little Marie.